Modernising Governance

Modernising Governance

New Labour, Policy and Society

Janet Newman

SAGE Publications
London • Thousand Oaks • New Delhi

First published 2001

SAGE Publications Ltd
6 Bonhill Street
London EC2A 4PU

SAGE Publications Inc
2455 Teller Road
Thousand Oaks, California 91320

SAGE Publications India Pvt Ltd
32, M-Block Market
Greater Kailash – I
New Delhi 110 048

British Library Cataloguing in Publication data

A catalogue record for this book is available from the British Library

ISBN 0 7619 6990 X
ISBN 0 7619 6989 6 (pbk)

Library of Congress catalog card number 2001–131842

Typeset by Mayhew Typesetting, Rhayader, Powys
Printed and bound in Great Britain by Athenaeum Press, Gateshead

Contents

Foreword

Writing a book about the politics and policies of new Labour that goes to the printers around the time of a general election is a hazardous process. By the time you read it, many things will have changed. If Labour is returned to power, its approach will move on – it will have drawn some lessons from its experiences of government, new ministers will be in office, and new crises or events will be requiring government attention. As the parties line up for the 2001 election some changes are already evident. Labour has begun to loosen the reins on public expenditure now that it assumes it has won the confidence of both the electorate and the financial markets as a prudent guardian of the economy. It has begun to allow the language of poverty and redistribution to re-enter its political lexicon. There is less focus on policy experimentation than in the early years of the 1997 Labour government, and more assurance in its handling of the long-term policy agenda. The latest round of health reforms (bringing greater delegation of decision-making) was presented by Alan Milburn, the Secretary of State for Health, as part of a critique of creeping centralisation, though evidence that this is a critique shared by others in government has yet to emerge. There is now less talk of the Third Way – the battle to establish a centre left against the strong forces of both the 'old' left and the new right are assumed to have been won – though Blair returned to this concept in setting out his stall for a second term of office (Blair, 2001). The preoccupations with retaining the support of the urban electorate while winning over 'middle England' have been partially sidelined by deepening crises in the rural economy.

These shifts mean that many of the policies and practices described in this book may rapidly become old news. But the book is intended to be much more than a description of specific policies or an assessment of government successes and failures. My story is of the way in which Labour attempted to respond to the challenges of governing a complex and differentiated society in the aftermath of two decades of neo-liberal reforms. At the centre of its response to these challenges was an attempt to transform the policy process and to modernise the public sector. These changes can be set in the context of deeper shifts in governance based on a re-imagination of the relationship between state and citizen, a new emphasis on the values of community and the role of civil society, the remaking of key areas of social policy, and the introduction of fundamental changes in the state itself through constitutional reform. My story also concerns a government increasingly frustrated by its power to make things happen and engaged in a struggle to exert tighter and tighter control from the centre. The tensions between these different narratives – on the one hand of renewal, trans-formation and innovation, and on the other of centralisation and the ratcheting up of control measures – forms a central thread in my account of the 1997 Labour government in office. The book also traces the lines of fracture and conflict which have repeatedly undermined Blair's attempt to install an image of Britain as a consensual nation, a nation in which old conflicts, and the inequalities on which they are based, have been resolved. Such tensions and conflicts are fundamental to the process of making public and social policy, and will continue to shape the experience of those responsible for delivering it, long after the life of this government. They are fundamental to the contemporary process of governance in modern societies.

To understand these processes the book draws on different strands of governance theory that help illuminate current shifts in the role and power of the state. But the insights offered by governance theory only take us so far. My own theoretical background has been shaped by cultural studies and feminist theory as well as social and public policy. The experience of working at the interfaces between theory, policy and practice has also led me to become fascinated by the processes of cultural and institutional change. My analysis has been based in part on the experience of those who have been actively involved in shaping, delivering and interpreting change: civil servants, health professionals, police and probation officers, local government managers and staff, those working in the voluntary sector and in community-based organisations, researchers and academics. I have drawn on these different resources to both critique and develop governance theory. The foundations of my analysis are set out in chapters 1 and 2, and I return to them in the conclusion. Those keen to get on and read about new Labour may want to skip lightly over these, but are encouraged to linger briefly over their propositions and frameworks (figures 1.1, 2.1. and 2.2) since these will help situate the arguments of later chapters.

Whatever the political shifts and policy changes that may continue to characterise Labour in government, it is clear that the fate and fortunes of the public sector will be at the centre of its struggle to retain public legitimacy and continued electoral success. As David Marquand has com-mented, 'Social democracy and the public realm are inextricably inter-twined' (*Guardian*, 20 March 2001: 19). The renewal of the public services, and the culture that sustains them, will, Marquand suggests, be a crucial part of the process of embedding social democratic norms in the public culture and the structures of the state in order to resist any threat of a resurgence of the right. The public sector is becoming better at evaluating its success in delivering policy goals and objectives. But the success or failure of specific reforms has to be set in the wider programme of political and institutional change with which this book is concerned.

Acknowledgements

Thanks to all those who have helped me to understand the politics and policies of the Labour government and how these are being interpreted and enacted on the ground. They include those who have given their time to be interviewed as part of research programmes, and delegates on management and leadership programmes I have run within organisations and at the School of Public Policy at the University of Birmingham. Special thanks are due to the delegates on the Public Leadership Programme, Public Service MBA and MSc programmes in the autumn of 2000, who commented on earlier versions of the models included in the book.

My thanks also to colleagues John Stewart and Chris Skelcher who read early drafts; to Sue Richards who shared her knowledge and insights; and to John Clarke, my co-author on *The Managerial State* and my continuing collaborator and critic.

List of abbreviations

CCT	Compulsory Competitive Tendering
DETR	Department of the Environment, Transport and the Regions
ESRC	Economic and Social Research Council
EU	European Union
GOs	Government Offices of the Regions
GP	General practitioner
HImP	Health Improvement Programmes
ICT	Information and Communication Technology
LEAs	Local Education Authorities
NHS	National Health Service
NICE	National Institute for Clinical Excellence
NPM	New Public Management
OFSTED	Offices for Standards in Education
PCGs	Primary Care Groups
PIs	Performance indicators
Quango	Quasi-autonomous non-government organisation
RDAs	Regional Development Agencies
SEU	Social Exclusion Unit
SRB	Single Regeneration Budget
SSI	Social Services Inspectorate

Introduction: new Labour and the question of governance

This book asks the question 'How far did the 1997 Labour government represent a shift in the governance of the UK?' Much of new Labour's[1] electoral platform had been based on a critique of the changes produced by the Thatcher and Reagan governments. Tony Blair set out a vision of the future based on a re-articulation of the language of community and citizenship, reciprocity and responsibility, justice and fairness. His government was presented as embodying a 'Third Way' between the market individualism of neo-liberalism and the collectivist, state-centred approach of Labour governments of the past. Did these political shifts mean that the UK was developing a new form of governance that transcended the neo-liberal approach of the 1980s and 1990s? In that period, the relationship between 'state' and 'society' went through profound transformations. The cumulative impact of neo-liberal policies both exacerbated a range of social problems and at the same time weakened the capacity of the state to respond to them. The public sphere became more fragmented as a result of the splitting-up of large state bureaucracies, the introduction of market mechanisms, the privatisation of state facilities and the proliferation of 'quangos'. Managerialism changed employment relationships within organisations and buttressed the spread of market and market-type mechanisms. Relationships between organisations and the users of their services were recast through the metaphor of the 'customer'.

Governance and new Labour

One view of the Labour government sees it as continuing this neo-liberal agenda, for example in its focus on equipping the UK workforce for the global economy and in its attempt to 'modernise' the welfare state. However, the picture is more complex in that Labour also attempted to establish – and sustain – a new set of political alliances. It sought to forge a consensus around an agenda of 'modernising' reforms designed to remedy deep-seated social problems such as poor schooling, ill health, child poverty, rising crime and urban decay – intractable areas of public and social policy to which the Labour government addressed electoral pledges. There was a partial retreat from the ideological commitment to market mechanisms as the driver of public sector reform and a softening of the approach to competition. The focus on 'joined-up government', public participation and partnership suggested important shifts of emphasis in the policy programme. The policies introduced in the first years of the new government also emphasised innovation, experimentation and policy evaluation designed to build the foundations for sustainable long-term change in public services. Nevertheless, in order to deliver on its electoral pledges, the government's modernisation programme also led to an intensification of many neo-liberal reforms. Targets and performance indicators continued to cascade from the centre. Audit and inspection regimes proliferated, now backed up by sanctions imposed on 'failing' organisations. Efficiency savings and 'value for money' reviews remained central to the experience of most public service organisations.

But new Labour's project involved a re-imagination of the social and cultural spheres that cannot simply be read as a functional corollary of a particular form of economic governance. The Third Way was a metaphor used in the USA and some other European states to help forge political settlements that combined a recognition of the increasing importance of the global economy with attention to the importance of social cohesion. It was not just about creating an alternative to the state and the market, but addressed issues of civil society and cultural values. It symbolised a break from the social and political ideologies of the new right, but also a recognition of the challenges faced by social democratic governments in conditions of globalisation. In the UK it can be understood as an attempt to retain the economic gains of Thatcherism, while invoking a set of moral and civic values through which Labour sought to reshape civil society. A new emphasis on issues of citizenship, democratic renewal and social inclusion appeared alongside a continued emphasis on economy and efficiency. There was an attempt to appeal to new constituencies – women, black and minority ethnic communities, disabled people, lesbians and gays, and especially the young – while seeking to shed the image of class-based politics associated with 'old' Labour.

The picture is still evolving, influenced by shifts in the broader economic, social and political context as well as by the changing fortunes of particular ministers and of the prime minister himself. The Labour government in office faced considerable difficulties in sustaining support for its political programme, and deep-seated tensions have become evident. Some of these resulted from the programme of devolution to Scotland and Wales and the difficulty of reconciling a centralised polity with the decentralisation of power. Some arose from tensions in the process of economic restructuring. Many of Labour's policies addressed the need to build a flexible, mobile and knowledge-based economy. At the same time, it confronted major problems in 'traditional' industries – shipbuilding, car production – which were politically embarrassing. The fuel crisis in the summer of 2000, during which oil refineries were blockaded and petrol shortages threatened the capacity of the state to keep basic public services running, presented one of the most serious challenges to Labour. This crisis highlighted the vulnerability of governments to global economic shifts and their dependence on actors (in this case oil companies) over whom they could wield little authority. In the UK the government's capacity to ensure that the police force took action to get the tankers moving out of the refineries was initially in doubt. The depth and scale of the protest also came as something of a setback to new Labour's attempt to build a consensual style of governance which could embrace widely divergent interests.

Other lines of fracture and social division also became evident. The Labour government had presented itself as the natural government for a modernised society in which gender and 'racial' conflicts had been settled. Economic and welfare policies were based on an assumption that women had both social and economic equality, yet many of the government's policies harked back to images of family and parenting based on traditional gender roles as the source of moral order. The initial expectation that new Labour represented a party which would deliver women-friendly policies was dispelled relatively early in its first term of office, and many of the new women MPs elected in 1997 decided not to stand for office at the next election. Conflicts around 'race' also beset the new government. Its discourse of 'multi-culturalism' suggested an inclusive, consensual form of citizenship that could encompass all, but the government was repeatedly beset by struggles over who was to be included. This was most notable in the political storms over asylum seekers, with the Transport and General Workers' Union and the Commission for Racial Equality, among others, attacking the racist implications of government policy. The consensual basis of multi-culturalism came under severe challenge with the response of black and minority ethnic communities to the Macpherson Report of 1999 following the enquiry into the death of the young black teenager, Stephen Lawrence. The limitations of the government's response were also emphasised by the Runnymede Trust's *Report on the Future of Multi-Ethnic Britain* (2000) and its political reception, issues to which I return in Chapter 8.

Conflicts and tensions within the modernisation programme for public services also became apparent. Teachers' Unions mobilised against Ofsted and the introduction of performance-related pay in education; while Chief Constables successfully rejected a prime ministerial proposal to impose on-the-spot fines for 'hooligans'. The National Health Service continued to serve as a symbolic indicator of Labour's difficulties in securing its intended reforms and delivering results fast enough to reassure the electorate that things were going to get better. The slowness and difficulty of delivering change might be understood as a result of the 'bloody mindedness' of particular ministers and civil servants, or in terms of cultural and institutional factors (see Chapter 2). Whatever the cause, by July 1999, Blair was talking of the 'forces of conservatism', which he saw as blocking the progress of change, and of the 'scars on his back' produced by the unwillingness of the public sector to innovate.

Key questions

Against this background, the book offers frameworks for analysing Labour's approach. It seeks to address two sets of questions:

- How far does Labour's approach represent a fundamental shift to governing the UK? How far does the complex pattern of continuity and change suggest a shift towards a 'new' mode of governance, involving the reconfiguration of relationships between the state and civil society, the public and private sectors, citizens and communities?

To help answer this set of questions, the book draws on contemporary theories of governance. At its simplest, governance refers to ways of governing, whether of organisations, social systems or the state itself. It embraces not only the actions of government but also the wide range of institutions and practices involved in the process of governing. Much of the literature argues that the governance of modern states is characterised by the increasing importance of networks in both the shaping and delivery of public policy. They represent a shift from the traditional forms of governance through state hierarchies and the neo-liberal focus on markets as a form of self-regulating governance. A variety of explanations are offered for this shift, but the literature agrees that network forms of governance represent significant challenges for the state itself in its attempt to exercise control over both its external environment and internal polity. Chapter 1 reviews this literature and the theoretical challenges it raises for understanding the flows of power and influence in complex, highly differentiated societies. Such theories highlight the way in which the state adapts to changes in its capacity to direct or influence events, and suggests the need to reconceptualise the role of state institutions and the channels through which democratic control and accountability are exercised

One of the features of governance literature is its focus on change, yet, paradoxically, questions of change in the mode or style of governance tend to be under-theorised. The second set of questions of the book, then, centres on:

- How can we best understand the dynamics of change?

Narratives of change which imply a clear distinction between past and present through a series of dualisms – as in 'from government to governance' or 'from competition to partnership' – present an over-simplified picture. What is rather more interesting is to explore what happens when different elements of new and old are packaged and repackaged as different models of governance are overlaid on each other. Governments do not rely just on one kind of policy approach but typically draw on several, not all of them readily compatible with each other. For example, Labour emphasised the importance of developing long-term solutions to complex social problems such as social exclusion, child poverty, ill health, poor education standards and crime and disorder. This long-term approach was based on funding long-term initiatives, fostering partnerships across traditional organisational or departmental boundaries, drawing the 'community' into the process of developing and implementing solutions, devolving responsibility to local projects and fostering evaluation and learning. At the same time, however, it put considerable energy into getting quick results on key issues linked to electoral pledges – such as cutting hospital waiting lists – often through highly centralised, top-down policy measures. The interaction between centralisation and decentralisation, 'enabling' and 'controlling' strategies, produced tensions and disjunctures as different sets of norms and assumptions were overlaid on each other. Such tensions were also evident in the political dynamics of change. On the one hand, a major programme of constitutional reform involving the devolution of power to Scotland and Wales was accomplished, while, on the other, the Labour government in office was linked to a strengthening of central control by the Prime Minister's office over Cabinet, Parliament and party.

How, then, can the process of change be conceptualised? The aim of this book is to explore the dynamics of change rather than to evaluate specific policies. To do so it draws on strands of new institutional theory and discourse theory. Chapter 2 sets out a framework for analysing institutional change and mapping the interaction of different models of governance, each with its distinctive pattern of relationships, form of power and authority, and assumptions about how change is to be accomplished.

Politics, policy and culture: outlining the approach

This book is an attempt to understand the shifts in public and social policy, public management and the role of the state introduced by Labour within this broader political and social context. It does not attempt a comprehensive analysis of the Labour administration. (At the time of writing the policy agenda is still being elaborated, the implementation process is uneven, and the political programme is in the course of being reshaped for the general election of 2001.) The focus on governance means that the book will not only explore the modernisation of central and local government, the NHS and other institutions, but will also highlight the way in which key relationships – between organisations in the public, private and voluntary sectors, between professionals and managers, and between the state, users and citizens – are being reimagined and re-drawn. The book offers critical interpretations of the core themes of partnership, performance, participation and inclusion in Labour's approach to social and public policy. It also attempts to unravel some of the complexities of the process of institutional change as new discourses are enacted and policies are implemented.

I have written this book for those struggling to understand or respond to the changing context of social and public policy across different settings: as workers in public services, as policy analysts and commentators, as students of politics, government, social and public policy. I have attempted to bridge the worlds of theory and practice by offering models and frameworks through which practitioners may reflect on their experience, while also drawing on a range of theoretical approaches to enrich the analysis and argument. The book analyses the changing institutions of the state and government, but is also concerned to develop a broader conception of the public sphere, embracing theoretical perspectives on social and cultural change. It draws on a range of theories. Governance theory is used to develop a series of propositions about shifts in relationships between the government, public services and the citizen. But the book also looks to the social policy literature to help analyse the changing conceptions of 'welfare' and 'the state' on which Labour's policies are based. It revisits work on the New Public Management and managerialism to tease out ways in which the modernisation programme may influence public sector organisations, their relations with users and their role in delivering public policy outcomes.

The book is about politics but is not located in the mainstream political science approaches to studying state institutions. Issues of discourse, ideology and culture are central to my analysis. As part of its attempt to forge a new politics, Labour has drawn on, and amplified, a range of discourses that had been submerged or marginalised during the Thatcher and Major administrations. The languages of democracy, citizenship, society, community, social inclusion, partnership, public participation, central to new Labour's discursive repertoire, can be understood as an attempt to reinstall 'the social' in public and social policy. My interest is in the implications of these new, and not so new, discourses for the practice of making and delivering policy. The book is also concerned with what happens on the ground as managers, professionals and staff struggle to deliver government targets and manage the dilemmas and tensions of institutional change.

To explore these themes, the book draws on forms of cultural analysis which have remained on the margins of political science, public policy and, to a lesser extent, social policy. Cultural analysis emphasises the way in which social arrangements are constructed as a result of the production of meanings and the repression, subordination or incorporation of alternative meanings. So, for example, much of Labour's politics and policies are based on an attempt to associate itself with an image of the modern. However, 'modern' is itself the site of contested meanings. In attempting to establish the supremacy of a particular image of the modern, Labour incorporated strands from earlier conceptions of the modern state, and developed some new political associations of modernity (as, for example, based on a pragmatic, 'what works' approach to public policy). At the same time, it attempted to distance itself from alternative images of modernity, such as those arising from the new left and the new social movements of the 1970s and 1980s.

Cultural analysis views public and social policy as fields which are socially constructed: that is, problems and solutions are formed within the framework of particular narratives, ideologies and assumptions. Successful narratives are those that come to be taken for granted or viewed as 'common sense'. 'Common sense' does not arise naturally but is forged out of struggles to establish certain ideas as dominant. The book attempts to integrate issues of meaning and identity as crucial links between the grand narratives of politics and policy on the one hand and the domain of social action and political struggle on the other. Notions of gender, ethnicity and nationhood were crucial points of disruption for Labour as it attempted to install a consensual, inclusive style of politics.

Cultural analysis is an all-embracing term which includes a wide range of theoretical and epistemological shifts in the social science, including post-structuralism, post-modernism, critical theory, discourse theory and theories of ideology and hegemony (e.g. Burr 1995; Carter 1998; Dean 1999; Hall 1997; Hall and du Gay 1996; Hillyard and Watson 1996; Leonard 1997; Taylor 1998). The application of such theory to traditional academic disciplines, sometimes termed the 'cultural turn' (e.g. Chaney 1994; Clarke 1999), presents challenges to core assumptions and methods which are often not easily accommodated. It is not my purpose here to enter into all the theoretical debates that might arise when cultural theory meets political science or public policy. Rather, I seek to draw on what appear to be helpful frameworks in the conceptualisation of governance as both a constructed and contested domain of ideas and practice. Cultural analysis emphasises the processes and practices through which ideas are produced, struggled over, and linked with each other in the formation of new narratives and political ideologies. But it is not 'just' about ideas – it is concerned with the link between ideas and practice. So, for example, the book addresses the way in which contesting ideas informed different strands of Labour's approach to governing, producing tensions between different political narratives, policy imperatives and forms of implementation practice. Such tensions, I argue, lie at the core of Labour's approach to modernising governance.

The material on which the book draws is derived from a number of sources. These can be summarised as sources 'from above', i.e. sources which set out what the government intends, and sources 'from below', i.e. sources which indicate what is happening on the ground in the process of implementation. Evidence 'from above' is based on textual analyses of the policy documents, consultation papers and reports of the government itself, together with the ministerial speeches or press articles used to explain and legitimate policy. These are supplemented by analyses of presentations at conferences and seminars by policy-shapers close to the modernisation programme, and by discussions or interviews with senior civil servants. While policy documents and reports are public documents, the presentations and discussions tend to be 'off the record' (conducted under what are often called 'Chatham House rules') so cannot be cited directly.

Evidence 'from below' is based on analysis of the experience of organisations and groups of practitioners engaged in the implementation of policy and/or the delivery of services. Some of this experience has been gathered during the course of funded research projects, including a study on market testing in the civil service as part of the ESRC Whitehall Programme; a study of organisational and management change in local government; a DETR (Department of the Environment, Transport and the Regions) study of innovation in local government; and an ongoing project on new democratic fora within the ESRC Democracy and Participation Programme. Additional material has been gathered from work with delegates on management education and leadership programmes run by the School of Public Policy at the University of Birmingham. These cover all sectors and tiers of government (health, criminal justice, civil service, local government, Government Offices of the Regions, the voluntary and community sectors, private sector providers, quangos). The insights gained through this work have been supplemented by findings from research on the impact of the change of government on different sites and sectors, for example through ESRC seminar programmes and academic conference papers. My thanks to all those who have helped me to get to grips with this emerging agenda and with how it is being interpreted and enacted at the problematic interface of policy and practice.

I do not pretend that the result is an exhaustive study of 'new Labour'. It presents an assessment framed by particular questions, concerns and issues. The book was completed during the period when the government was beginning to position itself for election to what it hoped would be a second term of office. But its focus is broader than the assessment of a single electoral cycle. My aim has been to illuminate the underlying processes through which governments wrestle with the problems of governing in complex and differentiated societies, societies in which notions of nation and citizenship are no longer stable, in which the local and the global interact in dynamic processes of structural change, and in which tensions around questions of culture, nationality and identity are becoming increasingly evident.

The structure of the book

Chapter 1: Understanding governance explores the relevance of theories of governance to an understanding of the changes in public policy and management introduced – or intensified – under Labour. It traces key theoretical debates about the changing role of the state and the nature of power and authority in complex societies, and goes on to set out a series of propositions derived from the governance literature. These propositions are examined in the thematic chapters (Chapters 4–8) exploring key themes in Labour's policy agenda.

Chapter 2: The dynamics of institutional change argues that change can best be conceptualised not as a process of state evolution or adaptation, nor as a rational process of policy development and implementation, but as a dynamic process in which different forces or imperatives interact. The chapter sets out my approach to analysing change, drawing on new institutional and discourse theory. It then introduces a framework for mapping the interaction between four different models of governance. This framework is used in later chapters to assess the dynamics of change in specific aspects of Labour's approach to governing.

Chapter 3: The Third Way: modernising social democracy highlights the ways in which the discourses of the 'Third Way' and of 'Modernisation' work to establish the necessity of change and to define a particular programme of reform. It traces the interconnections between social, economic and cultural dimensions of change within Labour's political discourse. It then considers questions of continuity and change in Labour's political strategies and programme of reform.

Chapter 4: Modernising government: the politics of reform begins to examine the politics and policies of new Labour in terms of how far they signify a shift in the mode or style of governance in the UK. It focuses on the modernisation of central and local government against the backcloth of narratives highlighting failures in previous programmes of reform. It traces a number of themes in the modernisation programme: the reframing of policy problems; the move towards a more inclusive policy process; the development of a pragmatic focus on 'what works' in public policy; and the modernisation of the state itself through the establishment of the Scottish Parliament, the Welsh Assembly and the London Assembly and Mayor.

Chapter 5: Modernising services: the politics of performance focuses on the strategies and techniques used by the government in its programme for the modernisation of public services such as health, education and criminal justice. It describes the different strategies used to secure the cooperation or compliance of public service professionals and managers in improving performance. It explores the interaction between regulation and self-regulation in Labour's approach to governing public service professionals, and draws out the implications of Labour's approach to managing change. The chapter highlights tensions in the process of public service modernisation which reflect and refract deeper tensions in the political conception of the Third Way.

Chapter 6: Joined-up government: the politics of partnership traces the importance of ideas of 'holistic' or 'joined-up' government in Labour's approach to governing, and discusses how far these represents a shift towards a network-based form of governance. The chapter analyses the contradictory influences on partnership working created by the tensions between centralisation and decentralisation in government policy, and suggests ways in which Labour's approach influences the internal dynamics of partnership. The chapter concludes by highlighting the role of partnerships in the dispersal and reconfiguration of state power.

Chapter 7: Public participation: the politics of representation focuses on Labour's emphasis on the need for public participation and democratic innovation, and asks whether this can be viewed as signifying a form of governance that is adapted to an increasingly complex and differentiated society. The chapter questions how far new developments in participatory democracy might result in the greater flexibility and responsiveness promised by advocates of co- and self-governance. It also examines ways in which contemporary theories about equality, diversity and the politics of difference have inflected debates about public participation.

Chapter 8: Remaking civil society: the politics of inclusion explores Labour's attempts to remake the relationships between state and citizen, government and civil society, in the search for a new social settlement based on the politics of the Third Way. The chapter traces the way in which Labour has drawn on ideas of 'community' and 'responsible citizenship' in the creation of an ethical and moral discourse through which the modernisation of the welfare state is legitimated. It explores the potential lines of fracture around issues of poverty, gender and 'race' in the attempt to establish a new social settlement, arguing that Labour has attempted to address structural lines of inequality in its social policies while also seeking to contain issues of equality within the discourse of social exclusion and the consensual image of a 'modern' people.

Chapter 9: Conclusion: the politics of governance begins by reviewing the arguments of the book for understanding the political project of new Labour, asking how far its approach represents a distinctive shift towards a new style of governance. It goes on to explore governance as a constructed and contested domain, highlighting the contribution of cultural analysis to the understanding of changing political reconfigurations and realignments of power. This opens up an assessment of Labour's attempt to forge a new political settlement. Finally, the conclusion returns to the idea of modernisation itself and offers alternative possible modernities through which the future might be imagined.

Note

1 I use the term 'new' Labour when discussing the ideologies and discourses associated with the Labour Party leadership's attempt to forge a new political settlement, but refer to the 'Labour government' when describing and analysing specific policies and approaches of Labour in office.

1 Understanding governance

Governance has become the defining narrative of British government at the start of the new century, challenging the commonplace notion of Britain as a unitary state with a strong executive.

(Rhodes 2000b: 6)

Why has governance become such a defining narrative? What kinds of political or cultural shift have shaped the increasing interest in this idea? Governance is an analytical concept, giving rise to questions about what forms of power and authority, patterns of relationship and rights and obligations might typify a particular approach to governing. But what most of the literature is interested in is change. As Rhodes puts it, 'governance signifies a change in the meaning of government, referring to a *new* process of governing; or a *changed* condition of ordered rule; or the *new* method by which society is governed' (Rhodes 1997: 46, original emphasis). Governance has become a shorthand term used to describe a *particular* set of changes. It signifies a set of elusive but potentially deeply significant shifts in the way in which government seeks to govern (Pierre and Peters 2000). It denotes the development of ways of coordinating economic activity that transcend the limitations of both hierarchy and markets (Rhodes 1997; Smith 1999). It highlights the role of the state in 'steering' action within complex social systems (Kooiman 1993, 2000). It denotes the reshaping of the role of local government away from service delivery towards 'community governance' (Clarke and Stewart 1999; Stewart and Stoker 1988; Stoker 1999).

These shifts are located in broader patterns of economic and social transformation. It is argued that the capacity of governments to control events within the nation state has been influenced by the flow of power away from traditional government institutions, upwards to transnational bodies and downwards to regions and sub-regions. The old mechanisms of 'control through hierarchy', it is suggested, have been superceded by the rise of markets during the 1980s and early 1990s, and by the increasing importance of networks and partnerships from the mid-1990s onwards. Growing social complexity, the development of greater access to information and other social changes have made the task of governing more difficult. Complex social issues (such as environmental change) elude traditional approaches to governing. The state, it is argued, can no longer assume a monopoly of expertise or of the resources necessary to govern, but must rely on a plurality of interdependent institutions and actors drawn from within and beyond government. Governments, the argument goes, must adapt by developing new strategies to influence and shape the actions of others: 'Governance recognises the capacity to get things done which does not rest on the power of government to command or use its authority. It sees government as able to use new tools and techniques to steer and guide' (Stoker 1998a: 18).

Forms of analysis: political, economic and social governance

Governance has become a rather promiscuous concept, linked to a wide range of theoretical perspectives and policy approaches (Pierre and Peters 2000; Rhodes 1997). Below I outline three of the main bodies of theory, then highlight some of the theoretical challenges raised. The chapter goes on to explore the relevance of governance theory for analysing Labour's programme of modernisation, outlining a set of propositions against which change might be assessed.

Governing the nation: globalisation, the 'hollow state' and economic governance

One level of analysis in governance theory explores the global political and economic shifts that have limited the capacity of nation states to govern. Rhodes (1994) talks about the 'hollowing out' of the state with power shifting outwards to international financial markets, to global companies able to move capital and other resources from one site of investment to another, and to supra-national entities such as the World Bank or European Union. Power has, it is suggested, also shifted downwards to the sub-national level of regions and cities. These changes have taken place in an ideological climate hostile to 'big government', leading to a series of reforms producing both a reduction in the size of the machinery of government and its fragmentation. Gamble (2000) traces a parallel set of shifts in the state's capacity to manage national economies. He argues that in the last thirty years of the twentieth century the assumption that the state had a major role to play in economic governance was challenged by a number of different forces: concern over a series of policy failures; the growing complexity of the policy process; the increasing importance of global economic trends; and the difficulty of managing national economies as discrete entities.

This latter point is of particular significance for Labour as it attempts to exert influence in the supra-national institutions of the European Union (EU) while also defending the sovereignty of Britain as a nation state. The balancing act is made additionally difficult given the centrality of Europe to party political conflict within the UK, with questions of sovereignty, nationhood and identity interwoven in neo-conservative ideology. Europe's capacity to influence the politics and policies of the UK is, however, ambiguous. Sbragia argues that the EU itself can be viewed as an example of the new governance; that is, as a network organisation rather than as a state in its own right. It steers and coordinates the activities of member states both by the exercise of influence and through older forms of governance based on the exercise of judicial authority through which policy norms are enforced (Sbragia 2000). Through such processes the autonomy of nation states is constrained.

Globalisation, internal devolution within states and the growth of supranational bodies challenge the capacity of nation states to control their environment. In turn, this has led to a search for alternative strategies through which states might pursue their objectives. In adapting to change, governments have increasingly come to rely on influencing a multiplicity of institutions and actors. New strategies based on informal influence, enabling and regulation have grown in importance. However this does not necessarily mean a decline in the role of the state. Forms of control through hierarchical, institutional channels continue alongside new forms of governance. Furthermore, the changing role of the state can be understood as an adaptation to its environment rather than a diminution of its power. Pierre and Peters, for example, adopt an explicitly 'state-centric' approach which emphasises the reconfiguration of state power, viewing governance as a process in which the state continues to play a leading role (Pierre and Peters 2000).

Coordinating economic activity: markets, hierarchies and networks

The idea that markets, hierarchies and networks form alternative strategies of coordination is a central theme in the governance literature. Gamble defines governance as 'the steering capacities of a political system, the ways in which governing is carried out, without making any assumptions as to which institutions or agents are doing the steering' (Gamble 2000: 110). Different modes of governance, including those based on markets, hierarchies and networks, are likely to coexist, with different institutional combinations in specific nations, but with networks becoming increasingly significant.

In the UK the postwar welfare settlement was based on the conception of the state as a direct service provider, with large, bureaucratic state organisations forming a public sector predominantly based on governing through hierarchy. This was partly dismantled under the neo-liberal political/economic regime of the 1980s and 1990s. The introduction of market mechanisms led to a more fragmented and dispersed pattern of service delivery and regulation – what Rhodes (1997) terms a 'differentiated polity' – that required new forms of coordination. Privatisation, contracting out, quasi-markets, the removal of functions from local authorities and the proliferation of quangos, the separation between the policy and delivery functions in the civil service with the setting up of Executive Agencies all meant that governments had to develop new forms of control. These included framework documents, contracts, targets, performance indicators, service standards, contracts and customer charters. While governments could still set the parameters of action (through funding regimes) and had the monopoly on certain forms of power (such as legislation), they increased their dependence on a range of bodies across the private, public and voluntary sectors:

> Central departments eroded their nodal position in the networks. Steering was more difficult. Some of the new actors, for example business, were even less amenable to central steering than Labour-controlled local authorities. Governance, or self-organizational networks, were a major unintended consequence, challenging central elites to substitute indirect management for control. (Rhodes 1997: 23)

Similar changes, it is suggested, took place at local level. Research carried out under the ESRC Local Governance Programme (1992–7) found that network-based patterns of interaction had become increasingly important, leading to the conclusion that local government had been transformed into a system of local governance involving a plurality of organisations across the public, private and voluntary sectors (Rhodes 1999). Local governance involved coordination through networks alongside, and partly displacing, the earlier regimes of coordination through hierarchy (in the postwar bureaucracies) and markets (in the neo-liberal transformation of the public sector). Coordination through inter-organisational networks and partnerships was not only a response to the diminution of local government powers, but also, it was widely argued, enhanced the capacity of local agencies to respond more flexibly to changing patterns of need, new funding arrangements, shifting political priorities and the increasing complexity of localities and communities.

Steering the social: responding to complexity, diversity and dynamic change

The contemporary focus on governance can be understood in part as a response to the challenge of governing complex and fragmented societies, and the difficulties faced by the state in attempting to solve complex and intractable social problems through direct forms of intervention. Kooiman and van Vliet link governance to the need for an interactive form of governing:

> The purpose of governance in our societies can be described as coping with the problems but also the opportunities of complex, diverse and fragmented societies. Complexity, dynamics and diversity has led to a shrinking external autonomy of the nation state combined with a shrinking internal dominance *vis-à-vis* social subsystems. . . . Governing in modern society is predominantly a process of coordination and influencing social, political and administrative interactions, meaning that new forms of interactive government are necessary. Governing in an

interactive perspective is directed at the balancing of social interests and *creating the possibilities and limits of social actors and systems to organise themselves.* (Kooiman and van Vliet 1993: 64: my emphasis)

Kooiman and his colleagues argue that in a society that is increasingly complex, dynamic and diverse, no government is capable of determining social development. It is important to recognise the specific ways in which the concepts of complexity, diversity and dynamics are used in Kooiman's model of the social system. Diversity denotes a diffuse notion of difference between actors within a system of interaction rather than more conventional understandings of social diversity. Complexity denotes the complexity of the system within which they interact, and dynamics refers to possible points of tension within the system itself. Together these concepts constitute the capacity of systems to be self-governing and to balance continuity and change.

Kooiman argues that there has been an attempt by governments – in the UK, the USA and across much of Western Europe – to shift the focus away from the state itself to various forms of co-production with other agencies and with citizens themselves:

There seems to be a shift away from more traditional patterns in which governing was basically seen as 'one way traffic' from those governing to those governed, towards a 'two way traffic' model in which aspects, qualities, problems and opportunities of both the governing system and the system to be governed are taken into consideration. (Kooiman 1993: 4)

No single agency, public or private, has all the knowledge and information required to solve complex problems in a dynamic and diverse society, and no single actor has the power to control events in a complex and diverse field of actions and interactions. Rather than government acting alone, it is increasingly engaging in co-regulation, co-steering, co-production, cooperative management, public/private partnerships and other forms of governing that cross the boundaries between government and society and between public and private sectors (Kooiman 1993: 1). The tasks of steering, managing, controlling or guiding are no longer the preserve of government but are carried out through a wide range of agencies in the public, private and voluntary sectors, acting in conjunction or combination with each other.

Theories of governance, then, operate at different levels of analysis (the local economy, civil society, the state, supra-national governance), and offer different theoretical perspectives (drawn from political science, public administration, political economy, systems theory, development studies). They are influenced by the national context in which theory has developed. The UK literature has tended to focus on the fragmenting effects of the New Public Management and the emergence of 'new' modes of governance. The idea of a shift from markets and hierarchies towards networks and partnership as modes of coordination is a dominant narrative. Rhodes and Stoker, for example, discuss the emergence of new forms of governance as a response to the fragmentation of the public realm and the proliferation of new, self-regulating processes of coordination. Rather different forms of theory have emerged in continental Europe, with work in the Netherlands and Scandinavia influenced by the strong tradition of dense networks of interests groups and a history of working towards consensus (Peters 2000). Kooiman and van Vliet (1993), for example, view government as only one of many actors in a field in which other institutions have a great deal of autonomy. The role of government is to address the problems of guiding and influencing, rather than making, public policy. Different forms or modes of governance – self-governance, co-governance (what Kooiman terms 'heterarchical' governance) and governance through hierarchy – are viewed as likely to coexist in any society. However, the features of what Kooiman terms 'cross modern' societies are most likely to require a pattern of state/society interaction based on 'co' arrangements – collaboration, cooperation, co-steering and co-governing. This form of analysis shifts the focus of attention beyond economic structures or processes towards a much broader concern with issues of citizenship, concepts of community, and social and cultural formations.

Theoretical challenges

Governance has become a hard-working and somewhat overused concept. Rhodes, for example, notes seven different meanings, Hirst five versions of the concept, while Pierre suggests its relevance to a range of different theoretical approaches to understanding the changing role of the state in the coordination of social systems (Rhodes 1997, 2000a; Hirst 2000; Pierre 2000). Governance acts as a descriptive *and normative* term, referring to the way in which organisations and institutions are (or should be) governed. For example, Rhodes suggests that the language of governance offers a new way of engaging with change in public services which goes beyond a narrow managerialism:

> . . . we provide a language for re-describing the world and the (ESRC) Local Governance Programme has played no small part in challenging the dominant, managerial ideology of the 1980s and arguing for a view of the world in which networks vie with markets and bureaucracy as the appropriate means for delivering services. (Rhodes 1999: xxiv)

Governance is also a concept that signifies *change* – in economies and societies, politics and management. Here again it is both descriptive and normative. Empirically, studies have illustrated the increasing importance of networks and partnerships in the coordination of public services. But governance also symbolises a number of normative values, emphasising the primacy of network-based collaboration and coordination in complex societies. Networks are viewed as desirable in that they are more flexible and responsive than hierarchies, and capable of avoiding the 'anarchic' disbenefits of markets. Self-government is viewed as superior to government by the state. Public involvement is viewed as a means of building social capital and thus strengthening civil society. Democratic innovation is viewed as enabling societies to respond to the problem of accountability in complex societies in which the dispersal of power means that representative bodies can no longer control decision-making (Peters 2000). The focus on civil society, institutional renewal, democracy and citizenship can be viewed as a reaction against what is perceived to be the narrow reform agenda of neo-liberalism.

The concept of governance thus links normative hopes for a move beyond the fragmenting and dislocating market reforms of the 1980s with an analysis of the complex interactions and interdependencies of government institutions, communities, citizens and civil society. It shifts attention beyond the state itself while setting out new conceptions of the tasks and roles of governing. However, the very breadth of the concept produces difficulties. This section explores problems in the narratives of change on which some theories of governance are based, and highlights the tension between descriptive and analytical usages of the term. It goes on to identify tensions within theories of governance around notions of the state and conceptions of power.

Narratives of change

The first difficulty relates to the conception of change and the view of historical processes on which assumptions about the emergence of a new, network-based governance are based. These often appear to involve a mis-remembering or over-simplification of the past and an overly tidy view of the present or future. The view that we are shifting from hierarchies to markets and then to networks 'forgets' a number of important changes which complicate the picture of a 'from–to' dualism of past and future. For example, significant changes had taken place in hierarchies under the aegis of managerialism, producing a complex interaction between professional, bureaucratic and managerial regimes (Clarke and Newman 1997: Chapter 4). The use of market mechanisms in public services did not begin with Thatcher and Reagan, and the changes that were launched in the 1980s were in any case uneven and incomplete. The ways in which markets were introduced by government, and adapted or resisted by managers, varied widely between sectors and between individual organisations. Some versions of governance theory suggest a past in which the government could impose its will through the direct exercise of power and through the dominance of hierarchical channels of control. But public policy has long been shaped by a wide range of actors, both inside and outside government, and the idea of elite networks having a major influence on policy development is certainly not new. It is, then, unclear whether the idea of policy networks designates new systems of coordination and influence, or a new concept to designate a long-standing phenomenon.

Theory and practice

Some of the governance literature is based on empirically grounded accounts of practice, for example studies of public/private partnerships in economic development or of the role of networks in urban regeneration (e.g. Stoker 1998b, 2000). Other work develops models or theories that bring new insights into established areas of study, for example the literature on policy networks (Marsh 1998; Marsh and Rhodes 1992) or the analysis of state–society interactions as complex systems (Kooiman 1993, 2000). Is, then, governance linked to the development of new means of coordinating activity or to the emergence of new theory?

> Have we discovered a new hybrid form for the collective organisation of public life, largely informal, going beyond formal organisational boundaries and governmental borders, flowing, flexible, varied and reticulist? Is it a new, postmodern structural form that has come to substitute or at least complement traditional market arrangements and state bureaucracies? Or is network analysis a new, or at least different, way of looking at and analysing traditional government and public sector structures, thus discovering new patterns or at least different ones? (Bogason and Toonen 1998: 205)

There is undoubtedly a complex relationship between theory and practice. The idea of governance appears to have entered the discourse of practitioners as well as academics, reflecting aspects of their changing experience of delivering policy and managing public services. However, it also offers important analytical tools for understanding the interaction between state and civil society, governments and citizens, and the institutional complexity of the public sphere. This book is concerned with both. That is, I discuss governance as a narrative of change, tracing how far the changes introduced by the Labour government reflect a set of propositions about governance shifts. These are outlined in the next section. However, I also draw on different theories of governance, along with other theoretical approaches, to analyse issues of power and control in the 'modern' state, to discuss the discursive construction of 'modern' society and to highlight tensions and paradoxes in the process of institutional change.

The role of the state

A third set of theoretical problems in contemporary theories of governance clusters around the role of the state. It is possible to detect at least two different propositions here. The first is based on the decline of state power. It is argued that the process of globalisation has reduced the capacity of states to manage their own economies, while challenges from within the nation – from regions, often based on sub-national ethnic or cultural patterns of identification – have challenged the political legitimacy and integrity of the nation state itself. Attention shifts to the interaction of multiple sites of action in complex networks and partnerships operating at different levels. Kooiman distinguishes between three different levels or orders of governance: 'First order governing aims to solve problems directly, at a particular level. Second order governing attempts to influence the conditions under which first order problem solving or opportunity creating takes place; second order governing applies to the structural conditions of first order governing' (Kooiman 2000: 154). This is a helpful distinction, highlighting, for example, the importance of the way in which state and non-state institutions influence and shape partnership activity. Kooiman's third order – or meta-level of analysis – comprises 'the total effort of a system to govern itself: governability is the outcome of this process' (Kooiman 2000: 160). The state is viewed as having a role in shaping coordination at this meta-level of governance, in solving problems of coordination rather than directing everything from the centre. But the instruments available are characterised by 'weak power' (Mulgan 1994), based on guiding and steering rather than on command or authority. Kooiman offers important conceptual tools to analyse interactions within dynamic systems, but the role of the state as actor is diminished and it is not clear what the driver of change might be.

A second form of analysis suggests that what we are witnessing is a reconfiguration of, rather than a decline in, state power in order that the state may face new challenges. Pierre, for example, views governance as a process of state adaptation:

> These emerging forms of governance should be seen as alternative expressions of the collective interest which do not replace but supplement the pursuit of collective interests through traditional, institutional channels. Contemporary governance also sees formal authority being supplemented by an increasing reliance on informal authority. . . . The emergence of governance should therefore not, prima facie, be taken as proof of the decline of the state but rather of the state's ability to adapt to external challenges. (Pierre 2000: 3)

Hirst (2000) argues that the state, rather than being 'hollowed out', has become merged with non-state and non-public bodies (public agencies, quangos, companies) through which power and control are exercised, and that this decentring of state power has implications for issues of account-ability and democratic control.

Others question how far state power has become decentred. For them, new forms of governance interact with, rather than displace, the regulatory and distributional activities of the state. Jessop, for example, argues that the state retains its capacity to decide how and where to use different coordinating mechanisms, and regulates the interaction between different systems (for example, deciding when, and through what mechanisms, to replace a state-run service with one delivered through the market, or to implement its policy programme through partnership rather than through existing hierarchies). It decides how far and in what ways to provide material and symbolic support for proposals emerging from the complex pattern of policy networks, from 'self-organising' tiers of government or from public participation exercises. It not only 'steers' but also plays a much more directive role (Jessop 1998a).

Conceptions of power

Much of the work on governance tends to dissolve notions of power and agency. The index of a recent collection containing contributions from Kooiman, Gamble, Rhodes, Stoker, Pierre and other key theorists contains no entries under the heading of power (and this is not the result of poor indexing). Theories of governance that focus on the self-steering capacities of networks and partnerships tend to marginalise issues of agency and individual, institutional and state power. Rhodes (1997, 2000a) draws on notions of power dependence and games theory to explain what happens *within* networks, in relationships between those involved in collaboration and partnership. But the predominant narrative is that of the emergence of organic processes of coordination. As Peters puts it:

> If the old governance approach creates a straw person of the unitary state as motivator of the action, the decentralised, fragmented approach of the new governance appears to have little to force the action. Something may emerge from the rather unguided interactions within all the networks, but it is not clear how this will happen, and there is perhaps too much faith in the self-organising and self-coordinating capacities of people. (Peters 2000: 45)

This is a generic weakness of the cybernetic and systems-based theories on which much of the writing on governance is based. While it is helpful to highlight the dispersal and fragmentation of power, this does not mean that it should disappear from the analysis.

A rather different perspective on power is offered by post-structuralist theory. Rather than debating whether the power of the state has been 'hollowed out', or dispersed through a plurality of agencies, this directs attention to the kinds of knowledge and power through which social activity is regulated and through which actors – citizens, workers, organisations – are constituted as self-disciplining subjects. Much of this theory is directed towards understanding the shifts associated with the rise of neoliberal political ideologies in the UK, the USA and elsewhere. The break-up of large bureaucracies, the introduction of market or quasi-market mechanisms into the delivery of services and the privatisation of many functions previously viewed as the responsibility of the state itself were accompanied by the development of new patterns of control directed towards the construction of 'self-regulating', autonomous actors. As Rose and Miller comment, 'relocating aspects of government in the private or voluntary sectors does not necessarily render them less governable' (1992: 200). Rather than the reduction of government promised by neo-liberal regimes, such changes can be understood as the dispersal of governmental power across new sites of action, augmented through new strategies and technologies: 'the complex of mundane programmes, calculations, techniques, apparatuses, documents and procedures through which authorities seek to embody and give effect to government ambitions' (Rose and Miller 1992: 175). Power is viewed as residing in plural agencies and processes:

> [The state] emerges as one segment of a much broader play of power relations involving professionals, bureaucracies, schools, families, leisure organisations and so forth. In Foucault's terms, the various institutions and practices of the state operate as part of a 'capillary' of relations in which power continually circulates and re-circulates. Accordingly, post-structural interest is as much directed to the local dole office as the central policy-making bureau, and to the doctor's surgery or social worker's office as the Departments of Health and Welfare. (Barnes et al. 1999: 8)

Different governance regimes are viewed as drawing on specific forms of political rationality. For example, in the Thatcher and Reagan years the neo-liberal theories of Hayek and others offered a form of knowledge and 'claim to truth' which displaced the rationalities of Keynesian economics and which underpinned the attempt to transform the state around market mechanisms. This was accompanied by the partial displacement of professional forms of knowledge and power by managerial forms of rationality and control. Post-structuralist theory illuminates the processes through which new forms of knowledge and power become linked to individual subjectivities:

> Government concerns not only practices of government but also practices of the self. To analyse government is to analyse those processes that try to shape, sculpt, mobilise and work through the choices, desires, aspirations, needs, wants and lifestyles of individuals and groups. . . . One of the points that is most interesting about this type of approach is the way it provides a language and a framework for thinking about the linkages between questions of government, authority and politics, and questions of identity, self and person. (Dean 1999: 12–13)

Claims to truth or rationality carry with them the capacity to constitute subjects: power is treated as productive. So, for example, the neo-liberal reforms of the 1980s were linked to productive forms of power which constituted subjects in new ways, with professionals recast as managers, and citizens recast as the consumers and customers of services. Such strategies were not necessarily successful and the outcomes of the reforms are still debated. But post-structuralist forms of theory are important to my analysis because of the way they direct attention beyond the state and the operation of formal political authority. They highlight the complex apparatuses and strategies involved in the construction of new regimes of governance. Such theories transcend the normative emphasis of much governance theory in that they focus on the modes of power underpinning new technologies, including those based on the apparent 'empowerment' of subjects to regulate themselves. They help to conceptualise the forms and flows of power involved in 'governing at a distance' and to disclose the multiplication of strategies. As such, they provide a sharp contrast with the normative view of the 'self-governing subject' or the 'self-regulating network' as autonomous social agents.

New Labour, new governance?

Governance, then, seeks to explain a whole series of realignments and offers a range of explanatory tools. The structure of this book is driven by a concern to bring these approaches together to explore the process of modernisation under the Labour government elected in 1997. This necessarily involves more than a descriptive account of what Labour has done, or how successful it has been in delivering its policies and promises. The literature on governance highlights important intellectual challenges:

- how to understand the processes of governing within and beyond the government;
- how to conceptualise the complexity of the patterns of relationship involved in both the policy process and in the delivery of services; and
- how to analyse the flows of influence and accountability in plural and fragmented systems.
- how to conceptualise the indirect forms of power which flow through and beyond the state itself.

Jessop talks about governance in terms of 'a shift in the centre of gravity around which policy cycles move' (1998a: 32). How far does new Labour represent such a shift? The different perspectives reviewed in this chapter can be used to suggest key issues for analysis: the making and delivery of public policy; the relationships between sectors; and the government's conception of its relationship with citizens, 'communities' and civil society. Subsequent chapters examine the processes through which the new government sought to steer, direct, lead and coordinate actors both within and beyond government, and across the public, private and voluntary sectors, in the struggle to deliver its political objectives. In doing so the book draws on governance both as a multi-stranded *narrative of change* and as a set of *theoretical approaches* to unravelling state/society interactions. Governance as a narrative of change argues that the state has adapted to external and internal challenges to its capacity to govern. It has done so by alternative or complementary strategies designed to coordinate and steer the making and delivery of public and social policy. The development of networks and partnerships as a mode of coordination reflects the emergence of new economic and social conditions and a number of problems which cannot be managed by top-down state planning or 'market mediated anarchy' (Jessop 1998a: 32). The shift to network modes of coordination is associated with more fundamental shifts in the public realm (fragmentation, complexity) and in the way in which the state seeks to govern public services (through steering rather than by exerting direct forms of control). This network prescription, as Stoker notes, in a rather utopian extract,

> . . . argues for the development of longer-term, non-hierarchical relationships which bring together service providers and users on the basis of trust, mutual understanding and a shared ethical or moral commitment. The emphasis is on empowering both providers and users so that they can work effectively in partnership to achieve shared goals. Quality in service delivery is a key goal. An interest in longer-term relational contracting is characteristic. (Stoker 1999: 3–4)

These arguments suggest a number of propositions about the kind of changes involved in a shift towards a new form of governance, captured in formulations such as from hierarchies and markets to networks; from a view of state power based on formal authority to one of the role of the state in coordinating, steering and influencing; from an interest in the actions of the state to an interest in the interplay of plural actors in both the shaping of policy (through policy networks) and the delivery of services (through partnerships).

The book seeks to identify how far new Labour represented a shift towards this conception of governance as it adapted to change and attempted to forge and sustain new political alliances. My aim is to examine the processes through which a new government sought to steer, direct, lead and coordinate actors both within and beyond government in the struggle to deliver its political objectives. Certainly Labour appeared to be engaged in a rather different process of state restructuring and transformation from those based on neo-liberal conceptions of the minimalist state under Thatcher. While the ideology of Thatcherism – at least in the later years – can be viewed as one which espoused markets and which denigrated bureaucracies (hierarchy) as wasteful and inefficient, that of new Labour promulgated a discourse of partnerships, participation, social inclusion and a pragmatic approach to the use of the market. Notions of reciprocity, inclusivity and partnership were all key ideas in new Labour's vocabulary, and implied the goal of establishing a more consensual basis for state/societal interaction. New forms of democratic practice, based on self-government through networks, partnerships, deliberative fora and associations in civil society (Hirst 2000), have powerful resonances with new

TABLE 1.1 *Governance shifts: propositions*

The literature suggests that we are witnessing:

1 A move away from hierarchy and competition as alternative models for delivering services towards networks and partnerships traversing the public, private and voluntary sectors.
2 A recognition of the blurring of boundaries and responsibilities for tackling social and economic issues.
3 The recognition and incorporation of policy networks into the process of governing.
4 The replacement of traditional models of command and control by 'governing at a distance'.
5 The development of more reflexive and responsive policy tools.
6 The role of government shifting to a focus on providing leadership, building partnerships, steering and coordinating, and providing system-wide integration and regulation.
7 The emergence of 'negotiated self-governance' in communities, cities and regions, based on new practices of coordinating activities through networks and partnerships.
8 The opening-up of decision-making to greater participation by the public.
9 Innovations in democratic practice as a response to the problem of the complexity and fragmentation of authority, and the challenges this presents to traditional democratic models.
10 A broadening of focus by government beyond institutional concerns to encompass the involvement of civil society in the process of governance.

Labour's normative discourse about inclusiveness, democratic renewal and public participation.

How far does this signify a shift towards governance through steering and coordinating rather than through direct forms of authority and control? To answer this question it is necessary to set out a rather tighter set of propositions about the shift from governing to governance, propositions which can then be examined in the light of emerging policy and practice. The argument that we are witnessing a shift from direct forms of governing to a process of governance exercised through a plurality of actors, sites and processes suggests an increasing reliance by government on informal forms of power and influence rather than formal authority. This has, according to the literature, a number of implications (see Table 1.1).

These propositions are set out to support my analysis of the actions and policies of the Labour government in the UK. I am not attempting to evaluate how far there might be evidence of an increase in new forms of governance (more participation, more partnerships, more collaboration, and so on). There is an emerging body of research on such issues (see, for example, the research conducted under the ESRC Local Governance programme, or Lowndes et al.'s research on public participation: Stoker 1999, 2000; Lowndes et al. 1998). My aims are more modest: to assess the policy framework of the Labour government in terms of its 'fit' with these governance propositions, and to explore issues and tensions which have arisen in the process of delivering its programme of modernisation. The propositions, then, are intended as a starting point for discussion of Labour's approach to governing, rather than as matters for empirical verification. Rather than questioning how much change or what kinds of change, my analysis sets out to explore the process of modernisation in a way which links political ideology, government policy and the process of implementation. The next chapter focuses on the dynamics of institutional change, and sets out a framework for mapping the interaction between different models of governance that might be found within the UK.

2 The dynamics of institutional change

> The institutional frameworks within which organisations are embedded
> may frequently contain quite divergent and contradictory pressures.
>
> (Clegg 1990: 154)

The previous chapter set out the governance narrative that describes a shift
away from old forms of governance based on hierarchies or markets
towards a new, network-based form of governance. This narrative presents
an over-simplified view of change in at least two respects. First, it tends to
over-read the extent and embeddedness of change and underestimate
important points of continuity with past regimes. So, for example, in
highlighting the prevalence of networks and partnerships in Labour's policy
approach, important aspects of its continued reliance on markets and
hierarchy may be overlooked. Secondly, narratives of change which imply a
general shift from the 'old' to the 'new' tend to tidy away some of the
complexity of the process (Lowndes 1999). Institutional change tends not to
occur through some organic and evolutionary process by which one regime
is steadily displaced by another. More typically, old and emergent regimes
interact, with different elements of the new and old being packaged and
repackaged, producing tensions and disjunctures as different sets of norms
and assumptions are overlaid on each other. In this chapter I suggest ways
in which this interaction might be conceptualised. I then set out a framework for mapping the multiple models of governance that coexist and
interact at the beginning of the twenty-first century in the UK.

Conceptualising change

'New institutional theory' highlights the importance of the formal and
informal rules, norms and conventions through which social action is
shaped. North defines institutions as:

> . . . the rules of the game in a society or, more formally, the humanly devised
> constraints that shape human interaction. In consequence they structure incen-
> tives in human exchange, whether political, social or economic. Institutional
> change shapes the way that societies evolve through time and hence is the key to
> understanding economic change. (North 1990: 3)

As well as the formal 'rules of the game', institutional theory stresses the
role of informal institutions, embedded in culture and tradition, through

which complexity may be simplified to smooth decision-making and action. Such rules and norms flow across organisational boundaries, and between different tiers of government. March and Olsen (1989) suggest that behaviour is shaped by 'logics of appropriateness', which are associated with norms and obligations rather than by rational calculations. They emphasise the continuity and stability of such norms, and highlight the difficulty of producing deliberate change. Efforts to restructure organisations, for example, are frequently deflected, diluted or absorbed so as to conform with prior norms and patterns of behaviour. Similarly, policy changes put in place by governments are mediated through, and possibly deflected by, deeply embedded norms and assumptions (see, for example, the study of the introduction of market testing in the UK civil service in the 1990s: Newman et al. 1998, 2000). While policies may be made and guidelines set, restructuring programmes put in place and incentives offered, governments are unable to exert much control over the combination of practices which are likely to result (DiMaggio and Powell 1991). However, although norms and customs cannot be changed by fiat, the introduction of radical change programmes tends to place new constraints on social action which, over time, influence patterns of decision-making on the ground.

There are many strands of argument and debate within new institutional theory, spanning political science, economics, sociology and organisational theory (see summaries in DiMaggio and Powell 1991; Lowndes 1996; Scott 1994). While the new institutional economics views institutions as the deliberate creation of instrumentally oriented individuals, sociological and organisational strands of institutional theory place more emphasis on the role of culture in shaping institutions (see especially Meyer and Rowan 1977). Change occurs as organisations seek to adapt to their environment by incorporating ideas about the proper way to go about things – 'logics of appropriateness' – in order to win external legitimacy. The adoption of new ideas may be undertaken as much to win external legitimacy as to achieve performance gains. This may result in a process of isomorphism, whereby organisations tend to adopt similar policies, structures and ideas. DiMaggio and Powell identify three forms of isomorphism. Coercive isomorphism occurs where the state obliges organisations to adopt certain practices, for example the current government's requirement that local authorities adopt one of three models for restructuring their political management processes. Mimetic isomorphism occurs where organisations voluntarily copy each other in order to be identified with prevailing norms of 'best practice' and so win external legitimacy. The adoption by organisations of quality accreditation schemes or any other of a host of management innovations might be viewed in this light. Normative isomorphism occurs as a result of professionally or occupationally derived norms. A classic example here might be the spread of a new form of clinical practice among health professionals. Normative isomorphism can also be used to help explain ways in which 'new' occupations – the Community Safety officer, the Youth Offending Team worker, the Best Value manager – develop norms about how best to inhabit their new roles, norms which gradually become institutionalised.

This notion of isomorphism adds a rather different perspective to conventional ideas about the relationship between policy and implementation. Organisations seeking to secure legitimacy may place great emphasis on changing their language and symbolic practices. The new language and symbols, however, may remain 'loosely coupled' to mainstream organisational practice. There may be loose coupling between formal and informal structures, between different organisational policies, and between policy and action (March and Olsen 1976; Weick 1976). For example, in the 1990s most public sector organisations adopted the language and technologies of strategic planning, though for many the result was the production of a document directed at external stakeholders and funders rather than a helpful guide to decision-making. They also adopted structures with clear demarcations between 'strategy' and 'operations', which were unsustainable in practice. Many areas of organisational policy – for example on equal opportunities – remained loosely coupled to organisational action. Currently many public sector organisations are adopting the language of modernisation, joined-up government, partnership, public consultation, and so on. But the link between structure (the institutional environment within which organisations operate) and agency (how they respond) is contingent. Clegg notes:

> Organisations are arenas in which some things will tend to hang together and be adopted by power-players as a bundle, while other forms of combination may be far less likely to occur as a coherent package, perhaps because they are less coherent or because the alliance which could make them so lacks a position in the field of power to be able to constitute the necessity of its choices. (Clegg 1990: 205)

This contingent relationship between organisations and their environments, and the interplay of power relations within organisations, suggest that there is likely to be considerable variation about which institutions are incorporated into organisational practice, and how deeply embedded they become.

Institutional theory, then, can illuminate some aspects of the process of change with which this book is concerned:

- the difficulty faced by governments seeking to introduce change which challenges institutionally embedded norms and practices;
- the capacity of organisations and groups to co-opt, absorb or deflect new initiatives;
- the processes of isomorphism through which organisations come to adopt new 'logics of appropriateness' from their environment;
- the stability of 'old' institutions (e.g. those associated with markets and hierarchies) alongside 'new' institutions (e.g. those based on networks and partnership); and
- the significance of culture in analyses of change.

This last point, however, suggests some of the limitations of the institutional approach. Cultural strands of institutional theory highlight the way in which institutions are formed out of theories, ideologies, discourses, prescriptions about how society should work (e.g. Meyer et al. 1994). But the theorisation of culture tends to be drawn from anthropological approaches which view culture as undifferentiated: societies or groups are viewed as having 'a' culture, conceptualised as a 'shared thought world' (e.g. Douglas 1987). Secondly, while the constitutive power of institutions to shape identities is recognised (e.g. Scott 1994), the individual is viewed as a unitary subject rather than as an actor discursively constituted within multiple and over-lapping discourses. Thirdly, cultural strands of institutional theory tend to overlook questions of power (but see Clegg 1990).

To understand the relationship between ideologies and discourses, the constitution of identity and social action it is necessary to turn to post-structuralist theory. I want to draw on one aspect of this – discourse theory – to illuminate the cultural dimensions of institutional change. Discourse refers to 'a framework of meanings which are historically produced in a particular culture at a particular time' (Watson 2000: 70) or 'a set of meanings, metaphors, representations, image, stories, statements and so on that in some way together produce a particular version of events' (Burr 1995: 48). Discourse theory views language, stories, metaphors and images not just as a means of communication but as inextricably linked to questions of power, social identity and patterns of relationship. As Fairclough expresses it:

> Discourse constitutes the social. . . . Three dimensions of the social are distinguished – knowledge, social relations, and social identity – and these correspond respectively to three main functions of language. . . . Discourse is shaped by relations of power, and invested with ideologies. (Fairclough 1992: 8)

Discourses are ways of organising knowledge, knowledge through which problems come to be defined in particular ways and through which particular solutions are privileged. For example, the new Labour discourse of 'social exclusion' is subtly different from the old social democratic discourse of poverty. It constructs its problem in terms of social and cultural processes (schooling, ill health, lack of access to training opportunities, possible racism) rather than in terms of lack of material resources. The solutions offered are quite different from the 'old' solutions (as we shall see in Chapter 8). A second example might be the shift in the discourse of consumerism that came to pervade public services during the 1980s and early 1990s. Recent developments within public services have incorporated the discourses of citizenship, community and public involvement alongside consumerism, signifying a partial shift in the way in which the relationships between organisations and the public are conceptualised and enacted.

We can begin to see, through these examples, how discourse as knowledge might be related to issues of power: both the power of the state to shape knowledges and practices, and the power of citizens, communities and the wider public to engage with state organisations. What matters is 'which people and institutions have the power to define the terms of the debate or the way in which the problem is to be understood' (Watson 2000: 70).

Discourses do not determine policy, but inform the way in which policy problems and solutions are conceived (Bacchi 1999). They may become institutionalised through state practice: 'Discourses shape and become institutionalised in social policies and the organisations through which they are carried out. This is not just a matter of the big policy ideas – the pressure to "do something about poverty" – but also the minute arrangements by which "something is done"' (Clarke and Cochrane 1998: 35). A focus on discourse, then, allows us to study shifts in language, practice and relations of power (Grant et al. 1998). Discourses offer particular forms of identity for social actors and provide legitimacy for specific kinds of decision-making. A classic example here is the discourse of managerialism which reordered relationships within public service organisations in the 1980s and 1990s, which offered new kinds of identity for professionals and bureaucrats, and which prioritised decision-making based on criteria of organisational efficiency and success (Newman 1998b). As Chapter 4 will argue, the election of a Labour government produced a significant shift in public policy discourses, with the articulation of new discourses – joined-up government, social exclusion, evidence-based policy, best value, public involvement and a bundle of others – interacting with the older discourses of managerialism, efficiency, quality and consumerism. A shift in discourse produces new logics of appropriate action which are disseminated through policy networks, become embedded in government guidelines and legislation and are institutionalised through practices such as inspection and audit regimes. New discursive practices are adopted by organisations in order to establish or retain legitimacy in a changing policy climate. These in turn produce shifts in power and authority within organisations. Different discourses are associated with different organisational regimes which constitute actors in particular ways, which preference particular forms of judgement and which are based on particular forms of power and knowledge (Clarke and Newman 1997: Chapter 4; Newman 1998b).

The focus on discourses, then, enables us to assess governance as a complex, contested domain: one in which multiple forms of knowledge and power interact, and in which multiple narratives, assumptions and expectations shape social action and guide decision-making. Different narratives, assumptions and expectations are likely to coexist, with more or less discomfort, in any governance regime. So, as noted above, markets did not replace hierarchies in the 1980s and 1990s. They were superimposed on them, with considerable discomfort for those operating across the boundaries of these different models of governance (for example, operating within bureaucratic norms of probity and accountability while at the same time taking risks to secure the maximum efficiencies offered in the market place). The coexistence of multiple models of governance creates particularly sharp tensions during programmes of reform as deeply embedded institutional norms and rules are challenged by new logics of appropriate action, but no new 'rules of the game' have yet been established in practice. This is precisely the situation which prefigured and followed the election of the 1997 Labour government, where new ideologies (e.g. the Third Way) were promulgated, new discourses (e.g. 'joined-up government' or 'social exclusion') were articulated and a range of new policies was promised. Many of these challenged established norms and practices, creating tensions in the process of institutional change.

Exploring tensions in the process of change

Rhodes (1997) acknowledges the presence of 'hybrid' forms of governance which combine elements of the old and new. This notion of hybridity is helpful but does not fully capture the ways in which different forms of coordination and control interact, nor illuminate possible tensions between them. In *The Managerial State* (Clarke and Newman 1997) we argued that the interaction between bureau-professional regimes and new managerial regimes produced a field of tensions rather than a hybrid form of coordination. Each regime was associated with particular forms of power (administrative, professional, managerial) which gave rise to particular criteria of decision-making and logics of appropriate action (Clarke and Newman 1997: Chapters 2 and 5). The interaction between these produced conflicting demands and expectations on decision-makers and staff. These tensions were partly resolved through processes of co-option, displacement, subordination and appropriation. That is, managerialism sometimes displaced other regimes, but more usually subordinated other forms of judgement and decision-making to the economic calculus of managerialism (Mackintosh 1997). Sometimes managerialism co-opted the norms and values of other regimes, constructing articulations between professional concerns and those of managerialism (for example, translating the professional's concern for client well being into the rubric of quality management). Sometimes, however, the discourse of managerialism itself was appropriated by managers, front-line staff and even users to pursue goals and interests that conflicted with managerial norms.

The rise of New Public Management (NPM), then, led not to a complete closure around a new paradigm but to an 'unstable settlement' between bureau-professional power and the new managerialism (Clarke and Newman 1997: Chapter 8). Significant tensions were created between bureaucratic and consumerist models of accountability, between political centralisation and managerial devolution, and between older, neo-Taylorist styles of management and the new managerial focus on culture, excellence and entrepreneurship (Newman 2000a). Managers in the public domain did not have an unfettered 'right to manage', free from political interference, because of the nature of accountability and the political process itself. The most famous example of the limits to the supposedly devolved power of managers in Next Step Agencies arose when the then Home Secretary came into direct conflict with the then head of the Prison Service (Lewis 1997). Many of the dilemmas which organisations had to work with stemmed from oscillations between different political imperatives, or from contradictory performance measures flowing from different government departments. Tensions also arose from the incomplete closure around the goals and values underpinning NPM. Many workers expressed unease at what they felt to be the erosion of public service and professional values. Others, however, welcomed the 'modernising' thrust of change, viewing it as a source of innovation and a potential challenge to the paternalism, protectionism and parochialism that had characterised the 'old' public sector. This kind of analysis can be applied to current processes of change, producing an account of change as dynamic and contested rather than as linear or evolutionary.

Some of the governance literature acknowledges tensions in the inter-action between 'old' and 'new' approaches. For example, Rhodes notes that fragmentation and centralisation coexist: 'There is a persistent tension between the wish for authoritative action on the one hand and dependence on the compliance and actions of others' (Rhodes 1997: 15). Pierre suggests that 'emerging forms of governance should be seen as alternative expressions of the collective interest which do not replace but supplement the pursuit of collective interests through traditional, institutional channels (Pierre 2000: 3). That is, the process of realigning and dispersing state power is likely to interact with, rather than simply displace, other forms of power and control. The interesting question then becomes how do different processes – of centralisation and dispersal, of enabling and controlling, of loosening and tightening – coexist, in what relationship, and what might the consequences be?

Jessop (2000) explores such questions in his analysis of economic development partnerships which, he argues, are faced with a series of strategic dilemmas or tensions: between competition and collaboration; between openness and closure; between governance and flexibility; and between accountability and efficiency. Later chapters of this book will suggest that parallel sets of dilemmas or tensions are to be found in attempts to develop more 'inclusive' or 'joined-up' forms of policy-making, in the programme of modernisation for mainstream public services, in initiatives designed to enhance public participation and in the modernisation of central and local government. Different policies and initiatives give rise to different sets of imperatives, rules and norms, some of which are likely to conflict. The way in which organisations, individuals or groups seek to balance competing pressures or resolve the dilemmas they face is an important aspect of institutional change. The effects of change programmes do not flow directly from the intentions of those designing modernisation programmes or specific policy initiatives, but from the way in which competing pressures are resolved on the ground. Tensions and dilemmas, then, are not of mere academic interest but provide the key to understanding the lived experience of public sector staff and the dynamics of institutional change, processes which are of central concern in this book.

Mapping models of governance

This section develops a framework for mapping the potential disjunctures between different models of governance. There are a number of approaches to mapping different cultural values and practices, and exploring the tensions between them. For example, Dunleavy and Hood (1994) and Hood (1998) elaborate a 'grid/group' metaphor through which issues in public management and models of regulation in the public sector can be analysed. A rather different approach, and one on which I draw in this book, is based on the work of Robert Quinn (1988). Quinn developed a framework for mapping the contradictions of organisational life, identifying four different models or approaches: the rational goal approach, the developmental or open systems approach, the consensual or team approach, and the hierarchical or internal process approach. These can be adapted to suggest different models of governance, each with its characteristic form of power and authority, pattern of relationships and assumptions about change.

In Figure 2.1 the models are mapped on to a framework which represents two dimensions of difference. The vertical axis represents the degree to which power is centralised or decentralised, with high centralisation corresponding to the structural integration of governance arrangements and high decentralisation with strong elements of differentiation with the governance system. Few aspects of governance belong at one extreme or another: a more usual pattern is one of oscillation between these extremes, with the decentralisation of some forms of power (e.g. the management of schools) matched by the recentralisation of others (e.g. control over the curriculum). The horizontal axis represents the orientation towards change. Governance arrangements may be oriented towards the creation of continuity, order, stability and sustainability, or towards bringing about innovation in order to respond to new economic pressures or shifting public expectations. The intersection of these two axes produces four models of governance.

The *hierarchical model* is oriented towards predictability, control and accountability. It corresponds to the much-discredited form of governance in which the state exerts direct control over policy development and implementation through bureaucratic hierarchies. This model is characterised by bureaucratic power and vertical patterns of relationships flowing up and down hierarchies. Change is slow, brought about by altering legislation, rewriting the rules or guidelines, or producing new standards and procedures, all cascading down the vertical hierarchies of the governance system. Although delivering low flexibility, this model offers the strongest possibility of accountability, with formal accountability flowing upwards to democratic bodies. Accountability for process – for example probity of expenditure and decision-making procedures – tends to be high. The model

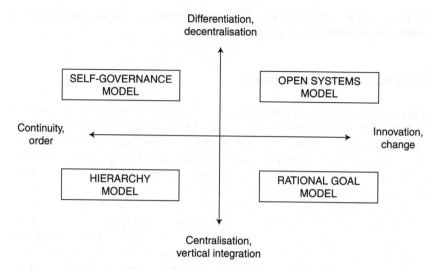

FIGURE 2.1   *Models of governance*

reflects the classic features of bureaucracy, being process-oriented (what matters is doing things correctly or properly) and oriented towards continuity rather than change. It values security, order, standardisation and the minimisation of risk. Policy development and implementation are functionally differentiated and formalised, and once policy is made there is little scope for feedback or adjustment during the implementation process. Government will tend to specify in detail the structures and processes through which policies are to be implemented. New problems (or problems given more political priority than in the past) are likely to be met by the setting-up of new structures or the establishment of new organisations.

The *rational goal model* reflects a focus on shorter time lines and the attempt to maximise outputs. Power is dispersed across a wide range of agencies rather than concentrated in monolithic hierarchies. This model is characterised by managerial, rather than bureaucratic, power. Change is brought about by altering incentives, with rewards (or at least the absence of penalties) attached to the delivery of targets and policy goals. Responsibility for delivering goals and targets is devolved to local managers who are held to account through contractual or quasi-contractual relationships with government (gaining resources or organisational legitimacy in return for performance). Despite this apparent devolution, this model of governance reflects a centralised approach with goals and targets cascading from government, against which performance is tightly monitored, inspected and audited. Policy is based on the assumption that organisations will behave as rational actors, responding to incentives such as competitive funding, the publication of league tables, or the promise of extra freedoms or flexibilities for good performance. This model is cross-cut by a mix of vertical and horizontal relationships. However, horizontal relationships tend to be short-term and pragmatic, with collaboration as a calculated means of competing more effectively (e.g. in the process of bidding for funds under specific government programmes). Accountability for outputs is high, linked to performance-monitoring and inspection, but accountability for detailed expenditure and the probity of decision-making would be lower than in the hierarchy model. The model is characterised by a strong means–ends orientation and a pragmatic, instrumental approach. It reflects many of the characteristics of the New Public Management with its emphasis on efficiency, economic rationalism and managerial authority.

The *open systems model* is oriented towards network forms of interaction and iterative processes of adaptation. Power is dispersed and fluid, based on the interdependence of actors on the resources of others to pursue their goals. Relationships are dynamic, constantly being reshaped to respond to new challenges or demands. The focus of action is experimentation and innovation. This model encompasses multiple inputs and 'reflexive' processes of development in which decisions can be adjusted in the course of new information. The system both influences and is influenced by the environment. It is fluid, fast and highly responsive. In terms of governance theory, this approach corresponds most closely to the 'network' model of governance described by Rhodes, Stoker, Kooiman and others (see Chapter 1). Networks cut across organisational boundaries, weave in and out of hierarchies and are highly dynamic. Government might attempt to steer or influence action, but it is unable to exert direct control. Differentiation is promoted through the decentralisation of power, enabling experimentation and innovation. In this model, the boundary between policy and implementation becomes more fluid, allowing feedback and learning during the policy cycle. Accountability is low but sustainability high. Change is accomplished by autopoeisis: through self-organisation and self-steering rather than as a result of external intervention (Kickert 1993; Kooiman 2000).

The *self-governance model* is oriented towards long time lines, focusing on building sustainability by fostering relationships of interdependence and reciprocity. It acknowledges the role of civil society in governance, highlighting the relationship between state and citizen rather than limiting notions of governance to the actions of the state. Governments, including the current Labour government in the UK, may seek to work in 'partnership' with citizens, for example to draw them in as co-producers of health and welfare services, or as partners in the development of sustainable solutions to social problems. They may also attempt to create social integration by fostering civic, familial and communitarian values that emphasise mutual responsibility. They may seek to extend their legitimacy by creating a strong consensus for their political programme by inviting the public to participate in decision-making as citizens or as the users of services. The model spans a range of conceptions of the relationship between state and citizen, from a focus on the ideological role of the state in producing social integration and cohesion to a focus on citizens and communities as agents of political change. It encompasses models of democratic innovation. These include participative and direct democracy, and what Hirst (1994) terms 'associational' democracy in which civil society takes on functions previously performed by the state.

Governments in liberal democracies tend to operate across all four quadrants, and the current Labour government has policy approaches that correspond to each model. However, each is based on distinctive values and assumptions, definitions of 'effectiveness', constructions of the problems to be solved, and institutionalised norms and expectations. These are often in conflict. Let us take as an example the range of governance models that might be involved in tackling social exclusion or the regeneration of 'deprived' communities. Each model offers a different lens through which problems would be defined and is characterised by different forms of power in the solutions generated. The *hierarchy model* would tend to construct the issue as a series of separate problems – housing, employment, etc. – refracted through the functional lenses of different government departments, each cascading guidelines for action down through existing hierarchies. Where the need for working in partnership was identified, new structures would tend to be established, institutionalising any emergent partnerships in order to ensure proper controls and accountabilities. The *rational goal model* would tend to break the problem of social exclusion or 'deprived' communities down into more manageable chunks (e.g. school truancy, rough sleepers). Government would set goals, but responsibility for acting would be devolved to the local or regional level, with funding linked to targets and output measures. Where the need for working in partnership was identified, this would be fostered through measures such as competitive bidding for resources, with bids being required to demonstrate evidence of partner involvement.

The *open systems model* would tend to view the problem in a holistic way and focus on delivering longer-term outcomes. Actions would flow from self-generated local or regional networks of groups, agencies and companies with a mutual interest in the regeneration of the area or in overcoming social exclusion, each dependent on the resources of others to achieve its own goals. The *self-governance model* would, following Labour's concept of social exclusion, be closely linked to communitarian ideas, with an emphasis on delivering sustainable solutions by developing the capacity of communities to solve their own problems. Mainstream agencies operating in localities would be expected to establish consensus and local 'ownership' around regeneration goals through persuasion, influence and commitment-building, with some devolution of power to community actors. Communities (of locality, interest or identity) might define the problem rather differently, not in terms of capacity-building but as the need for greater devolution of power and resources to self-managing groups or associations, or as the need for social rights and justice for groups stigmatised by government policies on deprivation or social exclusion. Traces of this model can be found in the reports of the Social Exclusion Unit and in initiatives such as the Sure Start programme (designed to address the social and health needs of young children and families), or the National Strategy for Neighbourhood Renewal. Although these programmes also draw on the rational goal and open systems models, there is a strong emphasis on community capacity, social entrepreneurship and on drawing community actors into self-help or partnership-based initiatives.

Each model offers specific definitions of the problems to be addressed and different sets of assumptions about the nature of change. This means that the models are not readily compatible. Taking a pinch of one model (say the rational goal model) and adding a soupçon of another (say self-governance) will not deliver a coherent strategy since the logics of appropriate action generated by one may well undermine the requirements of the other. The initiatives linked to Labour's modernisation programme tend to draw on a mix of approaches – delegation *and* central control, long-term capacity-building *and* short-term targets – producing tensions in the process of institutional change. The most significant lines of tension arise between the diagonally opposite quadrants of the model. One operates between maximising outputs (rational goal model) on the one hand and building sustainability (self-governance model) on the other since rational practices tend not to generate the inclusive and flexible approaches required to engage citizens and communities in the long term. For example, the enhancement of managerial power is not readily compatible with the devolution of power to associations and communities. A second major line of tension operates between the consolidation and continuity associated with hierarchy on the one hand, and the adaptive, dynamic and outward-oriented focus of the open systems approach. In the former, rules and procedures – how things are done – matter a great deal, while in the latter, fluidity, flexibility and experimentation are valued. The hierarchy model stresses proper procedures in order to ensure accountability, while the open systems model works through fluid networks where accountability is hard to pin down.

The dynamics of change

An important feature of the framework in Figure 2.2 is that it is dynamic. Each quadrant has its own pulls that act as pressure on the other models. For example, in the *open systems model* the pull is towards flexibility, expansion and adaptation. This model pulls those in the lower quadrants to loosen control in order to foster the greater degrees of adaptation required by growing complexity, diversity and dynamic change. Concepts of the 'learning organisation', 'holistic government' and of the 'network organisation', derived from this model of governance, have been incorporated into managerial discourse as espoused frameworks for delivering enhanced performance. The imperatives of 'whole systems' approaches to governance and the current focus on the delivery of longer-term outcomes are leading to some adaptations of the techniques of rational management (e.g. the

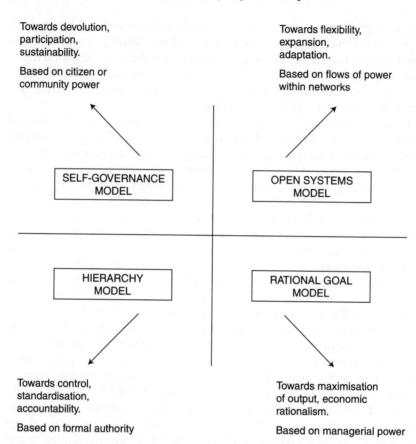

Towards devolution,
participation,
sustainability.

Based on citizen or
community power

Towards flexibility,
expansion,
adaptation.

Based on flows of power
within networks

SELF-GOVERNANCE
MODEL

OPEN SYSTEMS
MODEL

HIERARCHY
MODEL

RATIONAL GOAL
MODEL

Towards control,
standardisation,
accountability.

Based on formal authority

Towards maximisation
of output, economic
rationalism.

Based on managerial power

FIGURE 2.2 *The dynamics of change*

development of cross-cutting performance indicators and outcome-based evaluation tools). At the same time, the fluidity of the open systems model is constrained by demands for accountability which pull it back towards hierarchy, and by requirements for funding support from the state or from European bodies which exert pulls towards the rational goal model. Despite these pulls, however, the models cannot be collapsed into a single model of governance: each is based on a characteristic mode of power and distinctive logic of appropriate action.

Rather than a single governance narrative of a shift to networks and partnerships, this chapter has suggested that governance comprises multiple and conflicting strands. It involves simultaneous upward and downward flows of power. More significantly, it is constituted by disparate forms of power/knowledge. Some are vested in the formal powers of the state (including authority-based and coercive power). Some are embodied in managerialism as a means of coordinating a dispersed field of action. Some flow in and between organisations as they negotiate relationships of competition, collaboration and interdependence. Some spring from social and political action as the relationship between state and civil society is reshaped under new conditions. The power of government is constantly challenged by actors in state and non-state agencies seeking to enlarge managerial power or to test the limits of institutionally embedded norms and regulations. State power is also confronted by pulls towards greater rights and freedoms by social and political actors. These confrontations can be viewed as a struggle between autonomy and incorporation. Governance power involves cultural and ideological forms of influence overlaid on the apparently rational and technical focus of public policy discourse.

While governance in liberal democracies is always likely to be characterised by multiple and potentially conflicting models, my concern in this book is with the ways in which a specific government – 'new Labour' – has attempted to shift the point of balance between models. Its distinctive emphasis on devolution, partnership, policy evaluation, long-term capacity-building, public participation and democratic renewal suggests an emphasis on the open system and self-governance models. However, this emphasis is cross-cut by residues of, and even an intensification of, other styles of governance. In subsequent chapters my analysis of change is deliberately multi-faceted rather than linear. Different elements of policy and practice are overlaid on each other in complex ways. New elements of policy interact with institutionalised norms and practices established under earlier administrations, producing struggles between old and new ways of working and problems for a government determined to deliver fast and visible change to satisfy the electorate and secure re-election. All of this produces tensions in the process of institutional change and dilemmas for those working in public service organisations. The framework for exploring the dynamics of change set out here is revisited in later chapters to explore specific elements of the modernisation programme.

First, however, I want to explore the political settlement that new Labour has attempted to construct around discourses of the 'Third Way' and 'Modernisation'. Governance cannot be viewed as a free-floating phenomenon, understood simply through the lens of universal trends such as globalisation or growing social complexity. The approach to governance that can be found at a specific time, in a specific place, has to be understood in the context of particular political conjunctures. The next chapter explores the political project of new Labour and the formation of new ideologies and discourses through which the public realm, and the process of change, is symbolically constituted.

3 The Third Way: modernising social democracy

Modernisation is an updated version of the idea of progress, but now framed more as necessity than as triumphal march.

(Rustin 1999b: 93)

The image of a Third Way was used to mark out Labour's departure from the politics of the social democratic state, signifying a reconfiguration of relationships between economy and state, public and private, government and people. Modernisation was a label attached to a wide range of institutional reforms, including those of government, party and the political process itself. This chapter seeks to unravel how each of these discourses worked both to establish the *necessity* of change and to offer a *particular programme* of change which excluded alternative political possibilities in the 1997 Labour administration.

Constructing the Third Way

The politics of new Labour reflected an attempt across much of Western Europe and in the USA to forge a new political settlement fitted to the new conditions of a global economy but attentive to the importance of social cohesion. Its political position was marked out as distinct from the social and political ideologies of the new right, but also recognised the challenges faced by social democratic governments. It had strong associations with the 'new' governance outlined in Chapter 1, being linked to indirect, rather than direct, forms of state control:

The Third Way suggests that it is possible to combine social solidarity with a dynamic economy, and this is a goal contemporary social democrats should strive for. To pursue it, we will need less national government, less central government, but greater governance over local processes. (D'Alema, Italian Prime Minister, cited in Giddens 2000: 5)

The Third Way is commonly linked to the US Democratic Party in the Clinton era (Corera 1998), not least as a result of the dialogue on Third Way politics held in Washington in April 1999. But it can also be located in political debates in Europe about the future of social democratic parties.

Jospin, Prime Minister of France, argued that there was a need to wrest the idea of modernity away from the dominance of new right thinking, and to set out a new, explicitly socialist form of politics based on the regulation of economic policy in a globalised world, state-led measures to combat unemployment, equality of opportunity and other principles:

> The illusions of the neo-liberals have been shed. Social democracy has found new leaders and has started to rebuild its political identity. This work is far from complete, but I am confident about its outcome. Part of it is being carried out at a European level, as is only logical: for socialism is a European idea, born in Europe and shaped by European thinkers. (Jospin 1998: 5)

In a speech to party colleagues in October 2000, Gerhard Schroeder, the German Chancellor, explicitly linked German social democracy to a version of the Third Way. He identified the central task facing his party as 'to find a place for social democratic and government policy in the triangle represented by the market, civil society and the state' (quoted in *The Guardian*, 20.10.00: 17). However, the trajectories of reform in continental Western Europe and the UK showed important differences. The political context of the UK – the dominance of class politics, the rise of Thatcherism, the conflict between the state and trades unions in the 1980s, and the long failure of Labour to gain electoral success – shaped Labour's attempt to forge a new political settlement. Here, the Third Way can be viewed as an attempt to carve out a territory which distanced 'new' from 'old' Labour while rejecting the worst excesses of the neo-liberal politics of the 'new right' (Driver and Martell 1997, 1998, 1999; Glennerster 1999; Hay 1999; Perryman 1996; Powell 1999; Rustin 1999a). Driver and Martell highlight the negative or relational characteristics of the Third Way in which the rejection of the past was more significant than the elaboration of the future. The idea of a Third Way exaggerates the newness of new Labour while downplaying continuities with both the 'old left' and with Conservative policy-making in the 1980s and 1990s – 'except of course where it suits New Labour to appear "tough", on inflation or trade unions, for example' (Driver and Martell 1999: 5). This relational approach is also central to the writings of Giddens, a sociologist whose work is closely associated with the genesis of Labour thinking. He presented the Third Way as transcending the ideologies of both the old left and the new right (see Table 3.1).

Giddens argued that distinctions between left and right were unhelpful in addressing contemporary problems, and that social democratic parties needed to transcend old ideologies in order to address 'the anxieties that worry ordinary citizens' (Giddens 2000: 5) – anxieties such as crime and family breakdown, issues on which the 'old' left was viewed as weak. The Third Way, he suggested, differed from the 'old' left in its emphasis on the modernisation of the welfare state, but also from neo-liberalism in its emphasis on social investment and the need to build a flourishing civil society. Civil society, government and the economy were viewed as

TABLE 3.1 *The Third Way*

Social democracy (the old left)	Neo-liberalism (the new right)	Third Way (the centre left)
Class politics of the left.	Class politics of the right.	Modernising movement of the centre.
Old mixed economy.	Market fundamentalism.	New mixed economy.
Corporatism: state dominates over civil society.	Minimal state.	New democratic state.
Internationalism.	Conservative nation.	Cosmopolitan nation.
Strong welfare state, protecting from 'cradle to grave'.	Welfare safety net.	Social investment state.

Source: Giddens 1998b: 18.

interdependent. The importance of sustaining the family, re-invigorating community, supporting voluntary and charitable activity and overcoming exclusion were linked to economic as well as moral arguments. This meant constraining the power of the market and its fragmenting effects, but also constraining the power of government. The old 'nanny state' was to be eradicated by building 'responsible citizens', willing to take charge of their own fortunes and take up the new opportunities offered rather than expecting continued dependency on the state. The new politics was to be constructed around a new social contract that emphasised rights as well as responsibilities.

Citizens and welfare were positioned within a super-ordinate economic discourse. People and communities became 'capital (human and social)' central to economic success (Giddens 2000: 52). Education became a form of 'investment' in the future. Equality was reconstructed as equality of access to education and employment opportunities. The welfare state was reconceptualised as a 'social investment state'. While economy, government and civil society appeared as equivalent in Giddens's trio of 'elements of power', the economy took on a pre-eminent importance because of the need to reposition Britain in the global economy. Traditional left values and commitments – about citizenship, welfare and society – were re-articulated within, but subordinated to, a globalised economic discourse.

Conceptions of a Third Way as transcending old ideologies and marking out a new political terrain were used extensively by Blair and others to distinguish new Labour from the positions it was displacing. Labour's approach was delineated against narratives of past failure in both political speeches and in early consultation documents and policy proposals: 'Our task today is not to fight old battles but to show that there is a Third Way, a way of marrying together an open, competitive and successful economy with a just, decent and humane society' (Blair's speech to a meeting of the European Socialists conference in Malmo, Sweden, June 1997). Such constructions were frequent in early policy documents of the Labour government. For example in *The New NHS: Modern – Dependable* (1997), the Third Way was used to define Labour's programme of reform against two failed pasts:

> In paving the way for the new NHS the Government is committed to building on what has worked but discarding what has failed. There will be no return to the old centralised command and control systems of the 1970s. That approach stifled innovation and put the needs of institutions ahead of the needs of patients. But nor will there be a continuation of the divisive internal market system of the 1990s. That approach which was intended to make the NHS more efficient ended up fragmenting decision making and distorting incentives to such an extent that unfairness and bureaucracy became its defining features.
>
> Instead there will be a 'Third Way' of running the NHS – a system based on partnership and driven by performance. . . . It will be neither the model from the late 1970s nor the model from the early 1990s. It will be a new model for a new century. (Department of Health 1997: 10–11)

The idea of the Third Way as transcending the old alternatives of state and market was not the only theme. This document also contrasts centralised command with devolved responsibility:

> Health Authorities will devolve responsibility for direct commissioning of services to new Primary Care Groups as soon as they are able to take on this task. Such an approach provides a Third Way between stifling top-down command and control on the one hand, and a random and wasteful grassroots free-for-all on the other. This Third Way builds on the successes that commissioning groups and fund-holders have achieved over recent years. (Department of Health 1997: 27)

These examples show how this White Paper constructed its own context, narrating past failures in order to create the space for the Third Way. The failures of hierarchical governing – 'stifling top-down control' – were juxtaposed against the failures of the internal market, and contrasted with the successes of a more devolved approach based in part on networks (primary care commissioning groups). A later policy document on health, *Our Healthier Nation: A Contract for Health* (1998a), used the idea of a Third Way slightly differently, identifying other failed, or at least discredited, positions:

> To achieve these aims, the Government is setting out a Third Way between the old extremes of individual victim blaming on the one hand and nanny state social engineering on the other. . . . Our Third Way is a national contract for better health. Under this contract, the Government, local communities, and individuals will join in partnership to improve all our health.
>
> In the past, arguments about health ranged between two extremes – individual victim blaming on the one hand and nanny state social engineering on the other. The broad majority who just wanted a normal healthy life for themselves and

their families were ignored. In a modern society these old positions must become obsolete. Health is not about blame, but about opportunity and responsibility. Everyone has a part to play – Government, national organisations, local services, communities, families and individuals. Our Healthier Nation sets out a Third Way of tackling the problems of ill health that our country faces. (Department of Health, 1998a: 5, 28)

These two positions are related to, but not the same as, the state/market distinction made above. They are identifiable as political positions on health policy: the 'nanny state' (itself a term appropriated from neo-liberal ideology) being associated with 'old' Labour, while 'victim blaming' is identified with the new right. So the Third Way represented 'progress' beyond these old politics but also stood for moderateness, in contrast with the extremism of the other two positions. Their extremism is registered by the way that they ignored the 'broad majority who just wanted a normal and healthy life for themselves and their families'. Modernisation and moderation went hand in hand in Labour's vision of reform, embodying a non-ideological, pragmatic approach to the use of markets and an emphasis on the language of 'partnerships' and new contractual forms.

The Third Way was also used to delineate early thinking on welfare reform. The prime minister set out the approach in his introduction to the 1998 Green Paper, framing the identification of two flawed alternatives between which a new route must be constructed:

> We must return to first principles and ask what we want the welfare state to achieve. This is the question this Green Paper seeks to answer. In essence, it describes a Third Way: not dismantling welfare, leaving it simply as a low-grade safety net for the destitute; nor keeping it unreformed and under-performing; but reforming it on the basis of a new contract between citizen and state, where we keep a welfare state from which we all benefit, but on terms that are fair and clear. (Prime Minister's introduction, Department of Social Security 1998: iv)

The Green Paper delineated alternative welfare futures for the UK:

> The welfare state now faces a choice of three futures:
>
> - a privatised future with the welfare state becoming a residual safety net for the poorest and most marginalised; or
> - the status quo but with more generous and costly benefits; or
> - the Government's Third Way – promoting opportunity instead of dependence, with the welfare state for the broad mass of people, but in new ways to fit the modern world. (Department of Social Security 1998: 2)

The Third Way functioned at two levels in these statements. The first involved the construction of specific sets of old/extreme/failed alternative views, choices or policies. These were represented as unreasonable, unrealistic or unlikely possibilities. The Third Way is thus produced as the only viable or reasonable political option. The second level, however, implicitly referenced the wider realm of political differentiation: neither old Labour nor new right; neither the state nor the market. This newness was, of course, how new Labour represents itself. Freed from the burdens of ideologies of right and left (constructed as 'extreme' or 'dogmatic'), it could proceed pragmatically and popularly. The Third Way thus acted as a framing device through which the discursive field of welfare policy was ordered and organised in the pursuit of a dominant position for the new Labour programme. The emphasis was on a new *contract* between citizen and state appropriate for a *modern* world, themes which will be developed further in Chapters 8 and 9.

Many have questioned how far the Third Way represented a distinctive political programme or policy direction, and this book continues that debate. However, examining the Third Way as discourse shows that its practical function was to define the impossibility of alternatives, rather than to identify a specific programme of reform. How did it do this? Many formulations of the Third Way were expressed as a 'both'/'and' form of linguistic structure, as in 'fairness and enterprise', 'rights and responsibilities'. In his pamphlet for the Institute of Public Policy Research, Blair set out a number of oppositions that the Third Way sought to reconcile:

> My vision for the twenty-first century is of a popular politics reconciling themes which in the past have wrongly been regarded as antagonistic – patriotism *and* internationalism; rights *and* responsibilities; the promotion of enterprise *and* the attack on poverty and discrimination. (Blair, 1998a: 1, original emphasis)

Fairclough (2000) terms this the 'language of reconciliation' in which seemingly oppositional values are magically resolved. He provides a cogent analysis and critique of the discourse, including a commentary on the way in which the social democratic terms – in the above quotation 'internationalism', 'rights' and the 'attack on poverty and discrimination' – went through subtle shifts of meaning in the process of being coupled with a term from the neo-liberal lexicon.

The Third Way was deliberately a concept capable of accommodating a range of views and policy proposals. White (1998) notes two important lines of division within the Third Way, one between 'leftists' and 'centrist' views of opportunity and equality, and another between 'liberal' and 'communitarian' conceptions of civic responsibility. As Labour's policy programme developed, it became clear that left/liberal conceptions had been marginalised. Critiques from the left highlighted the failure to break with neo-liberal economic policies, the marginalisation of questions of social justice, the conservatism on issues such as crime and the family, and the way in which the Third Way was constructed to appeal to 'middle England' (Coote 2000; Hall 1998; McLaughlin and Muncie 2000; see also Chapters 8 and 9 of this volume). A rather different set of critiques concern the difficulty – or impossibility – of transcending the politics of left and right (Dahrendorf 1999; Mouffe 1998). Jospin was scathing about the 'politics of in-betweenism' that characterise such formulations of the Third Way:

> If the Third Way lies between communism and capitalism, it is merely a new name for democratic socialism peculiar to the British. If, on the other hand, the Third way involves finding a middle way between social democracy and neo-liberalism, then this approach is not mine. As I have already argued, there is no longer a role for such a politics of 'in-betweenism'. (Jospin 1998: 4–5)

Dahrendorf has argued that the Third Way was an unsuccessful attempt to develop a 'big idea' for our times, an attempt which spoke of the need for hard choices but then avoided them by trying to please everyone (Dahrendorf 1999). Social policy analysts such as Lister (1998) and Williams (1999) have suggested that the framing of welfare reform in this context has served to displace a whole set of challenges to the welfare state that sought expansive transformations (in rights, access, quality of benefits and services, participation and so on) into the category of 'old thinking'. The Third Way was discursively constructed in opposition to the class politics of the old left, obscuring, denying or selectively appropriating other forms of politics arising out of the 'new social movements' of feminism, anti-racism and gay liberation (Rustin 1999a; see also Chapter 9 of this volume). The Third Way, then, can be viewed not as a coherent political programme but as a discursive strategy that aimed to build new coalitions and establish a consensus around new Labour as a political party and government. While broad enough to draw in a wide range of interests from which a new political coalition might be built, it specifically excludes alternative political responses to the 'failed pasts' of both social democracy and neo-liberalism. It was a discourse characterising a particular political moment but remained important in Blair's presentation of Labour's approach in the run up to the 2001 election (Blair, 2001).

Modernisation: putting the 'new' into new Labour?

The Third Way attempted to forge a new political settlement by drawing selectively on fragments and components of the old, and reconfiguring these through the prisms of a modernised economy, a modern public service and a modern people. It is important to view modernisation as a *strategy* which was embedded in a particular political project rather than working towards a clearly defined end state termed 'modernity' – a specific cultural form or historical period giving way, some would argue, to post-modern forms in the late twentieth century. Modernisation did not of course begin with the Labour administration in the UK – previous cycles of reform, going back to the introduction of universal suffrage or to the Northcote–Trevalyn reforms of the civil service, can be seen as attempts to modernise the British state and its institutions. Cochrane (2000) identifies three separate phases of modernisation since the 1960s. The first – modernisation as 'big business' (1965–75) – restructured the welfare state in the image of big private sector corporations. Modernisation in this phase was based on a belief in the value of technical expertise and state planning. The organs of the welfare state were restructured into larger bodies (e.g. the combination of old government departments into 'super ministries', the creation of Regional Health Authorities, the reorganisation of local government, the establishment of Social Services Departments, the development of comprehensive schools). This, Cochrane argues, was an attempt to reform the social democratic state in its own terms by strengthening and developing its structures. A second phase of modernisation (1976–90) was linked to the dismantling of this social democratic state. The 'waste' and 'inefficiency' of large bureaucracies came under extensive criticism and restructuring was based on a belief in the superiority of markets as the best form of economic and social organisation. This period saw an extensive programme of privatisation of national utilities, the introduction of Compulsory Competitive Tendering (CCT) in local government, market-testing in central government and the internal market in the NHS. Council housing was offered for sale to tenants, schools became locally managed and the power of LEAs (local education authorities) constrained. This period challenged the fundamental assumptions about the role of the state as a provider of services and established new forms of governance based on the coordination of services provided by the market, the voluntary sector and by families themselves through self-provision. In relation to local government, for example, Cochrane argues that:

> The moves to an enabling authority, towards an increased role for a strategic core capable of managing a mixed economy of care and towards governance (rather than government), in which stress is put on the management of networks rather than the delivery of direct services by councils, had become a new orthodoxy at the start of the 1990s, ready for reinterpretation in the next wave of modernisation. (Cochrane 2000: 129)

The 1990s onwards are linked to a third phase of modernisation, based on managerialisation. Different forms of managerialism can be linked to each of the previous phases, with a belief in rational, scientific management, characterising the reorganisation of the welfare state on Fordist principles, and a belief in the application of business ideas to drive efficiency savings underpinning the Thatcher reforms (Newman 2000a). The period of modernisation from 1990 onwards saw a continuation of both forms of managerialism, but overlaid on these was the growth of consumerism in public services. John Major's 'Citizen's Charter' sought to drive up performance by sharpening accountability to users. League tables began to appear as a means of creating more informed consumers. The dominant managerial discourse emphasised the role of managers in bringing about 'culture change' in central and local government in order to deliver greater responsiveness to users and to improve the quality of public services. A multitude of 'quality' programmes bloomed across the public sector. Labour continued this managerial form of modernisation in a range of initiatives designed to improve performance, drive up standards and enhance responsiveness to consumers (see Chapter 5 of this volume).

Modernisation, then, is a loose term applied to widely different programmes of reform or restructuring. However, the term gained a salience within the Labour Party in opposition and in government that went far beyond any specific programme of reform. Modernisation took on a normative inflection as it was used to designate ways in which the institutions of party, government and public services *must* change. As a political process, begun under the leadership of Neil Kinnock and subsequently John Smith, the modernisation of the Labour Party enabled it to achieve electoral success in 1997 as new Labour under the leadership of Tony Blair. Labour's ideological reworking of modernisation suggests a number of strategies. First, it discursively establishes the need for change ('getting rid of the old-fashioned ideas and practices of the past') in the context of globalisation. Secondly, the need for modernisation is situated in the rise of the 'sceptical citizen-consumer'. Thirdly, it positions new Labour as transcendent, as beyond what are claimed to be the 'ideological' politics of the past. This theme runs through the discourse of the Third Way and the pragmatic and eclectic approach to social and public policy which has characterised Labour in office. It is linked to a programme of reform for public policy and public services that emphasises rational and scientific practices (managerialism, evidence-based policy, measurement and audit). These three strategies are considered in turn below.

Modernisation and globalisation

Modernisation is situated in a number of structural forces – globalisation, competition, and meritocracy – that are collapsed into a single unifying theme (Bewes 1998). Globalisation occupies a special place at the core of a series of narratives that construct an imperative to change. These narratives cut across the economy and the institutions of civil society:

> The driving force behind the ideas associated with the Third Way is globalisation because no country is immune from the massive change that globalisation brings. . . . What globalisation is doing is bringing in its wake profound economic and social change, economic change rendering all jobs in industry, sometimes even new jobs in new industries, redundant overnight and social change that is a change to culture, to life-style, to the family, to established patterns of community life. (Blair speech in South Africa, January 1999)

The concept of globalisation at the centre of these narratives has, however, come under both practical and theoretical criticism. There are different views about the depth and significance of transnational economic processes and about the extent to which governments can regulate or control global free markets (Held et al. 1999; Hirst and Thompson 1999; Jessop 1998b). The discourse of globalisation was structured to make it appear as a natural, inevitable and unresistible phenomenon: a state which has been accomplished, and to which states have to adapt or respond, rather than a complex overlaying of many different political and economic processes (Clarke 2000; Fairclough 2000; Jessop 1998b). Such differences were reflected in political discourses: Jospin suggests that the modernisation process in the UK is more 'globalised' than that of other European nations, is less willing to take on the role of an active state, and is less willing to regulate capitalist economic processes (Jospin 1998).

The rise of the sceptical citizen-consumer

The sceptical citizen-consumer has remained a central reference point in Labour's discourse of modernisation:

> Society has become more demanding. Consumers expect ever-higher levels of service and better value for money. . . . Three trends highlight the rise of the demanding, sceptical citizen-consumer. First, confidence in the institutions of government and politics has tumbled. Second, expectations of service quality and convenience have risen – as with the growth of 24-hour banking – but public services have failed to keep up with these developments; their duplication, inefficiency and unnecessary complexity should not be tolerated. Third, as incomes rise, people prefer to own their own homes and investments. (Department of Social Security 1998: 16)

This narrative was evident in the introduction to Labour's 'annual report' of 1999:

> Over the last two decades there has been a dramatic decline in the public's trust in government – indeed in the whole system of political institutions and the politicians who run them. A trail of broken promises and under-performing public services has left a legacy of cynicism and resignation towards the apparently inevitable failure of public bodies. By exposing its promises to public view, setting out measurable targets to be achieved, and seeking explicitly to be judged on them, this Government is attempting to stem the long-term decline in public trust. (Jacobs 1999: 3)

This image of the consumer underpins Labour's focus on modernising services. As Clarke et al. comment, 'The consumer forges a story about the past and future of public services' (2000: 261), a story which helps establish the necessity of reform and modernisation. It conflates a number of different ideas. One is of the consumer as an active agent, exerting choice in the market place of public services. This was the dominant theme in the market models of public service and social welfare provision under the

Thatcher reforms, though consumers were only rarely able to exert choice as they might in the commercial world. The idea of consumer choice underpinned a set of quasi-market relationships and purchaser-provider splits through which proxy customers (public bodies acting as purchasers) purchased services on behalf of service users. The idea of consumer choice also underpinned the later developments of the Citizen's Charter under John Major, with consumers supposedly able to select schools, health providers and other services on the basis of league tables and other performance data. Once again the capacity of users to choose was constrained by a number of factors. However, the idea of public services being directly accountable to their users, and of consumers as the agents through which standards of performance would be enhanced, are significant points of continuity between the Major and Blair governments.

From 'dogmatism' to 'pragmatism'

The modernisation programme of Labour was based on an espoused politics of pragmatism. This can be contrasted with a more visionary and expansive use of the idea of modernisation in the postwar years (Blackman and Palmer 1999) and with the ideological politics of Thatcherism. The idea of 'pragmatism rather than dogmatism' was explicitly used by Labour in its approach to the choice between state- and market-based delivery of public services. The emphasis on pragmatism in making choices about whether to locate services within the public or private sectors is found in the Better Quality Services programme in central government, which replaces Conservative policies on market-testing, and the shift from Compulsory Competitive Tendering (CCT) to Best Value in local government. This pragmatism was set against the ideological preference for market solutions in the Thatcher and Major administrations, and the ideological preference for retaining services within the public sector in the 'old' Labour Party.

The shift implied a move away from competition as a politically imposed strategy to the presumption that competition is one of the *managerial* tools through which performance can be improved. It was linked, in principle, to a decentralised approach in which there was scope for managers to make purchasing and contracting decisions according to the requirements of their business. In local government, the 'compulsory' element of CCT was removed, enabling local managers or politicians to make strategic choices about who should provide public services without necessarily going through the ritual of competitive tendering. This was, however, tempered by the assumption that private sector suppliers would 'normally' provide the best solution. The capacity of managers to make strategic choices is constrained by an emphasis on demonstrating the negative case that competition would not deliver better value. The view was that services should not be retained in-house where the commercial or not-for-profit sectors offered more efficient alternatives (Hughes and Newman 1999), and the government showed its preparedness to bring in private contractors to run organisations which did not meet the required performance standards. In health, GP fund-holding was replaced by a GP-led commissioning model based on Primary Care Groups (PCGs) of general practitioners and other professionals such as community nurses. These were able to make their own purchasing decisions within the strategic framework of the local Health Improvement Programme (HImP) produced by the Health Authority, to which they were accountable. Provision was made for changes in the degree of autonomy enjoyed by individual PCGs, from simple advice to the Health Authority on the purchasing of its services to the management of devolved, cash-limited budgets covering all hospital and community health services for an area. Experienced PCGs could become Primary Care Trusts responsible both for commissioning services and providing community and health services.

These changes represented a refinement of the use of the market as a lever for institutional reform rather than its eradication. But the emphasis on collaboration and long-term partnership in the proposals were important. Relationships between purchasers and providers were viewed as more collaborative, with year-on-year contracts replaced by contracts running for a minimum of three years. In local government there was a more cautious move towards longer-term, relational contracts and partnerships. But while softening the approach to competition, the Labour government's reforms broadened the competitive approach to reach to those parts of the primary care system which had not opted into the previous fund-holding arrangements, and to those local government services not previously subjected to CCT.

Despite the emphasis on non-ideological pragmatism, the Labour government's approach to public service reform has many points of continuity with the Thatcher and Major regimes. There was a continued focus on market mechanisms. Labour retained an emphasis on competition as a lever both for seeking greater efficiency and quality in the delivery of services and as a means off securing investment for innovation. The use of the Private Finance Initiative (re-labelled as Public Private Partnerships) to draw on private sector investment to build new hospitals and other public facilities was expanded rather than curtailed under Labour. It might be argued that the pragmatic, 'what counts is what works', emphasis in public policy under Labour masks the continuance of an underpinning neo-liberal agenda.

But Labour's project is one that appears to transcend politics and ideology. The discourses of globalisation, consumerism, pragmatism and managerialism combine and reinforce each other to produce a profoundly apolitical form of politics. The actions of government were presented as rational and common-sense responses to inevitable forces beyond the control of any individual state. The emphasis was on a rational goal-led form of politics and a managerial style of government: 'New Labour shares with new managerialism the obsession with achieving outcomes at the micro level, on the principle of "what matters is what works", where "delivery, delivery, delivery" is the name of the game' (Andrews 1998: 18). It is, perhaps, unsurprising that a government in office should be concerned with delivery and should attempt to move from theory to pragmatism. However Labour appeared to draw eclectically on different – and sometimes contradictory – elements of managerialism. One strand was the scientific rationalism of goals and outcomes, targets and measurement. Another was the concept of 'empowerment': of communities and citizens, of public sector managers and front-line workers, all constituted as active agents in a process of co-governance. The tensions between these reflected deeper tensions in Labour's political approach to delivering its programme.

Modernising governance?

Modernisation, then, was a programme of public sector reform around principles closely linked to the politics of the 'Third Way'. A reaction against state provision through large state bureaucracies was evident, and the result was an emphasis on the retention of the mixed economy of service provision but with a stronger emphasis on the importance and value of the 'third sector' in the mixed economy of provision. There was a softening of the rigidity of purchaser/provider splits and a new emphasis on the language of collaboration and partnership both within and between sectors. There was also a continued focus on consumerism and choice, though with a shift away from a reliance on market mechanisms alone as the guarantor of choice. Such shifts suggest an increasing importance of networks in relation to markets and hierarchies in patterns of governance highlighted in Chapter 1.

Labour attempted to distance itself from the outright assault on public services which took place under the Conservative administrations of the 1980s and 1990s (though not always consistently, as later chapters will show). Despite significant areas of continuity in the focus on performance and efficiency, the discourse of modernisation suggests some subtle shifts in relation to the New Public Management of the Thatcher years. Modernisation was presented as being not just about short-term efficiency but about longer-term effectiveness. The 1980s and early 1990s were characterised by a focus on institutional reform (introducing competitive tendering, quasi-markets and purchaser/provider splits). Modernisation was more strongly oriented towards the delivery of new policy agendas in health, education and social welfare, areas in which the delivery of policy outcomes was critical to Labour's continued political success. While the political ideology of the Thatcher and Major administrations focused on the benefits of competition, modernisation appeared to place more emphasis on collaboration both at the level of policy (in the rhetoric of 'joined-up government') and management (building partnerships and strategic alliances across the public, private and voluntary sectors). There was a new focus on inclusiveness in the policy process, with a proliferation of policy reviews, task forces and advisory groups set up in the early years of the new administration to involve stakeholders in policy formulation. There was also an emphasis on involving citizens and communities (not just 'consumers') in decision-making at a local level, and on ensuring the transparency and scrutiny of the actions of public bodies. The discourses also suggest shifts in the relationship between policy-makers (ministers, the senior ranks of the civil service and parliament) and the organisations responsible for the delivery of policy, whether in the public, private or voluntary sectors.

Globalisation, modernisation and consumerism were inextricably entwined in new Labour's discourse. They represented a set of narratives that constructed an imperative to change (the requirements of globalisation, enterprise and flexibility against the problems of parochial and bureaucratic inertia). Particular changes came to be legitimated in and through narratives that placed them in globalised contexts. The elementary structure of such narratives is familiar: the World has changed. . . . Britain has changed. . . . Consumers have changed. . . . We must change. . . . (see, for example, Clarke and Newman 1996). This cascade of change served to de-mobilise actual and potential sources of opposition, not least through its appropriation of the vocabulary of radicalism, leaving critics and opponents 'lost for words' (Blackwell and Seabrook 1993).

Labour appropriated this narrative in its legitimation of particular political/policy and organisational/managerial reforms. In the process, the discourse became enriched with supplementary signifiers – 'new', 'modern' and 'modernisation' – intended to bring extra potency. For example, the White Paper on the NHS announced its intention to create 'a modern and dependable health service for the twenty-first century' (Department of Health 1997: 4), promising that 'It will be a new model for a new century' (1997: 11). The 'changing world' was invoked as the reference point for organisational reconstruction:

> . . . in a changing world no organisation, however great, can stand still. The NHS needs to modernise in order to meet the demands of today's public. . . . In short, I want the NHS to take a big step forward and become a modern and dependable service that is once more the envy of the world. (Department of Health 1997: 3)

In relation to both health and welfare the meaning of modernisation went through subtle shifts as the programme of new Labour evolved, blockages to its intentions arose, and new agendas were set out. Much of the original reforms set out in the Green Paper of 1998 were not realised. The health reforms were slower to deliver than had been anticipated, and further cycles of modernisation were launched in each year of Labour's term of office. But there was, at the same time, an intensification of the *discourse* of modernisation. The discourse was deployed as both a means of legitimating change and as a convenient way of packaging what had been a rather disparate and eclectic series of reforms of government and public services into an apparently coherent programme.

Despite the emphasis on change, modernisation was also about continuity. Much of new Labour's electoral platform under the Blair leadership had been based on a critique of the Thatcher reforms and the setting out of a vision of the future based on a re-articulation of the language of community and citizenship, reciprocity and responsibility, justice and fairness. Indeed, the 'Third Way' can partly be understood as an attempt to retain the economic gains of the Thatcher years while also attempting to re-inscribe a set of moral and civic values that fitted rather uneasily with neo-liberal economics. In public services, the softening of the purchaser/provider split in health with the establishment of PCGs and the introduction of Best Value in local government suggested a shift of approach to the role of competition and market mechanisms. Changes were also evident in the emphasis on 'cross-cutting' agendas such as crime prevention or social exclusion, and organisations were encouraged to collaborate to deliver outcomes on key social agendas, for example through the 'zonal' initiatives in health, education and employment (see Chapter 4). However, modernisation can also be regarded as a continuation of the New Public Management type reforms in its focus on performance and efficiency coupled with an intensification of inspection and scrutiny regimes.

There has been much debate about how far modernisation constituted a distinctive political programme and how far it was merely a label under which disparate reforms were conveniently packaged. The concept was defined, in part, by its opposition to a discredited past, particularly that associated with the 'old' Labour Party. This broad usage robbed modernisation of much specific meaning – almost any change viewed as desirable might carry the label. At the same time, it carried a series of very specific meanings through which the political process itself was redefined:

> For Blair, 'modernisation' means integration, approachability and informality, the dissolution of barriers and the forging of 'connexity'. . . . Politics itself, as the representation of competing interests, is redundant. The political new modality is collaboration rather than antagonism, moderation rather than radicalism, and ideological flexibility rather than entrenched positions. . . . To be a moderniser means nothing more than to be a subscriber to a particular intra- (and increasingly, inter-) party politics. (Bewes 1998: 194)

The de-coupling of the idea of modernisation from earlier eras of reform and the establishment of Labour as part of a meta-narrative of modernisation as political as well as social and economic progress was one of new Labour's major ideological achievements. Subsequent chapters will explore the tensions within the Third Way and the modernisation programme between centralisation and decentralisation, and between hierarchical forms of control and governance through networks, beginning in the next chapter with the 'Modernising Government' agenda.

4　Modernising government: the politics of reform

People want government which meets their needs. . . . To achieve that, the Government's strategy is one in which the keystones of its operation are inclusiveness and integration:

- Inclusive: policies are forward-looking, inclusive and fair.
- Integrated: policies and programmes, local and national, tackle the issues facing society – like crime, drugs, housing and the environment – in a joined-up way, regardless of the organisational structure of government.

(Cabinet Office 1999a: paras 6 and 7)

The Labour government has put in place a wide-ranging programme of reform of both central and local government. This chapter examines these reforms in the context of previous phases of change. Its purpose is to identify how far Labour's policy approach signifies a move towards a different style of governance. The chapter begins with a brief assessment of the approach to governance established under the Conservative administrations of the 1980s and early 1990s and goes on to assess Labour's programme of modernisation. It argues that Labour has continued some strands of Conservative reform (such as the emphasis on quality and efficiency) but has also distanced itself from the consequences of the reforms of the 1980s. The chapter goes on to explore four themes in the modernisation of government: the reframing of policy problems; the move towards a more inclusive process; the development of a focus on 'what works' in public policy; and the dispersal of power to nations, regions and localities within the UK. Other themes – joined-up government and public participation – will be considered in separate chapters. These themes do not all suggest a similar trajectory of change in Labour's governance style. The interplay of different elements and forces is explored through the framework introduced in Chapter 2.

Neo-liberal governance

The neo-liberal reforms of the 1980s were characterised by a governance style based on what Pierre and Peters (2000) term 'de-centering outwards'. State functions were dispersed through market and quasi-market mechanisms, by the outsourcing of government functions to private sector companies and by the establishment of civil service Executive Agencies, NHS Trusts, GP fund-holding and the proliferation of quangos (Ferlie et al. 1996; Metcalfe and Richards 1990; Skelcher 1998). The splits between policy and implementation, between purchasing and providing, between commissioning and service delivery, which these reforms produced, express a set of distinctions fundamental to the New Public Management (Dunleavy and Hood 1994; Hood 1991; Pollitt 1993). The process of dispersal was coupled with a strengthening of central government control through performance targets, inspection and audit, and by the growth of managerialism as a mode of coordination (Clarke and Newman 1997: Chapter 2; Newman and Clarke 1994).

Despite the apparent focus on 'de-centering outwards', it is also possible to characterise the style of governance in this period as highly prescriptive and state-centred. This enabled the Thatcher governments to drive through change in areas where professionals, civil servants and administrators had succeeded in deflecting earlier reform initiatives. There was a shift in focus towards quality under the Major governments, with the introduction of Citizen's Charters and league tables. But none of these administrations did much by way of attempting to build support within the public sector for their reforms. They tended to look 'over the heads' of professionals and managers to the public themselves, seeking to form populist alliances between politicians and the public (as users and customers) against public sector staff. This strategy was reinforced by the demonisation of many groups targeted for reform, from 'self-seeking' and 'wasteful' bureaucrats to 'do-gooding' professionals, many of whom were viewed as the carriers of the 'permissive' values of the 1960s. This process of demonisation was especially sharp in relation to local government through caricatures of 'loony left' local authorities and the condemnation of local authority waste and inefficiency (Cochrane 1993).

The public sector was, throughout this period, viewed as a target of reform rather than as an agent through which social change could be delivered. The style of policy-making in relation to the public sector was non-consultative and action-oriented. Old stakeholders linked to the corporatist past were excluded from decision-making. Institutional reform was often initiated by reviews led by 'outsiders' from the business world (e.g. Rayner, Ibbs, Griffiths). There was a sharp move away from the consensus-building approach to change in, for example, the NHS, where earlier reviews had been based on wide consultation with the professions but policy changes now tended to be driven by political ideology.[1] The resulting programmes of reform were predominantly compulsory rather than permissive or enabling. There were some exceptions: the departmental structure of government and differences between ministers meant that the government did not exhibit a unified style. The sharpened separation between policy and delivery which was introduced with, for example, the setting up of Executive Agencies in the civil service meant that there was some discretion for local managers about the way in which reforms were to be implemented (e.g. which services to put forward for market-testing in the civil service, what structures to put in place to support the introduction of general management in the NHS, how to deliver efficiency savings in local or central government). There was also some experimentation: for example, under the City Challenge and later Single Regeneration Budget programmes the government sought to act as a catalyst for change by introducing competitive bidding for local authority urban programmes. But, despite some variation between sectors, devolution of responsibility to local managers was limited, and the institutional reform programme was tightly prescribed and controlled by the centre (Pollitt et al. 1998). The predominant style of policy-making and policy implementation was top-down, mandatory and prescriptive. There was little of the policy style Richardson (1982) calls 'de-centering down' – the devolution of authority to regions and localities.

The power of the executive was also enhanced. The monopoly of the civil service as advisors to ministers was challenged by the growth of 'think tanks', and a central policy unit was established to help the prime minister contest civil service advice (Campbell and Wilson 1995). New networks of business, academics and others were formed around neo-liberal and neo-conservative 'think tanks'. Executive power in local government was also enhanced as local authorities developed strong policy units at the centre, abandoning the traditional professionally-dominated corporate officer arrangements in favour of smaller boards of Executive Directors. This centralisation of policy was accompanied by an increasing managerialisation of government, local government and, albeit less successfully, the NHS. In the civil service, agency chief executives used their devolved authority to negotiate away 'inflexible' work practices and staff. Business management techniques became more widely adopted, partly as a result of market-testing, though the valorisation of policy over managerial work acted as a partial brake on the managerialisation of the service at senior levels (Metcalfe and Richards 1990). In the NHS, despite the limited purchase of managerialism following the introduction of General Management, the subsequent creation of GP fund-holders and NHS Trusts introduced a stronger business and commercial ethos (Pollitt 1993). In local government, the doctrines of strategic management, performance management and quality management underpinned the gradual transformation of many professional functions as a managerial calculus became devolved to lower and lower tiers of the organisation (Exworthy and Halford 1999; Keen and Scase, 1998). In both health care and local government, managerialism was promoted by the Audit Commission; by the growing use of consultants; and through the proliferation of management training, development and accreditation.

This strengthening of managerialism took place in a particular context: that of a strong focus on organisational, rather than system, efficiency. The unit of measurement and control, reflected in government performance indicators, Citizen's Charters and league tables, became the individual school, not the LEA; the individual hospital, not the NHS; the local government service, not the local authority. This focus was exacerbated by tight targets for efficiency savings and organisationally-focused performance indicators. This produced a particular form of managerialism: one oriented towards organisational survival, effectiveness and competitive success, and one concerned with vertical levers of control from government to the organisation, from managers to staff. The dispersal of the functions of government to a wide range of agencies in the public and private sectors, the introduction of market mechanisms, the sharper separation between policy and delivery and the organisational focus of the New Public Management, all led to a process of institutional fragmentation.

In terms of governance theory, such fragmentation is associated with a style of policy based on policy networks, and a style of delivery based on partnership. The role of the state becomes that of steering and coordination, and state power is exercised through leadership and influence, rather than direct control. However, the strengthening of executive power and the centralisation of control under the Conservatives appears to contradict this view. The Conservative style was anti-corporatist: the institutional channels through which government had consulted with businesses, trades union and interest groups were closed down. The increase in the use of think tanks and advisors to supplement or bypass an increasingly distrusted civil service was firmly linked to a centralised policy process where inputs were fed into the centre (Parsons 1995). The period of Conservative hegemony was, then, marked by a double process of centralisation and dispersal. Power was exercised through strong levers of financial control, coupled with the increasing dominance of neo-liberal ideology.

Neo-liberal ideology had as a central theme the elaboration of the past failure of the social democratic welfare state. It established links between the postwar expansion of welfare and the rise of the power of 'do-gooding' professionals and 'self-seeking' bureaucrats, producing problems of waste and inefficiency and spiralling welfare expenditure. Labour, in turn, has focused on the problems of social fragmentation and social exclusion produced, in part, by the policies of the 1980s and early 1990s, a theme to which I return in Chapter 8. Here I want to explore the ways in which Labour has focused on the problems generated by the reforms of the Thatcher and Major years in its programme for the modernisation of government itself.

Labour's modernisation of government

The *Modernising Government* White Paper (Cabinet Office 1999a) set out three aims:

- ensuring that policy-making is more joined-up and strategic;
- making sure that public service users, not providers, are the focus, by matching services more closely to people's lives; and
- delivering public services that are high quality and efficient.

These aims reflect the political agenda of the Third Way described in Chapter 3. The White Paper provides important points of continuity with neo-liberal reforms in its emphasis on quality, efficiency and consumer-centredness (see Chapter 5). But it also marks important changes. The White Paper highlighted the need to draw a range of agencies into partnership to develop more holistic solutions to complex policy problems. Like the Conservatives, Labour framed its governance approach and legitimated its reforms through narratives of past failure, highlighting in particular the fragmenting consequences of Conservative reforms. The White Paper, and the ministerial and prime ministerial statements around its publication, reflect and refract a number of critiques that had been developing among academics, senior managers and other stakeholders within the policy community around new Labour in opposition. Jervis and Richards (1997) summarise some of the major debates in a publication outlining what they term the 'three deficits' of public management. Drawing on the thinking of John Stewart and others, it was suggested that a 'democratic deficit' had resulted from the fragmentation of the public realm and the growth of quangos. The erosion of democratic accountability was linked to a possible decline in the legitimacy of decisions about public policy. A second deficit – the 'design deficit' – described the failure of the policy process to match the complexities of 'wicked issues'.[2] This phrase denotes the increasing importance of complex and intractable policy agendas, such as crime, the environment, public health, transport, poverty, community safety, and others. Problems are defined as 'wicked' when they are:

- subject to competing definitions about the nature of the problem;
- complex issues in which the relationship between different factors – say public health and the environment, or crime and unemployment – was hard to assess;
- issues on which interventions did not fit neatly into single-policy frameworks; and therefore
- issues for which effective intervention required collaboration in both policy formulation and delivery.

Collaboration to address wicked issues was hampered, it was argued, by a system of government organised around functional specialisms and the departmental structures within which policy was formulated and implemented. The capacity to collaborate at local level had been reduced by the increasing centralisation of policy decisions upwards to central government.

Jervis and Richards went on to highlight a third deficit, described as a 'development deficit' in public policy. This refers to the limited capacity of public sector organisations to innovate because of legislative and other restrictions constraining them from exercising the full strategic freedom that they would have in the private sector (e.g. constraints on risk-taking and competitive behaviour). Central to Jervis and Richards's argument was an analysis of the problems arising from the previous managerial focus of reform, in which emphasis had been placed on the efficiency by which services were delivered rather than, and at the expense of, a focus on the effectiveness through which policy was formulated and implemented.

Some leading thinkers within the civil service helped to shape the view that there was a need for a renewed focus on the policy process. Michael Bichard, then Permanent Secretary at the Department for Education and Employment, commented:

> The thing which surprises me is the way in which – over the past 20 years – the development of policy has not received much attention. Within Whitehall and beyond, all the focus has been on the way we manage executive agencies. I think the way we develop policy now needs a radical rethink. In the old days we said good policy is politically safe and intellectually clever. This government is now saying: 'No it's a lot more than that'. It focuses on issues not bounded by bureaucracy. It should be research based and properly evaluated. It is about including more people . . . in the development of that policy. That takes you towards social inclusion rather than away from it, as many current government policies tend to. More seriously, Whitehall has not been nearly as creative as it needs to be. (Bichard 1999: 7)

Similar forms of analysis and criticism emerged from political commentators. Writing in a Fabian discussion paper published in 1994, Wicks outlined principles for reforming social welfare under a future Labour government, the final section of which called for more attention to be paid to the process of 'governing social policy':

> the Labour Party should be aware of the problem of lack of coordination within the social policy arena itself. These seemingly dull questions of machinery are vital: many of the most crucial items of the policy agenda – the run down of the inner cities, the need for urban regeneration, family policy etc. – have characteristics and demand solutions which are not the province of any one department, central or local. Yet our whole system of government is riddled with specialism and departmentalism. Political reputations are made by civil servants defending departmental interests, safeguarding their budget and warding off intrusions from other fiefdoms. . . . The House of Commons Select Committee system mirrors, not challenges, this departmental slicing of the cake of governance. (Wicks 1994: 22)

Wicks also talks of the need for 'clear thinking based on past experiments' and of overcoming the problems of short termism in policy-making and budgeting. Each of these themes has been reflected in the writings of Mulgan, Perri 6 and others, in think tanks such as Demos which influenced the genesis and shaping of the Third Way. Perri 6, for example, highlighted the lack of coordination and fragmentation of public services and argued that 'problem-solving' and 'holistic government' was required to solve the complex social problems and to integrate government around the problems, solutions and outcomes that were important to citizens (Perri 6 1998a, 1998b; Perri 6 et al. 1999). An outcomes-based approach, it was suggested, would facilitate collaboration around social problems, and citizens themselves were to be viewed as part of the solution:

> The basic elements of the strategy are: shifting the balance of effort across government from trying to cure harms when they have already happened; integrating the accountability, financing and organisation of services around outcomes rather than activities; and putting as much [emphasis] on persuading people to think, believe, care and behave differently as on delivering services. (Perri 6 1998b: 52)

Such narratives were fundamental to the Labour government's presentation of its approach. The White Paper *Modernising Government* suggests that problems in the policy process had arisen in part as a product of earlier managerial reforms:

> This emphasis on management reform has brought improved productivity, better value for money and in many cases better quality services – all of which we are determined to build on. On the other hand, little attention was paid to the policy process and the way it affects government's ability to meet the needs of the people. . . . In general too little effort has gone into making sure that policies are devised and delivered in a consistent and effective way across institutional boundaries – for example, between different government departments, and between central and local government. Issues like crime and social exclusion cannot be tackled on a departmental basis. An increasing separation between policy and delivery has acted as a barrier to involving in policy-making those people who are responsible for delivering on the front line. . . . Too often the work of Departments, their Agencies and other bodies has been fragmented and the focus of scrutiny has been on their individual achievements rather than on their contribution to the government's overall strategic purpose. (Cabinet Office 1999a: Chapter 2, paras 4 and 5)

This quotation criticises the focus on managerial reforms at the expense of policy issues under Conservative governments, highlights the limitations of the organisational focus of the New Public Management and suggests that the opening-up of sharper lines of separation between policy and management had limited the input of managers to the policy process. Similar narratives of failure can be found in White Papers and policy documents relating to specific sectors. For example, the negative effects of fragmentation and of the separation of policy and delivery were noted in *Our Healthier Nation: A Contract for Health* (Department of Health 1998a). Several sectors were criticised for their failure to involve citizens and communities in decision-making on issues such as neighbourhood renewal (Social Exclusion Unit 1998a). The negative effects of viewing choices between the state and the market in ideological terms is a theme common to documents on health, local and central government, reflecting the emphasis on pragmatism in the Third Way (Cabinet Office 1999; Department of Health 1998a; DETR 1998). The failure to target resources based on evidence of effective practice was highlighted in relation to health, probation, policing and social services, and existing policies in these areas were viewed as failing to address the changing needs of the 'modern people'.

Commentaries on the policy process in local government took a rather different form. Audit Commission Reports (1990, 1997) had presented stringent critiques of the traditional committee processes and the lack of transparency and accountability in political decision-making outside committees. This analysis developed from earlier reports on local government through the postwar period (e.g. Baines Report 1972; Maud Report 1967) which repeatedly called for the streamlining of political decision-making processes. In contrast, the analysis emerging from local government itself tended to focus on the negative consequences of the Thatcher and Major reforms. Discussions and policy papers from local government associations prior to 1997 highlighted problems in the existing framework, most notably the impact of Compulsory Competitive Tendering (CCT) and the process of capping local government finance.[3] Local authorities strongly favoured more delegated responsibility for decisions on performance improvement and contracting represented in the promised shift to a 'Best Value' regime. Local authority arguments also reflected the idea that the changes of the 1980s and early 1990s had produced a 'democratic deficit' by transferring local authority powers to a range of non-elected bodies (Skelcher 1998). Underpinning all of these was a general concern about what was perceived as the strengthening of the powers of central government at the expense of local autonomy and control (Stewart and Stoker 1989).

Modernising the policy process

These analyses have been refined and refracted through Labour's programme for modernising the policy process. While the reforms of the previous decades had been predominantly concerned with institutional change (introducing competitive tendering, quasi-markets and purchaser/provider splits) in order to achieve organisational efficiencies, a strong thread running through the modernisation programme was the role of the public sector in helping to deliver policy outcomes on education, social exclusion and welfare reform, issues at the heart of Labour's political agenda. To achieve this, *Modernising Government* set out eight key principles, five of which focus on policy-making:

> *Designing policy around shared objectives and carefully designed results, not around organisational structures or existing functions.* Many policies are pursued by a single part of government. For 'New Labour', there is a need for a greater focus on outcomes, which will encourage Departments to work in partnership to secure desired results.
>
> *Making sure policies are inclusive.* This involves the design and development of policies that take full account of the needs of all those – individuals and groups, families and businesses – likely to be affected by them.

Involving others in policy-making. Rather than defending policies, Government should lead a debate on improving them. This means developing new relationships between Whitehall, the devolved administrations, local government, the voluntary and private sectors; consulting outside experts, those who implement policy and those affected by it early in the policy process so that we can develop policies that are deliverable from the start.

Becoming more forward- and outward-looking. This means learning to look beyond what government is doing now; improving and extending contingency planning; learning lessons from other countries; and integrating the EU and wider international dimensions into the policy-making process.

Learning from experience. Government should regard policy making as a continuous learning process, not as a series of one-off initiatives. We will improve our use of evidence and research so that we understand better the problems we are trying to address. We must make more use of pilot schemes to encourage innovations and test whether they work. We will ensure that all policies and programmes are clearly specified and evaluated, and the lessons of success and failure communicated and acted on. Feedback from those who implement and deliver policies and services is essential. We need to apply the disciplines of project management to the policy process. (Cabinet Office 1999a: Chapter 2, para 6)

These principles were far-reaching and, if realised, had the capacity to transform the policy process. They marked an apparent break with the strongly politicised and centralised policy process of the Thatcher years by talking about the need to include multiple actors in the policy process: those in local government, the voluntary and private sectors, staff and 'those affected by policy'. They acknowledged the need to take account of the new relationships between Whitehall and the Scottish Parliament and Welsh Assembly. They implied important cultural changes within Whitehall itself in the emphasis on partnership between departments, and on evaluation and learning.

The proposals on modernising the policy process were taken forward by a strategic policy-making team established within the Cabinet Office. This team produced a report setting out a model for what was termed *Professional Policy Making in the Twenty-first Century* (Cabinet Office 1999b). The model was based on a series of core competencies linked to the policy process:

- *Forward looking* – takes a long-term view, based on statistical trends and informed predictions of the likely impact of policy.
- *Outward looking* – takes account of factors in the national, European and international situation and communicates policy effectively.
- *Innovative and creative* – questions established ways of dealing with things and encourages new ideas; open to comments and suggestions of others.
- *Using evidence* – uses best available evidence from a wide range of sources and involves key stakeholders at an early stage.
- *Joined-up* – looks beyond institutional boundaries to the Government's strategic objectives.
- *Evaluates* – builds systematic evaluation of early policy outcomes into the policy process.

- *Reviews* – keeps established policy under review to ensure it continues to deal with the problems it was designed to tackle, taking account of associated effects elsewhere.
- *Learns lessons* – learns from experience of what works and what doesn't.

(Cabinet Office 1999b: para 2.11)

The report bases the model on its analysis of the need for change:

> The need for change is clear. The world for which policy makers have to develop policies is becoming increasingly complex, uncertain and unpredictable. The electorate is better informed, has rising expectations and is making growing demands for services tailored to their individual needs. Key policy issues, such as social exclusion and reducing crime, overlap and have proved resistant to previous attempts to tackle them, yet the world is increasingly inter-connected and interdependent. Issues switch quickly from the domestic to the international arena and an increasingly wide diversity of interests needs to be coordinated and harnessed. Governments across the world need to be able to respond quickly to events to provide the support that people need to adapt to change and that businesses need to prosper. In parallel with these external pressures, the Government is asking policy makers to focus on solutions that work across existing organisational boundaries and on bringing about change in the real world. Policy makers must adapt to this new, fast moving, challenging environment if public policy is to remain credible and effective. (Cabinet Office 1999b: para 2.3)

The language of this extract shows a number of remarkable similarities to the governance literature I outlined in Chapter 1. It talks of complexity, uncertainty and unpredictability, of interconnections and interdependencies, of diversity and coordination, and of dynamic change. Both the White Paper and the Cabinet Office Report appear to offer a model of policy-making appropriate to, and enabling the further development of, a new, network-based style of governance appropriate to this context. In order to explore this more fully I want to focus on three themes:

- the reframing of policy problems;
- the focus on an inclusive policy process; and
- the emphasis on 'evidence-based' policy.

Other themes – the modernisation of services, the importance of 'joined-up government' and the emphasis on public participation – are considered in subsequent chapters.

Reframing policy problems

Policy problems are social constructions: that is, they are perceived through a series of institutionally based, socially or politically derived lenses which construct reality in different ways (Bacchi 1999; Clarke and Cochrane

1998). The problems experienced by those living in run-down neighbour-hoods of inner cities, for example, may be perceived as a housing problem, an educational problem, a problem of poverty, or a cultural problem of low aspirations caused by deficient parenting by families locked in a 'cycle of deprivation'. Perceptions of the problem and possible solutions are likely to be constructed differently by different groups of residents living in the area, by workers from different professional groups, by different forms of com-munity or political activist, and by different departments of government. As the political climate shifts and new policy discourses are mobilised, prob-lems may be redefined and a new repertoire of policy instruments brought into play.

Pierre and Peters (2000) describe three broad ways in which policies may be framed:

- Framing by the function or activity of government, that is viewing problems through the lens of the formal structure of government departments (asking whose problem is it?) or of the instruments at the disposal of government (asking what instrument – e.g. regulation, subsidy – do we have available?).
- Framing by social factors (defining problems in terms of the target population or the relationships through which problems are shaped).
- Framing by political objectives (preventing political mobilisation or producing social change).

It is important to note that each reflects ways in which policy problems may be framed by policy-makers and government rather than by groups on whom policies are likely to impact. Nevertheless the typology is useful in highlighting the interplay between different ways of framing problems. To return to my example, the first form of framing would characterise the problem of inner cities through the lens of relevant government depart-ments, dealing respectively with housing, education, employment and other relevant issues which fit departmental or sub-departmental boundaries. Framing by social factors would highlight the problems experienced by those living in the areas concerned and would be more likely to see the interconnections between mutually reinforcing sets of problems, much as the Social Exclusion Unit did in its report on 'poor estates' (Social Exclu-sion Unit 1998a). Framing by political objectives might view the problem in terms of the political disaffection and potential alienation of certain groups.

Although all three forms of framing can be traced in Labour's policy programme, overall it represents a partial shift towards a reframing of policy problems by social factors. For example, Labour has sought to integrate services around the needs of target populations in the Better Government for Older People Initiative, the New Deal for Communities, the Sure Start scheme, and the work of the Social Exclusion Unit. This focus suggests the need for an integrated approach and a focus on policy outcomes, in which departmental outputs are reframed within a broader context. Some changes have already been introduced to encourage such a focus: for example, the reform of financial arrangements and the introduction of the three-year comprehensive spending review have introduced a longer planning cycle for public service organisations, linked to longer-term goals and targets. The Treasury also encouraged a shift to targets based on outcome measures in the 2000 Comprehensive Spending Review. A 'Public Services and Expenditure' committee of senior ministers in central jobs chaired by the Chancellor was established to monitor the delivery of Public Service Agreements and to take an overview on cross-cutting areas of the modernisation agenda, looking at the development of integrated budgeting and accountability frameworks.

However this reframing is only partial. Departmental power bases have remained strong and policy problems continued to be framed through the lens of departmental concerns and priorities, not least because civil service careers and ministerial fortunes depend on achievements against such priorities (Performance and Innovation Unit 2000a). Labour has been concerned with political objectives as well as policy objectives, especially the goals of mobilising support and defusing opposition. Its core political objectives have shaped choices about the policy process in the belief that a more inclusive approach would contribute to building support and legitimacy for Labour in office.

An inclusive policy process

The White Paper *Modernising Government* called for a more inclusive policy process which draws in a range of stakeholders. This implicitly acknowledged the growing importance of policy networks and communities, and suggested a commitment to developing more extended networks, incorporating new categories of actor. The idea of policy networks has formed a significant component of governance theory. The analysis transcends the traditional stark distinction between state and civil society: state and non-state institutions can be seen as linked by loose networks and by reciprocal connections, characterised by power/dependency (Rhodes 1997). It also overcomes the classic distinction between policy development and implementation (Hill 1997). More importantly in terms of my argument, states may have an interest in fostering policy networks because they facilitate a consultative style of government, make policy-making predictable and reduce policy conflict, thus making it possible to de-politicise issues (Jordan and Richardson 1987; Smith 1993).

Labour can be viewed as both incorporating existing policy networks – for example, through extensive consultations with local government associations, and NHS managers and professional bodies – and attempting to shape new ones. It established a large number of policy reviews, task forces and advisory groups, some 192 such groups being established in Labour's first year of office (Platt 1998). These included the major Comprehensive Spending Review, the review of access to Government Information, the

Better Regulation Task Force, a review of measures on Community Safety, the Prisons and Probation Review and the Disability Rights Task Force. Barker (2000) found that 2,459 'outsiders' (not ministers, political advisors or civil servants) sat on 295 task forces, advisory groups and fora in Labour's first eighteen months. By December 2000, 238 task forces, advisory groups and reviews had been set up (*Observer*, 31 December 2000, 7). Whatever the figures, the scale of involvement from people outside Westminster has been significant. The proliferation of new bodies, panels and networks continued the challenge to the civil service monopoly of policy advice under previous governments by giving professionals and others from outside government direct access to ministers. For example, in 1999 the Department of Health established a central board, comprising health managers, academics and others, to give policy direction to the modernisation of the NHS and to provide direct advice to the minister. Labour continued the tradition of bringing in business leaders to advise on government policy. But it also looked beyond the business world. The policy action teams set up by the Social Exclusion Unit comprise staff seconded from voluntary, business and community organisations, from local government, the health service and other sectors as well as civil servants. Initiatives on local regeneration placed a strong focus on both stakeholder participation and public consultation at a local level. As the first report of the Social Exclusion Unit noted, solutions to local problems which 'engage local communities' are more likely to be effective than those which are 'parachuted in' from government (Social Exclusion Unit 1998a). The Unit played a leading role in modelling a more inclusionary practice in the development of networks to help shape policy analysis, with particular emphasis placed on drawing in the voluntary sector, some 'community leaders' and practitioners drawn from front-line services as well as senior managers and civil servants.

Labour also showed a greater willingness to consult with local government than under the Conservative regime. Local authority networks had influenced the development of Labour's policy prior to the election, and after coming into office the government launched a series of regional seminars to engage local authorities in the process of modernisation. The new Local Government Association played a critical role in the debates, producing its own papers on modernisation and acting as a channel for consultation with government, while the Local Government Information Unit launched a collection of discussion papers designed to influence future policy (Kitchen 1997). Labour also set up a number of pilots to explore aspects of the modernisation agenda. Local authorities were invited to bid to become Best Value pilot authorities and to experiment with new political arrangements in advance of the legislation. A Modernisation Team was set up within the Department of the Environment, Transport and the Regions (DETR) to promote the programme of reform and spread 'best practice'. The emphasis appears to have been on communication, persuasion and the fostering of innovation in the run-up to, and the immediate period following, the publication of the White Paper on modernising local government. Parallel developments took place in health, with wide-ranging consultation linked to the new Health Action Zones and to the evolution of the NHS Plan of 2000.

Such strategies can be viewed as designed to strengthen the legitimacy of decisions. They enabled the government to bring those responsible for implementing policy into policy formation (including people from the voluntary and community sectors, business and local government). They may have helped to achieve support for policy changes before new measures were introduced. They also enabled government to draw on additional experience and expertise of 'what works' in a particular policy field, and increase the number of people from traditionally marginalised groups represented in policy discussions. As such they contributed to the building of a broad support base for Labour in office. Conflict over policy choices may be minimised where key interests are incorporated into the decision-making processes (Cochrane 2000). However, the focus on a more inclusive policy process raises a number of important issues about the transparency and accountability of the policy process, and about the representativeness of those included. New Labour has been criticised, following an investigation by the Public Appointments Commission, for the political bias of its appointments to the Boards of NHS Trusts, Health Authorities and other public bodies (*The Guardian*, 13 March 2000: 8). From a rather different standpoint, Falconer (1999) notes that, while the 'quangocracy' of new Labour has included a significant number of non-government members, at least half have been drawn from the private sector. The move towards a more inclusive policy process raises concerns about who is to be included, based on what form of legitimacy, at what level of decision-making, on whose terms, and with what form of accountability. It also raises issues about the possible co-option or incorporation of those who are included, a topic to which I return in Chapter 7.

At the same time as Labour has attempted to broaden participation in the policy process it has narrowed participation in decision-making within the Labour Party itself. Many commentators have talked of the stifling of debate within the party, both among MPs (who need to stay 'on message' to secure advancement), among Ministers (with Cabinet meetings reportedly lasting around thirty minutes) and in the wider party (with many party supporters protesting against the displacement of the National Executive Committee from a policy role and against party conferences becoming US-style political rallies directed to the media). Andrew Marr has suggested that:

Policy is made by professionals in London, behind closed doors; sold and attacked through the national media and debated on chat shows. A whole tradition of political participation, based around direct argument in school halls, trades union offices or front rooms, plus annual pilgrimages to seaside resorts to vote on policies, is dying away. (Marr 2000a: 28)

While dissent within the party has not by any means been eradicated – there have been a number of back-bench revolts – Labour has consistently attempted to centralise power.

This centralisation of power within the party reflects a wider process of centralisation pervading the modernisation process. A number of Royal Commissions and task forces set up by Labour to develop or review policy have now reported and many have seen their recommendations rejected in part or in whole, or not acted on. These include the Electoral Reform Commission, the Royal Commission on long-term care for the elderly, The Rogers Commission on urban regeneration and a task force on the regulation of football (*The Guardian*, 1 September 2000: 16). The reasons for rejection varied: some were due to the funding implications of the proposals; but many, including proposals on the introduction of proportional representation for national elections, can be attributed to party or prime ministerial preference. The move to a more inclusionary policy process needs to be located in this wider context of a tightly centralised process of political management under Labour. This cuts across the idea of a more consensual and inclusive style of policy-making. It also offers a post-ideological conception of the government as embodying a modernised, rational and managerial form of politics, a form of politics in which knowledge is translated into policy under the rubrics of 'what works' and 'evidence-based policy'.

Evidence-based policy

Political statements couched in the language of the Third Way repeatedly emphasise the need to retreat from the dogmatic, ideological politics of the past towards a focus on 'what counts is what works'. Initiatives linked to the *Modernising Government* agenda have affirmed the central importance of evidence in the policy process. The growth of interest in evidence-based policy is linked to a number of developments, including the explosion of data, developments in IT, the growth of a well-informed public unwilling to rely on professional judgement, an increasing emphasis on scrutiny and accountability in government and the growth in the size and capability of the research community (Davies et al. 2000). These developments have been complemented by the expansion of managerial approaches to the collection and use of evidence represented in programme evaluation, the proliferation of performance indicator systems and the increased use of inspection and audit as a means of collecting and using data on managerial practice and organisational performance. In some sectors, most notably medicine, the notion of evidence-based practice – a means of ensuring that interventions are based on the best available evidence – were already well established.

As the White Paper and Cabinet Office Report show, Labour has placed great emphasis on the need to develop policy based on evidence and to promote evaluation and learning to support this goal (Cabinet Office 1999a, 1999b). There has been a focus on setting up pilots and initiatives in order to allow experimentation, on evaluating the results, on assessing the experience of what works in other countries (especially in the USA) and on applying solutions to the UK. By such means, it is argued, resources could be targeted more efficiently and practice could be directed towards achieving effective outcomes. Resources spent on economic and social research across Whitehall increased massively under Labour (Walker 2000a) and some government departments pioneered a research-led approach to policy and practice. For example, the Department for Education and Employment set up, with the Economic and Social Research Council and the Higher Education Funding Council, a series of initiatives to bring researchers, ministers and civil servants into direct contact through research fora and seminars.

At the centre of government the search for a more rational, knowledge-based policy process has shaped the process of institutional reform. One of the roles of the Centre for Management and Policy Studies, set up by Labour and located within the Cabinet Office, was to develop a more evidential basis to policy-making, drawing on techniques of knowledge management. Government also supported the establishment of a new national Resource Centre for Evidence-Based Policy within the ESRC to support policy-makers and practitioners across different sectors. This was modelled in part on the Cochrane Centre at Oxford, whose role is to collate, assess and disseminate research evidence to medical practitioners. The newly established Performance and Innovation Unit and the Social Exclusion Unit within the Cabinet Office were strongly oriented towards developing policy initiatives in a more research-based way, involving experts outside government in cross-departmental, policy-focused task groups. These units represent 'important customers for high-quality research evidence and exemplify the new interface between policy makers and knowledge producers which will begin to unfold over the next few years' (Amman 2000: vi). Together, these initiatives symbolise an intensification of the attempt to apply quasi-scientific techniques to the policy process.

The intuitive appeal of evidence-based policy and practice is clear. However, it has been challenged from a number of different perspectives. One set of analyses highlights the problem in many areas of the social policy of collecting and using evidence based on a scientific model of research, especially in an era in which the scientific model is itself threatened by the acknowledgement that science is an uncertain and contested enterprise. The BSE crisis, the debate over GM food and concerns over the safety of MMR vaccine did little to sustain the idea that science could produce an uncontested and neutral body of evidence on which policy might be based. Furthermore, evidence-based policy tends to valorise techniques drawn from the natural sciences (e.g. randomised control trials) above qualitative methods, despite cultural barriers and ethical objections to the use of such experimental techniques in many areas of social care and criminal justice. Even in medicine – arguably a field in which scientific research methods are readily applicable – much evidence about treatment is incomplete or inconsistent, and the processes of weighing and evaluating evidence are not neutral or scientific but involve qualitative judgements (Raine 1998). Disputes about the nature of evidence in the social sciences are common, and the validity of data gathered in one political or ideological climate may be challenged in another (as in the re-examination of the findings of education research conducted in the 1960s and 1970s). The difficulty of collecting and evaluating evidence means that attention may focus on researching organisational outputs rather than policy outcomes.

A second set of issues relates to the interaction between political imperatives and evidence-based policy. As the editors of a recent collection suggest, 'Carefully designed research can be overtaken by political imperatives' (Davies et al. 2000: 8). They cite several examples of policy development under Labour which did not fit with available evidence, or which were based on 'flimsy' evidence. These included the introduction of the literacy hour in education, of NHS Direct in health and of elected mayors in local government. There have also been examples of the rejection of research evidence that is unpalatable to ministers, for example of the findings of research on the effects of homework by the Secretary of State for Education. Where there is a reliance on government-sponsored research it may be difficult to break out of the particular paradigm through which the problem to be researched is framed, as happened in the case of research oriented towards assessing future demands on the transport system in the 'predict and provide' era of transport policy (Terry 2000).

A third set of challenges to evidence-based policy focuses on the model of the policy process which underpins it. Rational models of policy are based on a clear separation between knowledge production (by experts) and knowledge use (by practitioners). Such models have been subjected to extensive critiques. First, the separation of policy formulation and implementation squeezes out the possibility of learning and adaptation during the policy cycle. Secondly, the rational model is suited to a centralised approach to policy-making, where all information is collated centrally and definitive judgements are formed. But the capacity of a single centre to collect, collate and analyse all available evidence is severely limited. An incremental model of policy, in contrast, acknowledges a plurality of interests, the validity of research evidence entering the policy arena through a process of advocacy, and of incremental adjustments to policy in the light of learning emerging during the implementation process. This still, however, raises the question of who has influence over the shaping of research questions and access to the data generated. '[A] problem arises when certain groups in society do not have access to research evidence, and, even if they did, their ability to use this evidence is restricted due to their exclusion from the networks that shape policy decisions' (Nutley and Webb 2000: 35).

The relationship between the move towards a more inclusive policy process and the collection and use of evidence is, then, ambiguous. It may be positive or negative, depending on the way in which evidence is gathered, disseminated and evaluated. Evidence may be gathered and shared in a way that promotes reflection and learning within a policy or practitioner community. Evidence-based policy has the capacity to drive network-based problem-solving within practitioner groups or local communities, and to extend democratic participation (by promoting access to data). Alternatively, it may be collated at the centre and used as the basis for an imposed programme of change based on best practice which narrows choices, constrains local experimentation, and displaces decisions away from democratically controlled bodies such as local councils or parliament itself. The use of evidence-based policy in Labour's approach to governance, in which evidence-based assessments of 'what works' is linked to the allocation of public funds through the Comprehensive Spending Review, suggests that the dominant model tends to reflect a centralised, programmatic approach rather than an 'open systems' model.

Modernising the state: towards multi-level governance

So far this chapter has focused on developments in the policy process at Whitehall and Westminster. However, this must be set in the context of profound changes in the UK system of governance that have been produced by constitutional change, the devolution of power to national and regional bodies, and by the changing relationships between central and local government.

Devolution to national and regional tiers of government

Among the most significant changes introduced by Labour has been the devolution of power to a range of new policy-making or policy-shaping fora, including nine Regional Development Agencies, a regional assembly with a directly elected Mayor in London, the possibility of further regional assemblies within England, and, most importantly, the setting-up of the Scottish Parliament and Welsh Assembly. The Scottish Parliament is able to enact laws on health, education, local government and housing, and to raise or lower the basic rate of income tax. The Welsh Assembly has fewer devolved powers but can influence legislation and is responsible for 'home affairs'. Hutton (2000) notes Labour's ambigious attitude to constitutional change. On the one hand, the prime minister wished to be viewed as a constitutional radical; on the other hand, to retain power in Westminster and assure critics that constitutional reform presented no threat to the Union. The modernisation of the state through constitutional reform, then, was underpinned by a double movement. On the one hand, it was characterised by what Pierre and Peters (2000) term 'de-centering down': the dispersal of power to subsidiary bodies and groups with large degrees of autonomy to take decisions, whether in the form of enacting laws, as in the Scottish Parliament, or of controlling substantial budgets, as in the case of the London Mayor. This dispersal was, however, accompanied by an attempt to centralise power in the hands of Whitehall and the political executive. This power may be exercised directly (as in Blair's attempts to influence the appointment processes for the First Minister for the National Assembly for Wales and for the Labour London Mayoral candidate) or indirectly (for example, through Treasury Public Service Agreements attached to devolved funding). Devolution, then, is a complex set of processes (rather than a single act). It involves contestation over the extent of power that is devolved, over the conditions under which devolved powers can be exercised, and over attempts to 'manage' the process (and personnel) from above. The exercise of central power over subsidiary bodies may be more or less successful. But the 'de-centering' of power added greater complexity to the field of policy-making in the UK, with distinct polices in Scotland (e.g. on tuition fees for university students or the payment of care for the elderly) influencing policy debates in the rest of the UK.

The establishment of new tiers of government can also be viewed as part of the emergence of a more differentiated governance, with a stronger focus on horizontal coordination through the Government Offices of the Regions, Regional Development Agencies and Regional Assemblies. Government Offices of the Regions (GO) were established in 1994 under a Conservative government to introduce a measure of coordination between the regional policies and programmes of four government departments: Employment, Environment, Industry and Transport. Despite the continued strengths of the vertical links upwards to parent departments, GOs promoted the development of regional networks and partnerships and can be viewed as an attempt to develop a more holistic or joined-up approach to governance at the regional level (Spencer and Mawson 1998, 2000). Regional Chambers, Regional Assemblies and Regional Development Agencies (RDAs) were introduced by Labour as new elements of regional governance. RDAs were created by legislation to improve regional economic competitiveness. Regional Chambers are public/private partnership bodies comprising indirectly elected local councillors and other regional stakeholders. Regional Assemblies comprise a new non-statutory political tier of government. The directly elected Regional Assembly in London, led by a high-profile Mayor, is likely to develop as a strong power base from which alternative policy agendas might be pursued. Pressure for the development of further Regional Assemblies is strong in some parts of the UK but government support for the establishment of further assemblies is uneven, with, reportedly, strong support from the deputy prime minister but resistance from the prime minister himself.

Regional Chambers and Assemblies represented a partial process of political devolution. The role of the Government Offices of the Regions was more ambiguous; they represented both a pull downwards (towards a greater focus on horizontal integration and embeddedness in local and regional networks and partnerships) and a pull upwards (towards ensuring that the interests of central government in the regions were pursued). They have tended to strengthen the position of central government in the regions rather than strengthening regional devolution or local government (Mawson and Spencer 1997).

The regional picture in the autumn of 2000 is confused. The experiments in constitutional change have led to increased pressure on government for devolution to the regions (through the extension of directly elected Regional Assemblies) and for strengthened regional and local account-ability. But Labour now seems unwilling to pursue political devolution: since the fiasco around the election of the London Mayor, no other Regional Assemblies have been proposed. The emphasis on the central-isation of power – in party and in government – remains high. The degree to which the devolution of power to Scotland and Wales genuinely con-stitutes an extension of multi-level governance is also ambiguous. Responses to the Queen's Speech in December 2000 from Scotland and Wales were highly critical about the dominant focus on issues of import-ance in English governance. But the effect of the creation of national and regional tiers of governance may challenge this centralising and (English) national focus by making it more difficult for government to hold a single line and to control the new institutions it has established. As Doreen Massey comments:

> The genie is out of the bottle. . . . Maybe the need to respond to – or at least acknowledge the existence of – 'local' complexities and challenges will open up debate under New Labour. And if this turns into something with an appearance of 'oppositionism', then New Labour will only have itself to blame. . . . One challenge will be to make differences and divergences symbolise not only difference from New Labour, but also the constructive proposition of viable alternatives. (Massey 2000: 8)

This quotation is a useful reminder that governance and politics are intri-cately entwined. New forms of governance represent not just a rational response to greater social complexity, the 'hollowing out' of the state and so on, but also reflect ongoing debates and conflicts within the dominant party and in the wider society. The dynamics of politics in the UK may be dramatically altered by the process of devolution, especially if, or when, the political administration in Scotland or Wales is controlled by a different party from that in power at Westminster. The introduction of proportional representation for elections in Scotland and Wales, and to the Greater London Assembly, has added an additional dynamic to the process, having potential consequences for the representation of minorities – including black and Asian groups – in the new fora (Gary Younge, Radio 4, 24 April 2000). Viewing the modernisation of the state as representing a move towards a more dispersed governance, then, is only part – and a small part – of the story. Many changes can be viewed in terms of a centralisation, rather than a dispersal, of power. But devolution and the consolidation of regional networks are likely to alter the political dynamics in the UK by strengthening regional and national identities and by shaping power bases from which oppositional and alternative political voices can be heard.

Modernising local government: central-local relations

Nowhere is the political nature of the delegation of power more evident than in the relationships between central and local government. Local government has traditionally played a strong role in shaping local and regional identities and has acted as a platform from which local politics can influence the national agenda. During the Thatcher years this role was severely constrained as functions were removed from the control of local authorities, some tiers of local government were abolished and as financial restraints bit into the capacity of councillors to pursue locally determined political goals. Central government introduced a range of measures through which tighter regulation and control of local expenditure and locally delivered services was exercised. Relations between central and local government became characterised by mutual hostility and mistrust. However, local government remained both a source of oppositional politics and a proving ground for policy innovations developed in the context of alternative political agendas.

Many of these innovations formed the basis of the development of Labour's policies in opposition and its policy programme in government. However, the climate of mistrust was not eradicated. Labour introduced a range of reforms which reflected the general thrust of its modernisation programme, aiming, for example, to bring local government more 'in touch with the people' (the subtitle of the White Paper *Modernising Local Government*):

> Modern councils succeed when they put people first, when they work and take decisions in a culture of openness and accountability to local people. They succeed when there is trust between them and their local community. Within this culture they build and support partnerships to develop a vision for their locality and to contribute to achieving it. They strive for continuous improvement in the delivery of services. (DETR 1998: para 1.3)

The reforms of local government fitted within the mixed economy and partnership ethos of the Third Way: 'councils, in partnership with Government, business, the voluntary sector and others, have a vital role to play in improving the quality of people's lives' (DETR 1998: para 1.2). The old regime of Compulsory Competitive Tendering was replaced by a new duty of Best Value on local authorities, coupled with powers for government to intervene in cases of service or performance failure. The White Paper also set out ways in which local authorities would be expected to consult within their local communities and with local businesses, including consultation on Best Value performance plans. The inclusion of local businesses as distinct (and implicitly coherent) stakeholders, and the devolution of responsibility for decisions about outsourcing or the setting-up of public/private partnerships to local authorities themselves, signify important elements of the 'post-ideological' and 'pragmatic' conceptions of the relationship between the public and private sectors that is central to the Third Way.

However, the main thrust of the reforms, and that which stimulated most debate and opposition, was the government's attempt to 'modernise' local politics in the image of the modernised Labour Party. This included a move towards strong, local political executives, viewed by government as having a greater capacity to drive through change than the structure of service-based committees. The White Paper picked up themes developed in critiques of local government in previous decades, the most significant of which had been the shortcomings of the traditional committee structure. The White Paper and subsequent Bill proposed a mandatory reform of political structures around one of three options (elected mayor plus cabinet, cabinet with a leader, and elected mayor with a council manager).[4] The option to do nothing was not available. A package of measures was also introduced to 'improve local democracy', with experiments designed to increase electoral turnout and the introduction of local referenda. Council decision-making was subjected to new disciplines in the form of scrutiny committees and the ethical conduct of councillors was to be monitored by standards committees backed up by an independent body able to investigate allegations that a council's code of conduct had been breached.

These reforms had important and wide-ranging implications which were viewed in very different ways by different stakeholders in the process. Government ministers viewed them in terms of a strengthening of local democracy by raising the profile of local politics, increasing electoral turnout and strengthening the accountability of decisions made within local party groups. A sub-text of the official view was that the modernisation of local government was a necessary part of the modernisation of the Labour Party itself, tackling some of the bastions of 'old labour' at a local level by strengthening the power of local political executives. Within local government, the modernisation process was viewed by some as a rational programme of reform following decades of criticism about the arcane workings of local democracy. A sub-text here was the advocacy of reform by strong local party members with political ambitions to become members of the executive or to hold mayoral office. Others within local government, however, viewed the concentration of political power as likely to lead to a weakening of local democracy. The reforms sparked a national campaign by Labour councillors who argued for a reformed committee system to be included as an option within the modernisation programme ('The Labour Campaign for Open Local Government'). The proposed reforms also elicited resistance from Charter 88 and the Campaign for the Freedom of Information on the question of the transparency of the decision-making process of the new executives, and new measures on public access were incorporated into the Local Government Bill. The new political structures are likely to transform the dynamics of the local political process, creating sharp distinctions between 'back-bench' and 'cabinet' roles, professionalising the role of members within the new cabinets and creating a stronger managerial ethos in the political governance of local authorities. A language of business efficiency previously embedded in understandings of organisational and managerial change – for example, talk of shorter meetings, better use of time, quicker decision-making, greater flexibility, sharper accountability – has been applied to the political process itself.

There are significant parallels to be drawn between the modernisation of local and central government. Both spoke of greater inclusiveness in the policy process and introduced ways of consulting beyond the traditional policy communities and of extending involvement in policy debates. However, both were also exclusionary in that the role of back-bench MPs and local councillors was curtailed as power became concentrated into stronger executives. This process has been unstated and emergent in central government while in local government it has been explicit and imposed from above. Local authorities were also captured in the governance dynamics of central government, occupying contradictory roles which reflect the tensions in Labour's approach to governing. Local authorities were required to act as the agents through which a set of prescriptive government policies would be delivered, with little scope to shape or retain local diversity. Walker suggests that this model of 'central command, local delivery' represented Labour's view of the new shape of local governance. But he also notes that local authorities remain indispensable in the government of modern Britain since central government only rarely has the instruments under its direct control through which to deliver policy locally (Walker 2000b). Indeed, this problem of control has underpinned the development of the new regional infrastructure of governance discussed above. At the same time, however, local authorities can be viewed as the experimenters, enablers and facilitators of systemic change at the local level, developing initiatives from which future national policy might be shaped as well as reflecting local expectations, needs, interests and aspirations. The Local Government Act of 2000 gave councils more freedom in the form of a power to promote or improve the economic, social or environmental well being of their area, and this may promote additional innovation. Local authorities played an important role during Labour's period in opposition: many national policies, from attention to cross-cutting initiatives to a focus on Best Value, emerged from local policy experiments. But how far local government can continue in this role, given the strengthening of regional tiers of government, threats about the further removal of functions from local authority control and increasingly tight control over performance, is open to question.

The modernisation programme raises a number of issues critical to an understanding of the changing relations between central and local government and the broader process of devolution. First, despite the emphasis on joined-up government, the much criticised 'silo' management is, in practice, reinforced by the vertical dynamics of relationships between central and local government departments, and between professionals and departmentally-based civil servants in Regional Offices. Secondly, the reform agenda for local government may have the consequence of reducing the diversity of ways in which local authorities organise themselves to respond to their localities (J. Stewart 2000). Thirdly, many of the policy changes being introduced speak 'over the heads' of local government direct to neighbourhoods and communities. The work of the Social Exclusion Unit, the zonal initiatives, the National Strategy for Neighbourhood Renewal and other projects designed to generate capacity at the local level both acknowledge the importance of *local* governance but also constrain – and in some cases marginalise – the role of local authorities within the partnership arrangements concerned. The modernisation programme also represents a continuation of the suspicion and mistrust with which previous administrations have viewed local government, despite the new language of 'partnership' which pervades new Labour's discourse of central/local relations (e.g. Armstrong 1998).

A new style of governance?

Chapter 1 set out a number of propositions against which the governance approach of Labour might be assessed. Evidence of a shift towards a 'new' governance style would be likely to include features such as:

- the devolution and decentralisation of power;
- the blurring of boundaries and responsibilities for tackling social and economic issues;
- the recognition and incorporation of policy networks into the process of governing; and
- the emphasis on the role of government in providing leadership, building partnerships, steering and coordinating, and in providing system-wide integration.

The language of new Labour policy documents and White Papers has been one of inclusiveness, participation, and other elements suggestive of a blurring of the boundaries between state and civil society. The approach to policy development suggests both a recognition of existing policy networks and an attempt to establish new ones, drawing new actors into the policy process. Constitutional change has led to the devolution of some powers to national and regional bodies. There is evidence of an 'enabling' style of governance in Labour's emphasis on innovation and experimentation in its first years of office, and the establishment of a host of initiatives requiring partnership working. All of this suggests an 'open system' style of governance, with elements of 'self governance'. However, Labour's style cannot be categorised so easily. Its approach is traversed by a number of tensions that can be mapped using the framework introduced in Chapter 2 (see Figure 4.1).

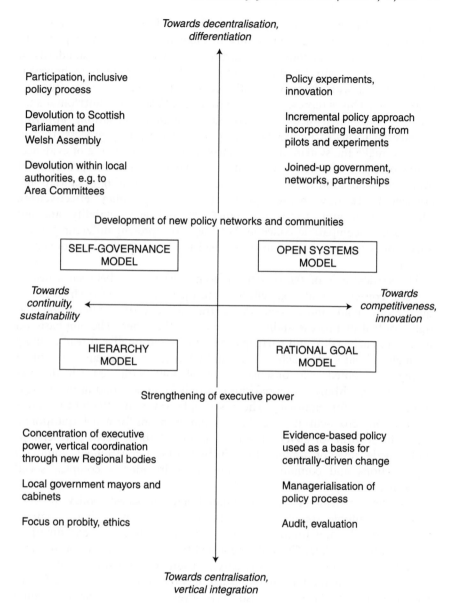

FIGURE 4.1   *Modernising government: models of governance*

The horizontal axis of the framework in Figure 4.1 represents the tension between democracy and accountability at one extreme and managerialism and efficiency on the other. The left-hand point of the axis – an emphasis on continuity and sustainability – directs attention to the importance of process issues: for example, to the standards of conduct in decision-making bodies, the transparency of decision-making and the representativeness of those included in policy task forces, fora and networks. Labour has attempted to sharpen accountability through the devolution of power to new bodies and by introducing measures designed to ensure standards of conduct in both central and local government. At the same time, however, it is obsessed with delivery – with securing tangible outcomes from its endeavours. This is represented at the right-hand end of the horizontal axis. Here it has intensified the process of managerialisation, applying managerial forms of knowledge and power to the policy process itself in order to make the system of governance more efficient. Its use of evidence-based policy, evaluation and audit have expanded and the processes of evaluation and audit (developed in the context of ensuring organisational efficiency) are now being applied to assessing policy effectiveness. Managerialism and democracy, efficiency and accountability are not necessarily incompatible concepts but they do represent different governance values that are not easily reconciled in a rapidly shifting domain of action.

The vertical axis of the model represents the tension between a decentralised, consensus-building, reflexive and open system approach to policy on the one hand, and a focus on centralisation, vertical integration and tight control of process and/or outcomes on the other. The emphasis on inclusion, partnership and participation reflects a distinctive thread running through Labour's approach, which can be located in an attempt to build a strong base rooted in a consensual form of politics (discussed in the previous chapter). Many of the reforms can only be understood in the context of this concern for legitimacy. There is also, however, an attempt to address deep-seated, 'cross-cutting' social issues and problems for which traditional, hierarchical forms of governance are unsuited. Labour needs partnerships with a wide range of organisations, including local government, voluntary organisations and community groups, to help address complex social problems.

The development of a differentiated and dispersed policy process, involving multiple stakeholders operating through increasingly complex policy networks and funding regimes presents problems of coordination. For example one Chief Constable reported that in policing, over a two-year period, there had been twenty-seven Audit Commisson and Police Inspectorate thematic reports published, incorporating over 3,000 different recommendations. There were also thirty-seven separate avenues of funding for development in local government and policing. He concluded: 'What is needed is effective "joined-up" national government, providing greater consistency of approach, better coordination and a focus on outcomes' (Pollard 1999: 34). There were numerous attempts to join things up from the centre, for example through the work of the Social Exclusion Unit, Performance and Innovation Unit and other units within the Cabinet Office. The Labour government's review of Government Offices in 2000 concluded that their role needed to be strengthened to overcome the fragmented pattern of regional arms of government departments. It also called for stronger ministerial and Whitehall coordination of policy initiatives and Government Offices in order to deliver a greater focus on the strategic outcomes of government initiatives affecting local areas:

> . . . the clear evidence from those on the ground and from the PIU's own analysis is that there are too many Government initiatives, causing confusion; not enough coordination; and too much time spent on negotiating the system, rather than delivering. Delivery of Government's priorities may be slowed down as a result. (Performance and Innovation Unit 2000b: para 11–12)

It was announced in April 2000 that a new Regional Coordination Unit was to be set up in Whitehall to link policy initiatives which straddle several departments, and Government Offices of the Regions were to take on a higher profile as 'one-stop shops', giving advice and support to councils and Regional Development Agencies over cross-cutting issues. As well as providing greater coordination, the location of this unit in the Cabinet Office provided a focal point from which regional policy across government could be coordinated.

This tension between dispersal and coordination, between centralisation and decentralisation presents one of the key paradoxes for Labour: the very systems of governance required to address complex and interlocking problems tend to reduce the capacity of government to control the delivery of its political programme. While aspects of the modernisation agenda emphasised greater openness and differentiation, this was limited by Labour's desire to exert control over its own party, over public expenditure and over the delivery of its political mandate in order to ensure political survival. This tension does not, however, mean that there has been no significant change. The development of the 'Modernising Government' agenda represented important shifts in the dominant policy discourses through which problems are framed and solutions sought. The 'new' policy discourses pervading Labour's speeches and consultation papers helped reframe 'old' policy agendas. The long-standing problem of poverty was reframed within the discourses of social exclusion and welfare to work. The twin discourses of 'cross-cutting problems' and 'joined-up government' have reframed the old (separate) policy problems of housing, urban renewal, health and education into the available mix of new solutions – local experimentation, targeting, community empowerment and partnership. In the process, responsibility for the solution to problems became dispersed. The proliferation of policies and partnerships coincided with a process of 'localising' problems and solutions. As Cook comments, citing the Home Secretary Jack Straw, 'In "putting crime in its place", crime is defined as an essentially "local problem, requiring local solutions"' (Cook 1999: 208). This process of making individuals, parents, communities and localities responsible for finding solutions to 'their' problems is a distinctive feature of new Labour's framing and reframing of policy problems (see Chapter 8 of this volume).

The processes of dispersal and localisation might appear to be an intrinsic aspect of the new governance, fitting closely some of the propositions set out at the end of Chapter 1. However, the power to establish the dominance of particular discourses and ideologies remains highly centralised. The state may have relinquished some of its responsibility for delivering services and may be sharing responsibility for solving social problems with a multiplicity of 'partners', but it has retained for itself the power to define the agenda and to shape the meaning of the 'evidence' that feeds the development of policy. In doing so it excludes alternative conceptions of modernisation. The success of Labour's conceptions of 'Modernising Government' is marked by the way in which the language of evidence, pragmatism and 'what works', of goals, targets and outcomes, of joined-up government and partnership now permeates the discourse of ministers and civil servants, managers and professionals, journalists and political commentators, and pervades the host of new policy networks and communities that influence the policy process. The new language, however, masks deep continuities in the practices through which policy is implemented. It also masks the intensification of reform processes begun under the Thatcher and Major administrations directed towards the transformation of the professions in health, social care, education, criminal justice and other sectors. This is the topic of the next chapter.

Notes

1 There were some exceptions: for example, Pettigrew, Ferlie and McKee comment that the Griffiths's findings tended to be consistent with much prior research (Pettigrew et al. 1992).

2 This term originated in the USA but in the UK is most closely associated with the work of John Stewart (e.g. Stewart 1990).

3 There was a widespread expectation within local government that legislation abolishing capping would follow in the first months following the election. Their response to CCT was more complex: some authorities had come to realise its benefits in terms of enhancing their capacity to deal with issues of poor performance.

4 A fourth option was later introduced following concerns raised by smaller local authorities.

5   Modernising services: the politics of performance

We believe in active government and we believe in public service, but if government is going to be effective at delivering services in the way people want them for today, it has to be modernised, it has to be updated and that's what this White Paper is all about.

(Prime Minister, cited in Cabinet Office 1999a)

Labour's programme of reform for the criminal justice system, the NHS, local government and other sectors were all packaged under the general label of modernisation, a term that, as I argued in Chapter 3, served to legitimate change. At first sight, modernisation presents itself as a rational and common-sense project to update public services in order to meet the expectations of modern consumers (who, for example, expect services to be organised around the convenience of those using them) and to meet the business requirements of the 'modern' world (for example, by drawing on developments in ICT). But it has a deeper significance when viewed through the lens of the governance propositions set out in Chapter 1. The Labour government's programme of modernisation continued the development of the mixed economy but with a more significant role for the 'Third Sector' of voluntary and community-based organisations. It softened purchaser/provider splits in some sectors and placed a stronger emphasis on colla-boration and partnership both within and between sectors.

But alongside this apparently flexible and collaborative approach, the modernisation programme can also be viewed as a continuance of neo-liberal reforms, aiming to open up those parts of the public sector that failed to be transformed by the market mechanisms and consumer ethos of the Thatcher and Major years. There was a continued focus on pursuing organisational efficiency and performance, and on the search for business solutions to social and public policy problems. Modernisation continued the attack on the 'producer dominance' associated with monopoly forms of provision, and sought to create new forms of accountability to users and local stakeholders. It did so not only through the use of market mechan-isms, but also through the regulatory capacity of the state. This was an extension of earlier strategies rather than a major change of direction, though with a shift of emphasis as Labour focused on enlarging the role of the state as a regulator of services, setter of standards and guarantor of quality. Ashworth, Boyne and Walker suggest that while the reforms of the

1980s centred on the promotion of competition, central government in the 1990s rediscovered the need to regulate public bodies such as local authorities, health authorities and schools: 'The invisible hand of the market has been replaced by the visible hand of the regulators. Political controls rather than market controls are prominent on the agenda of policy makers and researchers. In short, regulation is the new competition' (Ashworth et al. 1999: 1).

Whether this claim is justified or not, it is clear that regulatory constraints on public sector organisations increased in the latter years of Conservative government (Hoggett 1996; Hood et al. 1999; Power 1997). Labour has extended this process through its use of performance targets, standards, audits, inspection and quality assurance schemes, all backed by additional powers for government to impose mandatory measures on organisations deemed to be performing poorly. The idea that this can be treated as a shift from the market orientation of the Thatcher years back to hierarchical governance is, however, too simple. Hood (1998) and Hood et al. (1999) set out four 'ideal type' models of regulation inside government: competition (control through rivalry and choice); oversight (command and control techniques); mutuality (control through group processes); and contrived randomness (control through unpredictable processes or payoffs). Hood suggests that a combination of these multiple forms of control produced greater intensity and complexity of regulation since the 1980s, but with an increase in competition and oversight ('comptrol').

This chapter deals with the interplay between self-regulation (mutuality) and oversight (comptrol) in the modernising programme, and addresses Labour's approach to the management of change. It begins by exploring the relationship between Labour and the public sector, a relationship in which public services were simultaneously positioned as the partners of government and as its agents in a set of tightly prescribed quasi-contractual relationships. The chapter goes on to highlight the different strategies used by government in its attempt to secure the cooperation – or compliance – of professionals and managers in the delivery of Labour's modernisation goals. It explores the impact of these strategies on organisations and individuals, but also notes the possibility of resistance to, or appropriation of, the reform agenda. The chapter analyses the different models of change underpinning modernisation, and the conflicting imperatives for service managers that these may produce.

Public services: partners or agents?

Two conflicting discourses are in play in the Labour government's programme of public service modernisation. One is that of 'partnership', the other of 'principals and agents'. A partnership discourse was associated with the attempt by government to learn from and draw on developments arising within the public sector, to consult with its staff and include them in the development of policy, and to influence their actions through communication and persuasion rather than the exercise of direct control – all images associated with the propositions set out in Chapter 1 concerning the 'new' governance role of the state. A rather different, contractually-based set of discourses ran alongside these, which was designed to ensure that local managers delivered against central government goals and targets. The notion of a principal–agent relationship arises where one party (the agent) carries out work on behalf of another (the principal), where the interests of principals and agents may not coincide (Ross 1973; Walsh 1995). This 'principal–agent' form of relationship captures the way in which local services were mandated to deliver government policy but under conditions of tight monitoring and control.

A partnership model is implied in the way in which Labour responded to some of the concerns arising from within public services and incorporated these into its modernisation programme. These included the shift away from Compulsory Competitive Tendering in local government towards the Best Value regime; the increasing focus on primary care in health; and the commitment to redress inequalities in the standards of health care offered in different regions. The 1997 White Paper on the NHS proposed an evolutionary model of change rather than major restructuring. Its language of 'going with the grain' of emerging patterns of change (Department of Health 1997: 5) implicitly acknowledged the staff of the NHS as an organisational and social force that needed to be accommodated within the reform programme. Poole (2000) suggests that Labour's language was one of partnership and cooperation, with new pay and incentive packages for nurses and the promise of consultation and involvement as the main carrot for the medical profession. Images of a new partnership between government and local government were also repeatedly used by Hilary Armstrong, the Minister responsible for Local Government, for example in the introduction of Best Value (Stoker 1999).

Despite the espoused ethos of partnership, the forms of inclusion and consultation in the policy process discussed in Chapter 4 were not extended to the professions as a whole. Although key individuals were involved in task forces and policy discussions, the government tended to talk 'over the heads' of the professions to win the support of the public and political stakeholders. Professional knowledge was set against the 'common sense' of the public. For example, the Department for Education and Employment's homework policy, which received extensive criticism from some parts of the teaching profession, was claimed to be one which '[t]he vast majority of parents see . . . as straightfoward *common sense*' (Blunkett 1999: 7–8, my emphasis). Critics of the introduction of Early Learning Goals in nursery education were charged with 'misunderstanding early years education in central Europe and a failure to acknowledge the evidence from our own country. . . . Fortunately in the consultation exercise we conducted, 95% of respondents rejected this nonsense and stood up for *common sense*' (Blunkett 1999: 8, my emphasis). Reynolds, in a response to Blunkett, suggests that the government did not win the support of many teachers for the modernisation process precisely because of this approach. The publication of the 'list of shame' of failing schools after the 1997 general election, he argues, diverted attention from the causes of problems and tended to trivialise complex issues. Policies had not been portrayed in a 'teacher friendly manner', and the government was charged with prioritising presentation to a national political audience over the professional audience. 'In short, teachers have been presented as part of the problem, when of course policies dictate that they are also the solution' (Reynolds 1999: 13). The tendency by Chris Woodhead, then head of Ofsted, to view the teaching profession as part of the problem rather than the source of solutions produced considerable resistance to the government agenda. Teachers walked out on a ministerial speech at a conference in April 2000, and there were threatened strikes over performance-related pay (see Ozga 2000). The intensification of inspection and audit was viewed as increasing the pressure on staff and was exacerbated by a sharper sense of vulnerability to charges of failure.

The initial assumptions of cooperation and partnership between government and public sector professionals were short-lived. Blair's talk of the 'forces of conservatism' and the 'scars on his back' in July 1999 suggested a change of tone. Such representations were closely linked to the proliferation of control measures designed to ensure that 'agents' (organisations in the dispersed field of service delivery networks) delivered what the 'principal' (government) intended. This cut across the language of partnership in rather uncomfortable ways. Particular emphasis was placed on the regulation of professional work.

Regulating professional work

The regulation of the public service professions presents a number of difficulties. Such professions have a history of relative autonomy based on expert knowledge, though the degree of autonomy varies depending on the power base, knowledge claims and control over entry exercised by different professions. Their work is often complex and hard to measure so does not lend itself to standardised work processes and clearly definable outputs. Mintzberg (1983) argues that professional work is coordinated by the standardisation of skills and is governed by the professional body concerned. In practice, of course, most welfare professions work in bureaucracies and are subject to other forms of control. But the specialised nature of their skills and the relative autonomy of their practice produces difficulties in specifying and measuring the outputs of their work or controlling the process of professional labour (Cousins 1987; Johnson 1973). It has also led to problems for successive governments which attempt to reform the public sector but which are unwilling to launch direct assaults on regulatory bodies such as the General Medical Council or to attack the ethos of professional self-regulation (C. Davies 2000). However, the late twentieth-

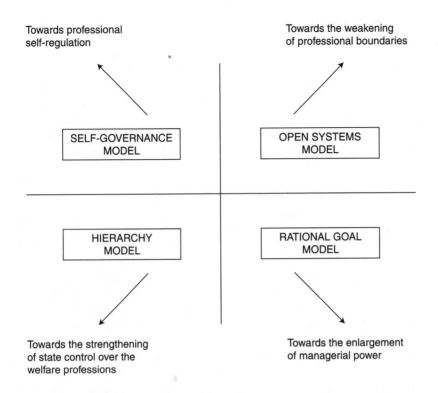

FIGURE 5.1 *Governing the welfare professions*

century rise of managerialism, together with the introduction of quasi-markets, saw significant shifts in the autonomy of professionals in health and social care. These shifts exerted a significant tension between the professional pull towards self-governance and autonomy of practice on the one hand, and the pull towards managerial control on the other. This dynamic tension can be mapped onto the framework of governance models introduced in Chapter 2 (see Figure 5.1).

Prior to Labour entering office, the dominant line of tension was that between self-regulation and managerial forms of power. This tension has continued as the Labour government attempted to extend control over both the *outputs* and *processes* of professional work. The former is represented in the expansion of targets, league tables and performance indicators; the latter in the tightening of the regulation of the labour process itself (the pedagogic practices of teachers, the clinical practice of doctors, or the nature of the interaction between probation officer and young offender).

Measuring outputs: governing by numbers

Performance indicators (PIs) are now viewed as an essential instrument of political control, their growth increasing with the greater accessibility and use of information technology (Carter et al. 1992). They are used in an attempt to sharpen the transparency and accountability of organisations, and have the capacity to shape managerial behaviour and to change strategies of control *within* organisations (Hoggett 1996). Debates about how PIs should be used, and indeed whether they should be used at all, have pervaded the literature for the last decade. PIs may be used as 'tin openers' (to help diagnose problems) or as 'dials' (to measure performance) (Carter 1989). The former opens up the possibility of feedback, self-regulation and reflexive performance management systems while the latter is associated with externally-applied systems of control.

The Labour government's use of PIs remains highly centralised, linked to the gathering of data at the centre rather than as a process of feedback and learning. However, Labour has attempted to shift the focus of PIs towards the measurement of outputs and outcomes rather than inputs and processes. The difficulty of setting such targets was highlighted in the run up to the 2000 Spending Review when the Chief Secretary to the Treasury admitted that those set in the first round had had serious shortcomings (speech to the Institute of Public Policy and Research, *The Guardian*, 5 April 2000: 15). The problems were identified as the setting of too many targets, some of them unworkable, and too great a focus on inputs rather than on outputs or outcomes. The subsequent round of Public Service Agreements show evidence of a shift towards fewer, more output-based and integrated targets but considerable variation between departments remained.

Labour also experimented with indicators that are designed to measure performance against 'cross-cutting' goals and targets. Practice here tended to lag behind the rhetoric due to difficulties in allocating responsibility for performance in complex systems where many organisations might contribute to any particular outcome. Nevertheless, the government set out a number of ambitious promises, such as reducing the numbers of children living in poverty by 25% by 2004, promises that require both joined-up policies and integrated action by public services (see Chapter 6).

The proliferation of targets and performance indicators was linked, under Labour, to the requirement that organisations in most sectors produce year-on-year plans reporting on past performance and outlining the way in which they intend to achieve improvements. Examples include Best Value performance plans, Health Improvement plans, School Development plans and a host of others. Many such planning processes became mandatory and subject to audit and inspection processes. There was some scope, however, for organisations to set self-determined goals and targets, based on consultation with users and other stakeholders. Despite this proviso, targets, performance indicators and mandatory plans can be viewed as strategies to focus professional effort and managerial activity around a government's priorities. They do not necessarily intervene in the professional task itself, but have consequences for the relationship between professional and managerial roles within an organisation. In contrast, greater *task* control is involved in the formalisation of standards for professional practice.

Specifying practices: regulating the labour process

The White Paper *Modernising Social Services* introduced its proposed reforms with the comment that:

> One big trouble social services have suffered from is that up to now no Government has spelled out exactly what people can expect or what the staff are expected to do. Nor have any clear standards of performance been laid down. This government is to change all that. (Foreword by the Secretary of State, Department of Health 1998b: 2)

Standards are the means of moving towards the eradication of inconsistencies in practice between different regions or organisations. For example, local variation in standards in health, social services and other locally or regionally controlled services was used by the Audit Commission and other bodies to indicate the need for reform. The introduction of common standards enables government to overcome perceived defects in the way in which delegated authority is used by local managers to control professional practice. Moves towards the standardisation of practice included the introduction of a mandatory 'literacy hour' and 'numeracy hour' in primary schools and a range of measures in Social Services and Probation. Even the strongest bulwarks of professional power, medicine and surgery, became subject to tighter regulation and the standardisation of performance norms following examples of surgeon error at Bristol Royal Infirmary and other scandals involving surgeons and general practitioners. The publicity surrounding these cases led to the government adding a clause to the 1999 NHS Bill, giving it wide-ranging powers to change the machinery of self-regulation in the health professions. National Service Frameworks were introduced to create greater consistency in the treatment of specific disease groups, placing constraints around the clinical freedoms of medical practitioners. The National Institute for Clinical Excellence (NICE) was charged with responsibility for making judgements on the value of new medicines and technologies. All of these developments undermined the tradition of professional self-regulation in the welfare and health professions.

Towards self-regulation: quality assurance

The development of standards can be linked to the increasing emphasis on quality in public services which developed through the Thatcher years but became particularly signficant with John Major's Citizen's Charter, relaunched under Labour in its Service First programme. Quality assurance is an all-embracing term covering a range of different meanings and practices (Kirkpatrick and Martinez Lucio 1995). Its importance increased under Labour in areas where competition was no longer viewed as the main driver of change. For example Best Value was based on a drive for continuous improvement in council and other services, with councils expected to show improvements in meeting quality targets for service delivery. In health, the 1997 White Paper emphasised the importance of quality and announced the introduction of national standards and guidelines. The long-term service agreements which replaced contracts were underpinned by explicit quality standards. The 'Quality Protects' scheme, which was introduced in social services, sets specific targets for improvement in the lives of looked-after children over a three-year period. Many organisations adopted a quality accreditation system such as the Business Excellence Model or began to participate in peer review schemes (e.g. that established for local government by the Improvement and Development Agency).

One of the most signficant developments under Labour was the introduction of a new system of clinical governance in health, defined as a 'framework through which NHS organisations are accountable for continuously improving the quality of their services and safeguarding high standards of care by creating an environment in which excellence in clinical care will flourish' (Department of Health 1998a: 3). Clinical governance is a comprehensive approach covering clincal audit, evidence-based practice and standard-setting. It places a statutory responsibility for quality on chief executives and requires each Trust or Primary Care Group to develop procedures for all professional groups to identify and remedy poor performance. In doing so it shifts the focus from external regulation by government or the professional body to the development of 'self-managing' organisational systems, procedures, guidelines and protocols. Clinical governance can be viewed as a strategy to strengthen systems of professional self-regulation, but accompanied by managerial mechanisms of quality control. Trust Boards were expected to establish a vision and implementation strategy for clinical governance which was then reflected in the performance targets of individuals and teams. A Commission for Health Improvement was charged with responsibility for clinical governance arangements and was given the power to tackle shortcomings. Clinical Audit might be viewed in terms of the exercise of greater control over activities that were previously the province of individual professional or managerial judgement. It might, on the other hand, be viewed as re-balancing of professional–manager relations. Some suspect that efficiency goals have played a role in these developments, alongside issues of clinical or professional effectiveness (Boseley 2000). But it is also closely linked to the 'what works' philosophy I described in Chapter 4, drawing on best practice and inscribing this into general guidelines and standards.

Towards external scrutiny: audit and inspection

Each of these instruments and strategies was reinforced by audit. Clarke et al. (2000) locate the growth of audit in the neo-liberal reforms of the 1980s, arguing that the new dispersed state form, in which provider organisations had enlarged autonomy for operational management, implied new issues of control for the centre. 'Audit has emerged as a generic feature of this new state form in the UK, although it combines in complex ways with a variety of arm's length control systems and practices: inspection, accounting, regulation, performance review, and processes of organisational development' (Clarke et al. 2000: 254). Labour's approach to modernising public services such as education, health, social services and probation was based on strengthening this external oversight through functionally separate agencies such as the Audit Commission, Ofsted and the SSI, each established under previous governments. Labour also expanded the range of bodies involved in scrutiny, inspection and audit. It established a new Commission for Care Standards in each region to regulate social care in domiciliary and residential settings. The role of the Audit Commission continued to expand and Housing and Best Value Inspectorates were established under its aegis. A new body – Her Majesty's Inspector of Probation – was introduced. The multiplication of inspection regimes was accompanied by additional powers for Secretaries of State in education, social services and elsewhere to remove services from organisations receiving poor inspection reports. The Commission for Health Improvement was given the power to intervene in the running of Primary Care Trusts alleged to be performing poorly. Ofsted inspections were backed up by powers for the Secretary of State to remove functions from local education authorities (LEAs) or to close schools and re-open them under the Fresh Start initiative.

Audit and inspection in the 1980s and 1990s predominantly focused on value for money. This is a continuing focus under Labour: the frameworks of performance indicators, standards and targets that have passed from policy into legislation strongly reflect the New Public Management focus on service costs and performance (Hughes and Newman 1999). However, there was an increasing focus on auditing the measures introduced by organisations to deliver the government's policy agenda. Measures of policy outputs and outcomes reflect an emerging agenda of joint audits, cross-cutting targets and outcome-oriented performance indicators. The partial shift towards auditing and inspecting outcomes was underpinned by an assumption of self-regulation: that is, that managers and professionals would find the best means of securing the desired changes. However, in case they did not, the government set in place a range of measures through which organisations could face the removal of some or all of their self-governing powers.

Sanctions and threats

The development of audit and inspection was linked to a wider discourse of failure and the growth of threats and sanctions against organisations deemed to be performing poorly. The language of threat and coercion became common:

> If you (local government) are unwilling or unable to work to the modern agenda, then the government will have to look to other partners to take on your role. (Blair 1998b: 22)

> The choice is not a new NHS or the current NHS. It is the new NHS or no NHS.
> (Dobson 1999: 18)

In the Health Service the language of partnership and 'going with the grain' gave way to more coercive strategies as the government became frustrated with the slow speed of change. In March 2000 it was announced that Blair would take 'personal charge' of the government's efforts to improve the NHS by chairing a new Cabinet Committee to monitor NHS improvements in England after admitting failure to deliver election pledges. This followed a budget announcement earlier in the same week of extra money for modernisation reforms. The extra resources were set against new measures to redress failure by withholding cash if performance targets were missed, and were accompanied by the threat to replace managers with 'hit squads' of managers from successful units. Blair spelled out a much harsher message for health service workers than that underpinning the earlier 'partnership' model, calling for a new realism on the part of health professionals and demanding that they 'strip out unnecessary demarcations, introduce more flexible training and working practices' (Blair, reported in *The Guardian*, 23 March 2000: 23). The division of local authorities, schools and other services into 'heroes' (or beacons for others to follow) or 'villains' ('failing' services) laid the foundation for the exercise of additional powers by Secretaries of State. Services deemed to be failing were required to produce action plans and demonstrate measurable improvements within a specific time period. Where these were not delivered, additional sanctions were available. For example, the Fresh Start scheme for schools enabled Secretaries of State to impose special measures and ultimately to close 'failing' schools and re-open them under new leadership and with additional resources. The model of change here was based on the presumed power of heroic leadership: the capacity of individuals to transform organisations by motivating staff and putting in place new management systems. Three such 'super-heads', however, resigned in the first months of 2000 (*The Guardian*, 15 March 2000: 4). These resignations, and the publicity surrounding them, raised concerns about the capacity of individuals to treat the symptoms of more structural problems in the education system by business recipes of organisational turnaround. The introduction of 'hit squads' in the NHS was, paradoxically, announced shortly after problems in the Fresh Start scheme in education became apparent.

The ultimate threat was that of privatisation. In April 2000 a private sector company took over most LEA services from Islington Council following a highly critical report from Ofsted in the previous year. Comprehensive outsourcing of LEA services was also threatened at Liverpool, again following an adverse Ofsted inspection. The consultants KPMG had been called in to plan the outsourcing programme and it was reported that Tony Blair conceived this as a 'demonstration project for a Third Way in education' (*Education Guardian*, 18 January 2000: 8), although the eventual decision here was to retain the LEA.[1] Threats concerning the removal of powers and functions also became a recurrent theme in local government. Discussions running up to the 2000 Spending Review included proposals to remove social service and education functions from local councils, with direct funding of schools and Health Authorities taking over care of the elderly. The outcomes of the discussions were more muted, with a strengthening of partnership working between health and social service departments and only a partial implementation of the proposals to fund schools directly, bypassing the LEA. However, the principle of 'front-line funding' – passing additional funding made available over a three-year period for health and education direct to schools and health workers – effectively short-circuited potential centres of professional resistance.

Shaping behaviour: regulation and self-regulation

What impact did all this activity have on those being regulated? The literature highlights a number of key concepts about the relationship between regulator and regulatee, including regulatory capture, resistance by regulatees and ritualised compliance (Ashworth et al. 1999). The literature also suggests the importance of models of power dependence in understanding relations between regulator and regulatee (Cope and Goodship 1999). Research evidence on the links between audit or inspection and performance is scant and inconclusive because of the difficulties of measuring the impact of inspection in relation to other variables. However, it has been suggested that audit and inspection may have a number of consequences for organisation and individual behaviour. It may lead organisations to focus on process rather than outcomes (e.g. ensuring that an organisation can demonstrate it has followed the expected procedure for conducting a Best Value review). Audit and inspection may lead an organisation to focus on the factors likely to be the subject of external scrutiny, or the factors measured in performance indicators, with possible 'perverse effects'. The anticipated visit of auditors or inspectors will almost certainly divert resources from mainstream activity and produce higher than normal degrees of anxiety and stress. External scrutiny may also lead organisations to focus their energies on the production of discourses of success – what Corvellec (1995) terms 'narratives of achievement' – to ensure survival in a competitive environment, at the possible expense of more realistic assessments of weaknesses and strengths.

Finally, audit and inspection may produce its own perverse incentives in the form of encouraging greater conformity with an expected norm. This is a point made by Boyne (1999) in relation to Best Value, which he suggests may lead to a 'dull conformity' as local authorities have their attention directed to the same performance indicators. Standardisation, peer review, inspection, audit, performance indicators and other measures may bring huge benefits in terms of eradicating the worst practice in public services and using the best as a benchmark for others to follow. However, they may also have significant consequences in terms of organisational isomorphism (see p. 27 in Chapter 2), squeezing out the diversity of practice within a particular sector. Such diversity is an important source of innovation and, ultimately, of new models of policy and practice for the future.

A related set of issues concerning the effects of the expansion of regulatory processes concerns the relationship between external regulation and self-regulation. Hood's model of regulation (see p. 84) implies a sharp distinction between 'comptrol' and 'inspector free' forms of regulation, although he acknowledges the importance of hybrid forms. He argues that:

> the distinction between 'comptrol' and 'inspector free control' is important, because the main lessons of cybernetic analysis for bureaucracy is that a system can be under control without having any identifiable overseers and that in any complex system control cannot be effected by simple steering alone, but must in large measure consist of self-controlling mechanisms. (Hood et al. 1999: 13)

This is an important point for arguments about the relationship between hierarchical governance and co- or self-governance. Public service professionals have never been entirely autonomous agents; they have always been subject to external regulation by professional bodies and/or the hierarchical disciplines of the bureaucracies within which they work. But the neo-liberal reforms of the 1980s and 1990s saw an explosion of new strategies of control. Managerialism subordinated many areas of professional judgement to an economic calculus, at the same time that contracts and service standards limited the extent of professional discretion (Clarke and Newman 1997: Chapter 4). The extent and nature of these disciplines varied between sectors, but all involved what Rose terms a shift to 'governing at a distance':

> In a plethora of quasi-autonomous units, associations and 'intermediate organisations', experts are allocated new responsibilities and new mechanisms are deployed for the management of professional expertise 'at a distance' – that is, outside the machinery of bureaucracy that previously bounded experts into devices for the government of 'the social'. (Rose 1996a: 350)

Rather than a clear distinction between 'comptrol' and 'inspector free' forms of regulation, the theories of governmentality introduced in Chapter 1 would assess the full range of strategies in terms of their capacity to constitute *self-regulating subjects*. Power (1994, 1997) argues that one consequence of what he terms the 'audit explosion' has been the construction of auditable organisations. He notes the shift of organisational resources from first-order to second-order functions, diverting resources from delivering the core business to the process of accounting for what is delivered. Audit and inspection also helps to construct new forms of professional self-regulation. As Rose comments:

... rendering something auditable shapes the processes that are to be audited, and the logics and technical requirements of audit displace the internal logics of expertise. ... These arrangements retain the formal independence of the professional while utilizing new techniques of accountability to render their decisions visible, calculable and amenable to evaluation. (Rose 1996a: 351)

This produces particular consequences for organisational behaviour as external scrutiny is translated into a myriad of internal forms of management control. The meeting of externally-set targets becomes a matter of managerial goals and priorities. Standards and norms become incorporated into the practices through which staff are recruited, trained and appraised. Peer review may be developed as a form of insurance against the possibility of 'failure' and the risk of external intervention. All of this produces an intensification of data collection and management within organisations, installing a 'calculative technology' in the enterprise (Rose and Miller 1992: 187) or a 'tyranny of numbers' which may stifle creativity and reason (Marr 2000b). Under Labour, there has been an intensification of external controls (standards, targets, audit and inspection), coupled with the emphasis on distinguishing between successful and failing organisations. But each has the capacity to produce a self-regulatory effect, albeit what in Vincent-Jones's terms would be viewed as 'enforced self-regulation' (1999: 282). The installation of a 'calculative technology' does not, however, necessarily induce commitment to the government's goals, nor motivate public service staff to work in new ways. This was one of the major dilemmas for the government: oscillations between commitment-building and control-based approaches to the management of change characterised its strategies for public service reform. This is the topic of the next section.

Labour's approach to managing change

Previous sections have discussed the range of strategies used by the Labour government to modernise public services. Commentators such as Ham (1999a) have noted the 'eclectic mix' of tools used by the Labour government. Indeed, the idea of a 'toolbox' became a common metaphor for Labour's approach to the modernisation of public services. The need for a mix of measures might be viewed in terms of a 'what works' pragmatism. Alternatively, it might be viewed as a 'belt and braces' approach, devolving responsibility and building commitment with one hand while strengthening central control measures on the other to ensure that strategies are delivered.

The Labour government's approach to modernising public services was based on a series of very different models of change. It encompassed strategies that were designed to support the professions and raise morale in areas facing recruitment problems (e.g. nursing, teaching and the police) at the same time as it encompassed strategies that were designed to exert pressure on recalcitrant workers to ensure policies were delivered. It included top-down measures (such as the specification of standards and targets) and decentralising measures (e.g. the empowerment of nurses and GPs in the new Primary Care Groups (PCGs) and the allocation of additional resources directly to schools and hospitals rather than to intermediary bodies). Accompanying the expansion of inspection, audit and other measures of control was an explicit emphasis by ministers on persuasion and influence – on attempting to secure support for change among professionals and managers in the public sector. There was also an attempt to encourage self-generated change – innovation – in the delivery of services. Some of the legislation introduced deliberately focused on setting frameworks within which managers, professionals and local politicians could choose how to implement reforms rather than on having a common template imposed from above. Threats of the removal of powers in examples of poor performance were offset against a programme of incentives. The modernisation programme included additional incentives for schools, hospitals, local authorities and other agencies to change in order to secure access to additional funds or powers. The 'incentive' elements of the programme included the devolution of responsibility to the new PGCs and Trusts, the Beacon Schools and Beacon Local Authority Schemes, and the launch of a host of new projects, pilots and initiatives. These enabled many public sector workers to act in more innovative ways and to be more proactive in shaping wider processes of change.

This eclectic approach drew on a range of different models of change that can be mapped onto the framework introduced in earlier chapters (see Figure 5.2). The top left-hand quadrant ('self governance') represents a focus on fostering commitment and ownership in order that public services professionals, managers and staff might take responsibility for delivering change. It also reflects a focus on capacity-building for the future, represented by Labour's attempt to resolve long-term problems of recruitment and the supply of trained professionals. The top right-hand quadrant ('open systems') reflects the government's emphasis on the need for innovation. This requires local flexibility and diversity and the devolution of responsibility for delivering policy outcomes. The bottom left-hand quadrant ('hierarchy') reflects an enhanced focus on standards and scrutiny of professional practice. The bottom right-hand quadrant ('rational goal') focuses on the delivery of outputs rather than on the achievement of outcomes. It reflects the panoply of targets, goals, plans and performance indicators cascading from the centre and the explosion of audit and inspection bodies. It reflects an approach to governance in which the state appropriates for itself the discourses and technologies of managerialism in an attempt to secure its goals in the context of a dispersed and fragmented system of delivery.

The model shown in Figure 5.2 can be used to highlight a number of emergent tensions within the implementation of the modernisation agenda.

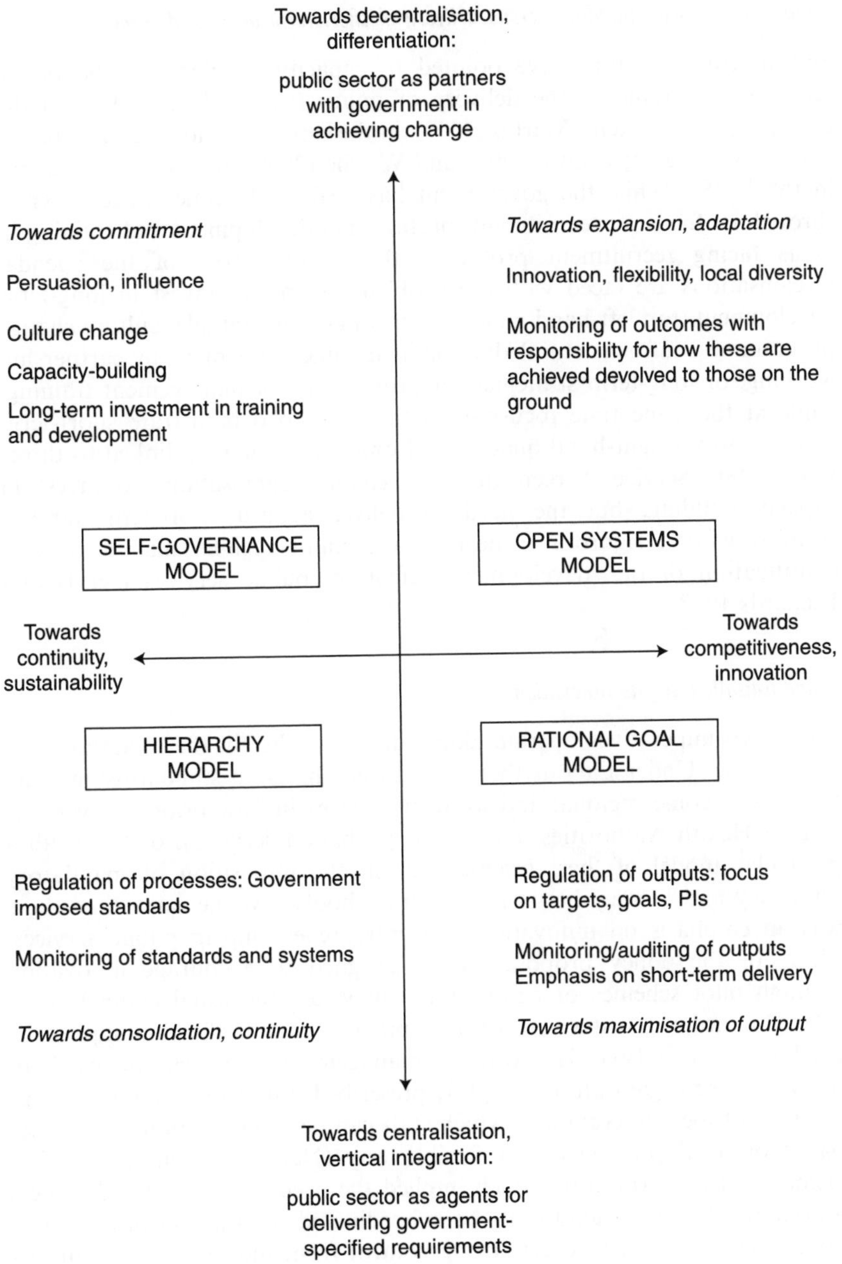

Towards decentralisation,
differentiation:

public sector as partners
with government in
achieving change

Towards commitment

Persuasion, influence

Culture change

Capacity-building

Long-term investment in training
and development

Towards expansion, adaptation

Innovation, flexibility, local diversity

Monitoring of outcomes with
responsibility for how these are
achieved devolved to those on the
ground

| SELF-GOVERNANCE | OPEN SYSTEMS |
| MODEL | MODEL |

Towards
continuity,
sustainability

Towards
competitiveness,
innovation

| HIERARCHY | RATIONAL GOAL |
| MODEL | MODEL |

Regulation of processes: Government
imposed standards

Monitoring of standards and systems

Towards consolidation, continuity

Regulation of outputs: focus
on targets, goals, PIs

Monitoring/auditing of outputs
Emphasis on short-term delivery

Towards maximisation of output

Towards centralisation,
vertical integration:

public sector as agents for
delivering government-
specified requirements

FIGURE 5.2   *Modernising services: models of change*

Long-term capacity-building versus delivery of short-term goals and targets

Several commentators have pointed to capacity problems in the public sector which influence the delivery of policy (e.g. Pollard (1999) on the criminal justice system; Martin (2000) on the capacity of local authorities to deliver Best Value; Ham (1999b) and Walshe (2000) on capacity problems in the NHS). While the government has dealt with some capacity issues through its focus on recruitment, professional development and training in areas facing recruitment problems, this is only part of the agenda. Organisations are faced with the problem of how to invest in long-term development (top left-hand quadrant) through, for example, culture change programmes, infrastructural development, time investment in partnership working, or long-term strategies for professional or management training, while at the same time focusing on the need to demonstrate short-term 'wins' (bottom right-hand quadrant). Longer-term funding linked to three-year Public Service Agreements may enable organisations to invest in capacity-building, but the need to deliver against short-term targets, coupled with a rigorous inspection and audit regime, may lead to a continuation of the 'development deficit' in public services (Jervis and Richards 1997).

Standardisation versus innovation

These two imperatives operate alongside each other in the modernisation programme. Under Labour there was an emphasis on standardising practice to overcome regional and local differences in how priorities were set (e.g. in Health Authorities, police and probation services), or to install a particular model of 'best practice' (as in the imposition of mandatory numeracy and literacy hours in primary schools). At the same time there was an emphasis on innovation and entrepreneurship in public services. Many of the policy proposals were designed to encourage innovation through pilot schemes or action zones in which the usual controls were relaxed in order to foster new forms of practice. Standardisation implies the need for a 'neo-Taylorist' form of management in which the work of individuals or organisations is tightly prescribed. Innovation implies a large measure of local discretion in which staff can develop solutions to service-based or local problems in a flexible way (Newman et al. 2000). The elements of modernisation which implied the need for flexibility and local autonomy, however, tended to be subordinated to other priorities for a government anxious to exert strong control from the centre to ensure its policy agenda and political project were carried through.

Commitment versus compliance

Over the last twenty years there has been considerable focus on the need for transformational leadership and culture change in the public sector.

Problems of implementation have frequently been linked to cultural barriers, and both politicians and senior managers have recognised the significance of culture and leadership in comments about the need to 'win hearts and minds' or to 'build ownership'. The strategies required to build commitment are, however, very different from those designed to exercise control, as recognised in the Human Resource Management literature (e.g. Legge 1995; Storey 1999; Storey and Sissons 1992). The expansion of performance indicators, targets, standards and other contractual modes of controls tends to induce compliance rather than commitment (Flynn 1994).

The language of decentralisation, flexibility and innovation pervaded new Labour discourse and suggested that there was a recognition of the need to build commitment and ownership. Local leadership was, in many documents, viewed as a solution to problems of poor performance in schools and other organisations (e.g. Scottish Office 1999), and as a source of culture change oriented towards the new agenda (e.g. Social Exclusion Unit 1998a). Devolution and innovation were mobilised as tools through which managers could deliver the results or outcomes government required. This form of managerialism, based on transformational leadership, culture change, entrepreneurial action and innovation, can be contrasted with the search for rational, mechanical levers of control, based on detailed guidelines and universal standards applied across different local contexts. Rather than devolved management and flexibility, the increasing requirement that organisations meet centrally-determined standards of performance tended to produce a neo-Taylorist form of internal management based on the standardisation of work processes (Pollitt 1993). These tensions were system-wide as well as organisation-specific. The tension between standardisation and flexibility was reflected in the problems experienced by government as it sought to reconcile long-term development through innovation, experiment and capacity-building with the delivery of electoral pledges relating to mainstream services such as health and education. The unwillingness of the government to release funds for significant investment in public services until three years into its term of office certainly exacerbated the problem of building capacity for the deep changes required by the modernisation programme.

Implementing change: trust and contract

The attention to how change was to be delivered – to the implementation of the reforms – tended to be a neglected element of the policy process. Change needs to be conceptualised rather more subtly than a simple contrast between government will and professional resistance. The implementation process is influenced by professionals and managers as social actors, making sense of the changing policy environment and learning to navigate the tensions between centralisation and decentralisation, empowerment and control. Issues of trust are central to this process. Trust mediates between the external stimulus (e.g. a new policy announcement) and individual or group perception (the meaning attributed to it). The difficulty with the eclectic mix of instruments used by Labour was that it invoked different forms of trust: calculus-based, knowledge-based and identification-based (Lewicki and Bunker 1996; see also Coulson 1998; Newman 1998a). Calculus-based trust derives from rational calculation and relationships of exchange. It invokes instrumental behaviour and game-playing, and is linked to the operation of incentives and the threat of sanctions. Knowledge-based trust is formed over time through experience of, and information about, the other party. It is based on a longer-term stake in the relationship which leads to 'give and take' and elements of reciprocity. Identity-based trust is formed through common patterns of identification and the principles of mutuality and loyalty. It is implicit, affective and long-lasting. Each of these forms of trust suggests different forms of behaviour and is associated with different costs and benefits. While calculus-based interactions tend to produce compliance, identification-based relationships tend to produce high levels of personal engagement and commitment. The former produces high transaction costs (the costs of monitoring compliance and exercising sanctions) while the latter is associated with low costs. Public services have traditionally operated on high levels of identity-based trust because of the commitment of workers to public service values, to their users and clients, or their identification with a profession or colleagues in a particular service. Identity-based trust may involve multiple and potentially conflicting identities, as when, for example, black police officers struggle to reconcile identification with both the police service and with local black communities. However, identity-based trust between the individual and their employing organisation has, in the past, formed a strong and unifying set of ethics based on public service values.

Such identity-based trust has, however, been eroded over the last twenty years. The New Public Management installed new patterns of control based on performance and contract displacing the collegial, professional and corporate forms of trust that characterised the postwar public sector. New forms of employment contract, market relationships and performance regimes led to a more instrumental set of calculations about the relationship between workers and employers, professionals and government (Newman 1998a). Audit and inspection processes installed new ways in which the public interest was represented, in place of trust in its professional and bureaucratic embodiments (Clarke et al. 2000). Labour's modernisation programme continued these trends. Knowledge-based trust was inevitably limited during Labour's first years in office, though some public sector staff carried expectations based on experience of working under Labour-controlled local authorities, or distant memories of a previous Labour government. Hopes and expectations were high, and many in the public sector identified strongly with the espoused goals of Labour, the new form of leadership and new freedoms which it was seen to represent.

However, the dominance of the 'principal–agent' model in Labour's approach to delivering change tended to produce a calculative form of trust based on compliance to a set of contractual relations. The modernisation agenda was implemented through a range of implicit or explicit contracts. These often took the form of exchange relationships such as the linking of the release of money for modernisation to delivery against staged targets, as in education: 'We are proposing money for modernisation – serious investment in return for necessary reform. The Government, supported by the wider public, cannot and *will not proceed without this fair exchange*' (Blunkett 1999: 11, my emphasis). More personal and constitutive forms of contractual relationship – what might be termed new psychological contracts – were also set out by government in place of the enforced restructurings of the past: 'I want to make sure that the people in the NHS have up-to-date and authoritative guidance, training and advice. *In turn, they must be willing to change* and be open to new ideas' (Dobson 1999: 18, my emphasis).

Here and elsewhere the government attempted to elicit a willingness on the part of public sector organisations and staff to pursue the modernisation agenda. New freedoms were offered to those performing well. In primary care, the achievement of NHS Trust status depends on demonstrating a systematic approach to monitoring and improving clinical standards in medicine and nursing. Local councils were invited to bid for Beacon status, exchanging 'exemplary' performance for financial flexibility and the relaxation of some legislative requirements. As noted earlier in this chapter, performance against contract was being tightly monitored by a range of inspecting and auditing bodies, and sanctions were being exercised where contracts are not delivered. But less formal modes of contract were also invoked. For example, the Best Value regime can be viewed as a form of implicit contract between government and local government in which, in return for abolishing Compulsory Competitive Tendering, councils were required to demonstrate continuous improvement in both costs and quality.

I noted earlier the eclectic mix of models in Labour's modernisation programme. The government oscillated between what, in ministerial language, is termed 'pressure' and 'support': that is, between strategies of direct control (quasi-contractual relations backed up by the exercise of new powers by Secretaries of State) and strategies designed to foster self-motivated change. This analysis suggests that, rather than these being aggregative and complementary – a 'belt and braces' approach in which one measure is intended to succeed if others fail – they may be mutually contradictory. The 'support' offered by government did not produce the expected levels of commitment precisely because it was backed up by, and in some cases preceded by, coercion. The behaviour of those to whom responsibility was delegated in 'enabling' parts of the programme was often shaped by a calculative form of trust (compliance, or at least the appearance of compliance) rather than engagement with the new agenda. The programme of incentives and threats tended to produce a focus on game-playing, information management and presentation rather than on the delivery of sustainable outcomes.

The mix of models was deliberate and was given a positive gloss by ministers. The former Secretary of State for Health, for example, claimed that the mix of what he terms 'pressure' and 'support' meant that the government was 'combining national standards for care with local flexibility. This really is a third way beyond old-style command and control and the pseudo market introduced by our predecessors' (Dobson 1999: 15). This was a key element of Labour's discourse on public service change. It resonates with the notion of a 'Third Way' and with ideas of the new governance outlined in Chapter 1 in that it claimed to transcend both hierarchy and market. The emphasis on national standards plus local flexibility appeared to reflect supposed shifts in the role of the state towards influencing and enabling rather than the exercise of direct control. But rather than a coherent model of change, the mix of models tended to produce confusing messages about the relationship between government, the professions and the public. As Celia Davies comments in relation to the regulation of the professions, central control remained dominant:

> Labour's reforms in health and social care retain regulation at the centre. . . . By a process of accretion, we now regulate persons, programmes and places. Little surprise, then, if consumers feel confused and professionals feel embattled. (C. Davies 2000: 288)

External forms of regulation and control result in a form of enforced self-regulation on the part of both individuals and organisations. The dominance of the principal–agent, contractual model of the relationship between regulator and regulatee, coupled with increased sanctions and threats, tends towards the production of low-trust compliance rather than a committed engagement with the modernisation process.

However, Labour's approach to managing change can also be understood through the lens of the theories of institutional change introduced in Chapter 2. The reform process undoubtedly had the capacity to produce shifts in the cultural formation of identity of professional and managerial workers. They became change agents, modernisers, leaders or standard-setters and a host of other possible identities, through which the outcomes of change were shaped. Generalised conclusions about the relationship between external regulation and self-regulation are not necessarily very helpful. Governance is, as Chapter 2 emphasised, a contested domain and each new control measure may be met by new strategies of appropriation or resistance – active or passive – on the part of those being regulated. Workers have a range of strategies for dealing with reforms, from resistance to compliance, co-option and appropriation. The impact of standards and quality programmes depends on how groups come to redefine these measures within a professional or service-based set of norms and meanings. For example, clinical governance might be viewed as a strategy used by government to introduce greater controls over costly treatments, or as a strategy directed towards professional self-governance, welcomed by the medical profession as representing a re-balancing of professional–managerial relations. Enforced self-regulation through targets, plans and audit may enable change agents to overcome past barriers to change, or may produce perverse effects as organisations focus more on compliance and presentation than on outcomes. Rather than viewing change as an evolutionary process in which professionals or managers simply adapt to new environmental opportunities and constraints, it is, then, necessary to study the strategies they use to win organisational or professional legitimacy in a contested field of governance.

Overall, however, the strategies of regulation and control that were evident in the programme of modernising public services described in this chapter invoked a centrally-driven, strongly managerial form of governance which can be contrasted with the propositions relating to a shift towards the network-based governance that were set out in Chapter 1. The next chapter goes on to consider areas of Labour's agenda which invoke the need for joined-up government and partnership, areas in which evidence of network-based forms of governance are more likely to be found.

Note

1 This followed a number of changes at senior management level and a programme of improvements which enabled the authority to head off the threat of outsourcing.

6   Joined-up government: the politics of partnership

> Above all, a joined-up problem has never been addressed in a joined-up way. Problems have fallen through the cracks between Whitehall Departments, or between central and local government. And at the neighbourhood level, there has been no one in charge of pulling together all the things that need to go right at the same time.
>
> (Social Exclusion Unit 1998a: 9)

The governance literature outlined in Chapter 1 suggests a move away from coordination through hierarchy or competition and towards networks and partnerships. This theme is strongly represented in Labour's approach. It formed a central element of the Third Way, which sought to transcend old ideologically-based preferences for delivering services through state bureaucracies on the one hand and competition on the other. It underpinned Labour's discourse of 'joined-up government' through which the government attempted to move towards a more holistic approach to public policy, an approach which transcended the vertical, departmental structures of government itself. Partnership also represented a powerful discourse of inclusion and collaboration which was central to Labour's attempt to forge a consensual style of politics.

This chapter traces these themes in Labour's approach to governing and asks how far they represent a move towards a network-based form of governance. It analyses the contradictory influences on partnership working that are created by the tensions between centralisation and decentralisation in government policy, and suggests ways in which Labour's approach influences the internal dynamics of partnership working. The chapter concludes by highlighting the role of partnerships in the dispersal and reconfiguration of state power.

Governing through partnership: a paradigm shift?

Attempts to create more joined-up government are not a new feature of public policy; there is a long-standing tradition of initiatives designed to bring about better integration of policies and services. The state corporatism of the Wilson, Heath and Callaghan governments produced earlier attempts to create integration through policy planning systems and the creation of super ministries such as the Department of Health and Social Security. Attempts to promote collaboration between statutory agencies such as the NHS and local authority Social Services Departments have a long history, with particular emphasis on the need for joint approaches underpinning successive policies on community care through the 1990s.

The idea of partnership as an emerging form of governance is rather different. It is associated with the 'hollowing out' of the state and the increasing fragmentation and complexity of the public realm. These developments, it is argued, have led to changes in the way in which the state seeks to govern public services, with an emphasis on governing by steering rather than by direct forms of control (see Jessop 2000; Kooiman 2000; Pierre 2000; Rhodes 1997, 1999; Stoker 1991, 1999). Jessop locates the rise of the new governance in the realisation that the market reforms of neo-liberalism had not delivered all that had been promised: 'market failures and inadequacies had not been eliminated, yet an explicit return to the state was ideologically and politically unacceptable' (2000: 11). The idea of networks as a form of governance was linked to the growing interest of governments in public/private, and other forms of, partnership.

Networks and partnerships grew in importance through the late 1980s and early 1990s, though the form and approach varied considerably. Conservative governments had introduced public/private partnerships as a way of unlocking the dominance of public sector power. These were viewed as a means of bringing in new investment for the development of public sector infrastructure and, later, the management of public services. The Conservatives had also set up a range of agencies (such as Training and Enterprise Councils and Urban Development Corporations) which brought together public and private sectors to tackle urban regeneration and economic development at a regional level. The City Challenge and SRB initiatives of Thatcher and Major developed a range of local partnerships through a policy approach based on competitive bidding. During the same period, local authorities actively developed local partnerships as part of anti-poverty strategies or to strengthen their broader role in urban regeneration and community governance (Alcock et al. 1998; Morgan et al. 1999; Stewart and Stoker 1988; Stewart et al. 2000). The 1980s and 1990s were also characterised by local collaborative developments around crime prevention, anti-drugs initiatives and community policing. The Morgan Report of 1991 recommended a multi-agency approach to community safety and, although not fully implemented, underpinned what Benyon and Edwards (1999) term the establishment of a 'community governance management of community safety' in the mid- to late 1990s.

The drive for partnership working, then, came from different directions. But a distinctive feature of Labour's approach was a more explicit focus on partnership as a way of governing. This focus was evident both in the strength of the partnership rhetoric and in the government's approach to the delivery of public policy. Labour introduced incentives for partnership working and emphasised the need to coordinate activity between health and social services, to enhance regeneration partnerships at a local level and to overcome departmental barriers in central government. Policy documents repeatedly stressed the need for the integration of policy to address cross-cutting policy agendas. They spoke of the need for culture change to overcome barriers to joint working across the departments of government and between central and local government, and they set out a range of proposals for integrating services, from pooled budgets to new arrangements for organisational governance.

In Jessop's terms this expansion 'is not meant to return Britain to a discredited corporatism . . . but, rather, to address the real limitations of the market, state and mixed economy as a means of dealing with various complex economic, political and social issues' (Jessop 2000: 11). Labour expanded the use of public–private partnerships, overcoming previous ideological barriers to partnership with the private sector (Corry et al. 1997). Partnership also became a significant theme in Labour's approach to tackling complex policy issues: neighbourhood renewal, social exclusion, community safety, child poverty and other 'wicked issues'. In such areas it emphasised the need both for better horizontal integration (partnership working between public sector organisations, voluntary sector bodies and private sector companies) and for stronger vertical integration (between central, local and community tiers of government). This emphasis reflected concerns about the hierarchical, 'silo' relationships built into the UK system of government and comparative weakness of horizontal relationships both in central government and at local and regional levels (see Chapter 4 of this volume). There was considerable interest in ways of addressing cross-cutting issues through a 'whole systems' approach to public policy (Pratt et al. 1998; Stewart et al. 2000; Wilkinson and Appelbee 1999). Labour also talked of the need for partnership between those involved in the shaping of policy and those affected by its delivery.

These developments have been linked to an emerging paradigm shift in the public policy system in the UK. The market-based paradigm of the Thatcher years supplanted a postwar paradigm based on state hierarchies. The problems of fragmentation produced by the market paradigm was now leading to the emergence of a new paradigm which was:

> . . . outcomes-focused, in that the design must be based on the best available evidence of 'what works'; it is holistic, the assumption being that many policy problems will be found not within the boundaries of single organisations, but on the interface between them, and the nature of the problem, rather than existing structural forms, should determine the delivery systems – 'form follows function'; prevention, or early intervention, is preferable and cheaper than cure or late intervention; and culture change highlights the notion that with many wicked issues, only the active involvement of the citizens trapped within the problem will secure a solution. (Richards et al. 1999: 10)

While in the Thatcher and Major years the predominant focus had been on the efficiency of organisations as discrete units, the modernisation agenda emphasises inter-organisational collaboration and policy coordination, both encompassed by the phrase 'joined-up government'. Changes in the Prime Minister's Office and the Cabinet Office were introduced to coordinate policy across government. A proliferation of central groups or task forces were charged with the task of integration (the Social Exclusion Unit, the Performance and Innovation Unit). A specific government minister was appointed to 'bash heads together' to overcome barriers (the 'Cabinet enforcer' role). There were also attempts to integrate funding and performance indicators through mechanisms such as the Fundamental Spending Review and Public Service Agreements. A number of 'Czars' were appointed to drive through change, give high profiles to policy agendas such as the government's anti-drugs strategy, and to coordinate policy implementation. The Cabinet Office report *Wiring it Up* provided a challenging analysis of the barriers to joint working in central government and proposed a range of strategies to address them in the longer term (Performance and Innovation Unit, 2000a).

The government placed particular emphasis on developing new policy initiatives through integrated local action. The Performance and Innovation Unit's report *Reaching Out* (2000b) listed thirty-two government-inspired, area-based initiatives requiring local partnership working. These included a series of zonal initiatives to bring local agencies together to develop holistic solutions to local problems, offering additional funding and greater flexibility in how funds were spent for successful bidders in order to foster local innovation. The first wave of Education Action Zones was established in 1998, bringing together local education authorities, voluntary organisations, businesses and schools to raise educational achievement in areas of low educational performance. Employment Zones similarly drew together a wide range of partners (including the private sector) in areas of high, long-term unemployment, while Health Action Zones aimed to reduce health inequalities by focusing the activity of different agencies – NHS bodies, local authorities, voluntary organisations and businesses – in areas of high need. Health Action Zones were based on the principle of recognising that health, social and other services were interdependent and needed to be planned and organised on a whole systems basis to deliver seamless care and tackle the wider determinants of health (NHSE 1999). The 'whole systems' emphasis on horizontal collaboration was present in a number of key documents and initiatives: for example, the introduction of multi-agency Health Improvement Plans, the Crime and Disorder Partnerships, the Sure Start programme, local economic development and neighbourhood renewal strategies, and the requirement that local authorities develop 'local strategic partnerships' with other agencies to coordinate action.

Holistic or systemic imagery also ran through a range of policy documents highlighting the need for *vertical* collaboration between central and local government, communities and users. The first report of the Social Exclusion Unit summarised the failure of past initiatives aimed at tackling the problems of 'poor neighbourhoods' as resulting from 'the absence of effective national policies to deal with the structural cause of decline; a tendency to parachute solutions in, rather than engaging local communities' (Social Exclusion Unit 1998a: 9). The need for 'bottom-up' involvement was also stressed in the *Service First* programme, which replaced the Citizen's Charter. A Department of Health discussion document, *Partnerships in Action*, criticised boundary disputes between health and social services and suggested a holistic, systems-based approach:

> We must deal with every link in the chain, from the strategic planners to people accessing services in their local community. Past efforts to tackle these problems have shown that concentrating on single elements of the way services work together . . . without looking at the system as a whole does not work. (Department of Health 1998c: 5)

The discourse implied a dissolution of hierarchical power relations as, for example, in notions of a new relationship between central and local government based on partnership, or of partnership between professionals and users.

Notions of holistic government are emblematic of the 'new' governance based on coordination through networks rather than markets or hierarchy. It is viewed in terms of plural actors engaged in a reflexive process of dialogue and information exchange. It is based on the idea of horizontal self-organisation among mutually interdependent actors, rather than hierarchical relationships. Network forms of governance must, then, be viewed as conceptually separate from partnership as structure (Lowndes and Skelcher 1998). Networks are informal and fluid, with shifting membership and ambiguous relationships and accountabilities. They may become formalised into official partnerships, but may also operate loosely across organisational boundaries. They are characterised by compromise rather than confrontation, negotiation rather than administrative fiat (M. Stewart 2000). The role of government is to enable, steer and coordinate rather than to control. Stoker, for example, argues that government requires a 'light touch':

> Steering involves government learning a different 'operating code' which rests less on its authority to make decisions and instead builds on its capacity to create the conditions for positive-sum partnerships and setting or changing the rules of the game to encourage what are perceived as beneficial outcomes. (Stoker 2000: 98)

There is an assumption that networks of actors will engage in finding solutions to problems and that organisations will develop strategies that incorporate the advantages and benefits of partnership working.

The limits of partnership

Labour's focus on delivering 'joined-up' or 'holistic' government led to a great deal of experiment and action. The government introduced new funding arrangements, common performance indicators, integrated ICT and other forms of infrastructural shifts to help overcome some of the barriers to collaboration that had impeded partnership working in the past. The policies directed towards fostering partnership working did, however, vary. Partnerships and joint working can have a number of objectives:

- to create an integrated, holistic approach to the development and delivery of public policy;
- to overcome departmental barriers and the problems of 'silo' management;
- to reduce the transaction costs resulting from overlapping policies and initiatives through coordination and integration;
- to deliver better policy outcomes by eliciting the contribution of multiple players at central, regional, local and community tiers of governance;
- to improve coordination and integration of service delivery among providers;
- to develop new, innovative approaches to policy development or service provision by bringing together the contributions and expertise of different partners; and
- to increase the financial resources available for investment by developing partnerships and joint ventures between the public, private and not for profit sectors.

It is difficult to generalise about how well the partnerships set up under Labour met these objectives because of the wide range of structures and relationships encompassed by the term. Partnerships range from loose networks to more stable groupings with defined structures and protocols. They involve relationships that range from a base of formal contracts to the more elusive processes of reciprocity and trust. Different issues are raised by attempts to overcome departmental boundaries in central government in order to develop a more integrated approach to policy (the usual meaning of joined-up government); the creation of partnerships between the public and private sectors; multi-agency partnerships between service delivery organisations (e.g. health and social services); and local partnerships involving voluntary and community sectors in, for example, regeneration initiatives. To add to the complexity, it may well be that formal bodies with well-defined structures and procedures are sustained by a loose network of key individuals who 'make it work'; or that a formal contract is underpinned by informal relationships of trust which help resolve conflict and reduce transaction costs.

Stoker (2000) notes a number of different steering techniques used by government: cultural persuasion, communication, finance, monitoring and structural reform. Cultural persuasion (promoting partnerships) is a relatively weak instrument but may create an enabling climate supporting local flexibility. Communication (facilitating learning and encouraging access) promotes capacity-building and can be used to support the development of local networks without threatening flexibility. New financial regimes or new structures may facilitate network modes of governance but may also create new rigidities: as one line of differentiation is overcome, new ones are delineated as boundaries are redrawn and interests regrouped.

My aim is not to distinguish between different types of partnership but to explore the ways in which they were overlaid on each other to produce a possible shift in the mode of governance. Labour's use of partnerships as a way of governing encompassed a range of approaches, only some of which facilitate the growth of network-based modes of coordination. Much of the early focus of the Social Exclusion Unit was on communication and persuasion in an attempt to build sustainable responses to the problems of deprived communities and social exclusion. The emphasis here and in the zonal initiatives was on new forms of funding, joint resourcing and the development of outcome-based evaluation linked to cross-cutting performance indicators. The initial aim was to promote flexible forms of collaboration, experimentation and innovation.

This initial emphasis on flexibility and innovation in these initiatives can be contrasted with the more prescriptive and formalised 'duty of partnership' within the Crime and Disorder Act (1998) and the Health Act (1999). The Crime and Disorder Act had at its core a statutory requirement for local authorities and police services to develop strategic partnerships to reduce crime and the public's fear of crime. New bodies which spanned the responsibilities of mainstream agencies – Youth Offending Teams – were established, with a new breed of worker (who may come from any of the agencies concerned) to manage them. Not only the structures but also many of the activities which such partnerships must undertake (e.g. crime and disorder audits) were specified in some detail and there was a strong element of vertical direction and control.

Such statutory partnerships may become bogged down in bureaucratic structures and power struggles, as happened in previous attempts to foster partnership working between Health Authorities and Social Service Departments. Joint structures set up following the Community Care reforms of the 1970s and 1980s produced little impact on the core organisations and tended only to produce short-term and piecemeal projects (Audit Commission 1986). The Health Act (1999) and other health reforms attempted further to institutionalise relationships between health and social services (e.g. through the governance arrangements of the new PCGs and Trusts) and to make collaboration mandatory (through Joint Investment Plans and Health Improvement Plans). At the same time, new flexibilities for pooled budgets in health and social services created the capacity for stronger network development as actors developed new ways of delivering services. Badged funding (as in the Social Services Modernisation fund) began to be used to promote longer-term preventative work. A focus on financing outcomes – rather than outputs – was a driver for the development of longer-term capacity-building activity. However, this was vulnerable to shifts in mainstream programmes as government priorities changed. Uncertainty about the future of earmarked resources tended to produce a focus on shorter-term rather than longer-term partnership goals (Glendinning and Clarke 2000).

These different approaches reflected differences between individual ministers and their departments, and oscillations in Labour's overall approach as it struggled to reconcile its long-term agenda of addressing intractible problems with the need to retain control over delivering its agenda. As Murray Stewart comments in his analysis of community regeneration partnership initiatives:

> The difficulty confronting the Blair government in managing this complex vertical/ horizontal system is that whilst in principle the aim is to devolve downwards to regions and local government, in practice the centre (ministers and officials) retains tight control. Whilst integration and joining up is embodied in the rhetoric of policy, in practice few of the interests are willing or able to concede the flexibility across programmes which genuine joint action requires. (M. Stewart 2000: 4)

Views from within government also acknowledged the difficulties, albeit from a rather different perspective. For example, Sir Richard Mottram, a civil service Permanent Secretary, noted how 'joining up' as a way of governing was cross-cut by other policy imperatives:

> The government has a number of desirable aims for improving our system of governance. . . . They include – in the jargon – seeking cross-cutting approaches with a long-term, outcome-based focus. The Government wants, and has developed, better patterns of cooperation with other levels of government and is seeking with them to build capacity at the community level. At the same time, as for all governments, there is the compelling need for (quick) results, the emphasis, wholly reasonably, is on delivery, delivery, delivery.
>
> These goals are not necessarily incompatible but nor are they without potential conflict. Thus the quickest way confidently to get results may be seen to be through top down command with the familiar plans, zones, targets and money coming down in tubes to match the various Whitehall silos. Some of the people at the centre can, in my experience, be just as keen on this sort of approach as some in departments and, if pressed on why, can point out – entirely correctly – that looser, more involving, less standardised and directed approaches have been tried in the past and found wanting.
>
> The ultimate test which will be applied with particular rigour is: 'What works?' Those keen – like me – for partnership working of various kinds and for more freedom of manoeuvre for those on the ground must show that it delivers more than the alternative. (Mottram 2000: 2)

This quotation highlights the possible tension between 'joined-up government' and more directive, hierarchical forms of governance. It also suggests tensions within the government's agenda. Labour had long-term ambitions for change which implied a shift towards governance systems based on networks and partnerships, collaboration and trust. At the same time, however, there was a political imperative to demonstrate 'quick wins' and to do so the government turned to more familiar recipes in order to exert greater leverage. These different imperatives created a number of tensions in the development and operation of partnerships. For example, Jessop (2000), J. Davies (2000) and other studies highlighted a number of difficulties produced by the positioning of local partnerships within central government policy agendas. They note how prescriptive and bureaucratic funding regimes tended to undermine local capacity. Problems were created by the attempt to impose best practice from above, as opposed to encouraging diversity and allowing horizontal communication and learning among partnerships. Tensions existed between the use of local partnerships to deliver centrally-determined policies and their capacity to be driven by local perceptions of needs and priorities. The focus of local partnerships was shaped by what is perceived to be a general centralising trend in government policy. The next sections explore ways in which such tensions were experienced within partnerships themselves.

The dynamics of partnership working

The 1990s also saw an explosion of 'how to do it' manuals and guidelines for partnerships and a number of more academic analyses of the difficulties of partnership working. While the former tended to highlight the importance of shared values, joint goals and other normative features associated with an optimistic model of partnership, the latter drew attention to a number of difficulties based on lack of trust, problems of accountability, inequalities, differences of power and the problems of the sustainability of partnership working over time (Huxham 1996; Huxham and Vangen 1996). Such problems are experienced within partnerships themselves but their origin may lie elsewhere: in the interaction between the external and internal collaborative environment created by such factors as the policy approach of government, the impact of funding regimes, and the cultures of parent organisations. However well a group may work at building collaboration and trust, it may nevertheless come unstuck because of external shifts or ambiguities. Such shifts took place in government priorities and strategies, and the purpose of partnerships was influenced by changing priorities in mainstream programmes. For example, as the programme of the Social Exclusion Unit developed over time, it became linked to a series of specific government targets – for instance on school exclusion – and the use of more prescriptive policy instruments linked to narrower forms of output, rather than outcome, measures. The experience of Education and Health Action Zones was of a shift to much narrower targets, more tightly linked to ministerial agendas, in place of their initial diverse and multiple policy objectives.

The dynamics of partnership were also influenced by shifts in partner organisations as they adapted to changes in national policy, changed strategic direction or adopted new structures and roles. Some private sector partners underwent significant changes in direction as they reassessed the risks and costs of public–private partnerships. The requirement that local authorities adopt new political structures based on elected mayors or Cabinet government began to influence the dynamics of local partnerships. The picture was also influenced by the sheer number of partnership-based initiatives launched by government. Many organisations became enmeshed in multiple and often interlocking partnership relationships, with different life-cycles and funding mechanisms adding extra sets of complexity and uncertainty to the work of the agencies and individuals concerned.

The combined effect of these processes was to create a series of dilemmas or tensions for partnerships (Newman 2000b). These were resolved in particular ways depending on the way in which external constraints or opportunities were interpreted by participants. Such (temporary) resolutions can be mapped using an adaptation of the framework introduced in Chapter 2. Four of the principal imperatives which influence partnership working are those of *accountability* (having proper structures, formalised roles and transparent procedures), *pragmatism* (getting things done, meeting targets), *flexibility* (adapting fast to changing conditions, expansion), and *sustainability* (fostering participation, building consensus and embedding networks to ensure long-term development). Each of these is likely to be present in any partnership, though the balance between them may be uneven and may shift over time. The model (see Figure 6.1) is intended as a way of capturing or mapping the balance between different imperatives within any particular partnership. The terminology (towards . . .) is deliberately meant to suggest pulls or trajectories of movement rather than static categories or ideal types.

The vertical axis of the model represents the way in which partnerships are positioned in or shaped by their external environment. The top quadrants suggest a focus on self-steering or co-governance, while the bottom quadrants are more directly influenced by policy directives and performance management systems. The horizontal axis of the model represents aspects of the internal dynamics of partnership. The left-hand end suggests a dominant focus on the internal structures and procedures which are needed to ensure accountability (lower left-hand quadrant) or to build long-term network capacity (upper left-hand quadrant). The right-hand end of the horizontal axis suggests a dominant focus on external adaptation, with much less regard to internal structures and processes. The focus may be on pragmatism in order to respond to government incentives or targets (bottom right-hand quadrant), or on developing flexible networks in order survive in a competitive and fast-changing environment (upper right-hand quadrant).

The different imperatives, each linked to a particular model of governance, are not necessarily reconcilable. For example, the kind of structural arrangements put in place to deliver accountability or ensure fair conduct may limit flexibility. The setting-up of clear operating procedures and accountable structures tends to create barriers to fast action. A pragmatic

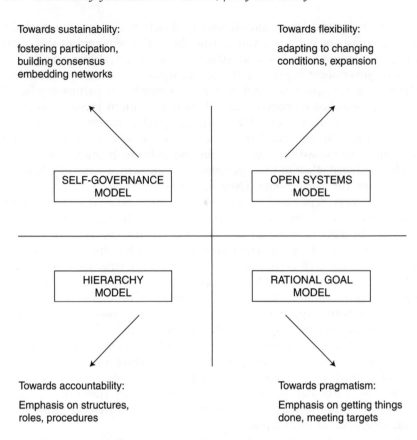

Towards sustainability:

fostering participation,
building consensus
embedding networks

Towards flexibility:

adapting to changing
conditions, expansion

SELF-GOVERNANCE
MODEL

OPEN SYSTEMS
MODEL

HIERARCHY
MODEL

RATIONAL GOAL
MODEL

Towards accountability:

Emphasis on structures,
roles, procedures

Towards pragmatism:

Emphasis on getting things
done, meeting targets

FIGURE 6.1   *The dynamics of partnership working*

focus on the delivery of short-term goals may limit sustainability by inhibiting capacity-building within partner organisations or with local communities. The inclusive and participative activities which help build sustainability are precisely those which may be sidelined under pressure to deliver a bid or an outcome to a tight deadline.

Few partnerships fall neatly into a single quadrant: most are based on some form of compromise or equilibrium between the different models. The equilibrium may change over time, perhaps with a focus on openness at the beginning being constrained as the need for delivery against time-limited goals becomes pre-eminent. Lowndes and Skelcher (1998) propose a life-cycle notion of partnership in which the early stages are characterised by relatively fluid membership and indistinct boundaries, the mid stages by closure and more formal arrangements, and the final stages by a return to networking as organisations negotiate ways of maintaining commitments. But partnerships may also experience 'institutional drift', leading to inappropriate patterns becoming embedded and reproduced. For example, a fluid, initially responsive network may drift towards structure in an attempt to create institutional stability, a stability that is inappropriate to an uncertain and unstable environment. The internal dynamics of partnerships or networks may also be influenced as they adapt to new requirements or shifting external conditions. Each model produces specific problems whose resolution may require a re-balancing to accommodate other values, as illustrated below.

Towards accountability: here the focus is on partnership institutions (e.g. joint structures, joint planning mechanisms, joint governance arrangements) designed to formalise the interaction between organisations and regulate decision-making processes. The focus on formal accountability through the following of 'due process' does not, however, necessarily deliver *democratic* accountability: 'Accountability is couched in terms of managerial and technical project and programme management rather than in terms of political accountability to community and electorate' (M. Stewart 2000: 6). The mechanisms through which partnership boards are accountable to parent organisations or the wider public may be obscure. Many mandatory partnerships, or partnerships where there is low trust between organisations, are pulled towards a strong emphasis on structures and procedures (e.g. the now superceded joint planning structures between health and social services, or the newer crime and disorder partnerships). A focus on structures, systems and procedures may mean that decision-making is slow, leading to pressures to move towards pragmatism or flexibility. However, formal structures or procedures influence, rather than determine, internal partnership dynamics. Many such bodies do deliver productive collaboration, though often this takes place despite, rather than because of, formalised partnership arrangements. That is, the formalised institutions may be largely symbolic with emphasis being placed on one or more of the other models in day-to-day decision-making.

Towards pragmatism: the emphasis here is on joint activity around specific – and often short-term – objectives. Collaboration may be 'thin', driven by external requirements or obligations, rather than self-generated. This thinness is often a result of compliant responses to external demands (e.g. delivery against government performance targets for which collaboration is required) or more proactive responses to opportunities (e.g. bidding for government, European or other funding to a tight timescale). An emphasis on this model can be viewed as a product of short-term shifts in policy, or the use of incentive-based policy instruments. Adaptiveness is high but the capacity to deliver sustained outcomes may be low. The emphasis is on getting on with the job, not necessarily addressing process issues, and the partnership may not significantly affect the core strategies or cultures of mainstream organisations. However, the networks that develop may have a longer-term impact, and create movement towards longer-term responses represented in the values of flexibility and sustainability. Where the demand for pragmatism produces behaviour that transgresses the informal or formal decision-making rules of parent organisations, however, there may be a call for a tighter emphasis on accountability and transparency.

Towards flexibility: here collaboration tends to be driven by longer-term goals. It is 'thicker' in that collaboration is entered into on a voluntary basis in order to pursue particular strategies or set up initiatives to adapt a fast-changing environment more quickly than parent organisations can move. Networks are dynamic and fluid, held in place by network members rather than statutory requirements or incentives. Collaboration is entered into in order to deliver mutual goals (e.g. local economic development) rather than comply with government requirements or partnership demands, though the goals may result from shifts in government policy. Adaptiveness is high because of the emphasis on fluidity and flexibility: partnerships driven by this imperative are less vulnerable to short-term shifts in policy so may have the capacity to deliver longer-term change. However, there may be tensions between the partnership and the mainstream cultures of the parent organisation since the pace and nature of change in each will differ. Problems may occur when there is a distance between joint, network-based projects and parent organisations which may leave projects in a kind of organisational limbo (Hardy et al. 1992). This may create a pull within the network towards greater sustainability, or alternatively a pull back by parent organisations to ensure stronger structures of accountability.

Towards sustainability: here the focus is on setting up processes through which the capacity of partners – organisations, communities, user groups – can be developed over time. There is likely to be a focus on 'empowerment' and 'participation', bringing in and supporting users, community members and front-line staff to generate momentum and take responsibility for actions and outcomes. Culture change and learning in participating organisations may be emphasised in order to embed new forms of activity. New sources of leadership in community initiatives or collaborative projects may be sought to provide continued momentum. However, tensions between long-term, sustainable goals (overcoming inequality, building community capacity, preventing ill health) and mainstream policies requiring delivery against short-term targets may be particularly sharp. Coupled with this, the difficulties of achieving long-term change may lead to temporary pulls towards pragmatic responses, or the abandonment of the goal of sustainability altogether. Where it is pursued with some success, on the other hand, there may be calls from previously excluded or marginalised groups for new structures or protocols that devolve power and provide greater accountability.

Power, trust and leadership

The framework described in the previous section can be used to help map some of the dynamics of power, the social relations of leadership and trust, and the patterns of inclusion and exclusion which may result (Newman 1998a). The economic models which underpin much of the analysis of partnership tend to focus on opportunistic power – the power of one party to take advantage of another. Yet power may be formal or informal; may be coercive, remunerative or normative. Power is also discursive. The discourse of partnership speaks of equality, shared values and high trust, creating an illusory unity which masks fundamental differences of power and resources and directs attention away from the need to engage with the gritty political realities of divergent interests and conflicting goals. Naïve or optimistic views of partnership focus on what the parties have in common and ignore power differences and inequalities. The history of relations between the voluntary and statutory sectors is littered with examples of the difficulties resulting from power inequalities.

Leadership, as a form of power, is often marginalised in discussions of partnership (but see Huxham and Vangen 1999). Where leadership is discussed, the emphasis tends to be on the need for emergent, participative and power-sharing approaches (see for example Luke 1998). This stands in stark contrast with the perceptions of many public sector practitioners of the reality of partnership working and the need for stronger, more directive leadership to bid for funding within short timescales or deliver the outputs desired by government performance requirements. Mapping issues of power, trust and leadership using the framework suggests the following:

Towards accountability: a tendency to marginalise difference through the setting-up of structures which regulate conflict and act as a control on power-bargaining. Leadership is positional, reflecting the positional power of the representative from the lead organisation (e.g. the local authority). Trust may be low but is institutionalised through mechanisms guaranteeing transparency and fairness. However, this may not succeed in winning the trust of groups marginalised by or excluded from formal decision-making processes.

Towards pragmatism: a tendency to marginalise difference in the search for a small, more tightly focused group which can work to a common agenda. The less powerful are likely to be left out of the process. Leadership tends to be based on personal power and influence, and tends towards being directive rather than inclusive. Decision-making is fast and informal. Trust is based on a calculation of risks and stakes involved in collaboration. There is little investment in building trust but a reliance on negotiation and bargaining or the direct exercise of power – what Hudson et al. (1999) view as 'economising on trust'. While transaction costs are initially low because of the speed and informality of decision-making, the low investment in trust may increase transaction costs in the long term by acting as a barrier to the development of self-governing, sustainable networks.

Towards flexibility: a tendency to ignore issues of power and to marginalise those at a distance from the network hub. Leadership may be vested in an individual at the hub of interlocking networks and with the capacity to mobilise external resources, but tends to be opaque (difficult to pin down, fluid). There may be considerable competition for leadership roles. Trust is based less on calculation and more on experience, knowledge, reputation and investment in personal relationships. This kind of trust reduces transaction costs but can be misplaced where changes in network member-ship or strategic shifts in partner organisations undermine the investments made.

Towards sustainability: a tendency to acknowledge difference and to draw on divergent interests and views in the development process. Differences may not be resolved but are viewed as an essential part of the dynamics of change. Leadership is inclusive and empowering. Trust is fostered through an investment in 'principled conduct' (Cropper 1996) based on fair dealing in the distribution and appropriation of benefits, and fairness in procedure. Such conduct will have the effect of creating a reputation for being a good partner, and contribute to the sustainability of partnerships. Sustainability may, however, be undermined where principled conduct by one party is not matched by the behaviour of others. For example, the use of partnership success by one party to enhance its own reputation and thus expand its own resource base can lead to a sense of betrayal on the part of its erstwhile partners, leading perhaps to a desire for formalised and institutionalised procedures in future ventures.

Voluntary and community sectors may be positioned as marginal players in partnerships developed by local authorities or the partnership boards of area-based initiatives. Their collaboration is required to add legitimacy to funding bids but they may experience particular sets of tensions. These are mapped on Figure 6.2. This highlights the way in which issues of power and patterns of inclusion and exclusion may influence the internal dynamics of partnerships and the strategies developed by individual players. Many local groups and small voluntary organisations now consider that their token involvement in partnerships set up by central or local government is not worth the time and investment required, and some have engaged in a tactical withdrawal from the partnership game. Others have undertaken a pragmatic repositioning to secure new sources of funding or to enlarge their role. The view from localities is that tight timetables and rigid frameworks are inimical to fruitful partnership. They act as constraints, limiting the number of actors drawn into the process, causing resentment among excluded groups (the very groups on whom the longer-term capacity to deliver project outcomes may depend). The pragmatism-versus-empower-ment line of tension is particularly sharply experienced by voluntary and community groups. Many express dismay at the tactics of mainstream agencies produced by their struggle to meet tight deadlines for bidding. Some adopt tactical responses of their own that may result in a loss of local credibility and the erosion of trust among community stakeholders.

The government's use of partnership cuts across all of the dimensions of the model. An emphasis on innovation in government policy, as in some urban policy initiatives, tends to foster networks which provide the degree of flexibility required to respond to new conditions, challenges and incen-tives. On the other hand, mandatory partnerships, in which structure and systems are specified in government guidelines, will pull in the opposite direction. A strong focus on performance exercised through tightly

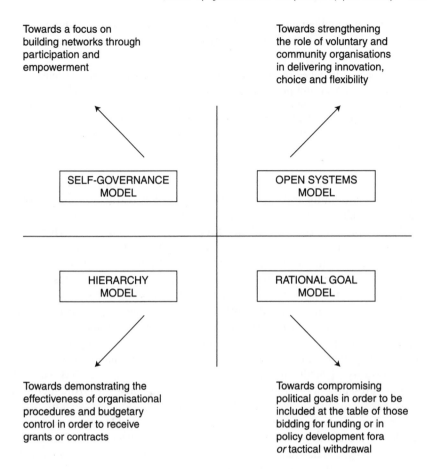

Towards a focus on
building networks through
participation and
empowerment

Towards strengthening
the role of voluntary and
community organisations
in delivering innovation,
choice and flexibility

SELF-GOVERNANCE
MODEL

OPEN SYSTEMS
MODEL

HIERARCHY
MODEL

RATIONAL GOAL
MODEL

Towards demonstrating the
effectiveness of organisational
procedures and budgetary
control in order to receive
grants or contracts

Towards compromising
political goals in order to be
included at the table of those
bidding for funding or in
policy development fora
or tactical withdrawal

FIGURE 6.2 *Dilemmas for community and voluntary sector partners*

specified, output targets, as in health and social care, will tend to pull partnerships towards the lower right-hand quadrant, with its emphasis on short-term pragmatism. Looser, outcome-based targets may, however, act as a catalyst for the development of more sustainable activity over a longer timeframe. The process of performance review, the promotion of best practice and threats of intervention for non-delivery will tend to force partnerships towards the bottom quadrants of Figure 6.1, imposing rigidities and acting as a constraint on the development of self-managing networks.

Overall, the dominant 'pull' exerted by the policy approach and performance regime of the Labour government has been towards the bottom quadrants of the model – towards vertical or hierarchical governing rather than horizontal, network-based governance. This has presented difficulties for promoting and sustaining collaborative activity. Clarence (1999) contrasts the collaborative discourse of government with the continuation of a performance management regime based on economic rationalism developed under previous Conservative governments:

> These two approaches run counter to each other and have created tensions in government policy and programmes. The tensions evident in the Labour government's agenda have had an effect on networking and partnership working at the local level and impacted upon the ways in which local authorities have responded to the opportunities offered by the expectations of central government. (Clarence 1999: 2)

Similar tensions are produced by the performance regime in mainstream services. Glendinning and Clarke (2000) suggest key features of the performance approach in health and social care which run counter to partnership working. One is the sort of evidence sought. The dominance of performance measures based on simple, accessible and ready-made indicators, and the pervasiveness of mono-organisational rather than system-wide or multi-organisational measures, militates against partnership effectiveness. In the struggle to overcome barriers to partnership working between health and social services a number of attempts have been made to align performance management systems. However, the flow of government policies – on social services modernisation, on the reduction of hospital waiting lists – have continued to exert considerable pressure towards a focus on core business. The centrality of health to the government's political agenda has led to an ongoing pressure for discrete targets. This suggests that a shift from hierarchy and markets towards governance through collaboration has been marginal, rather than central, to the modernisation agenda. Despite attempts to develop cross-cutting performance measures, the structuring of audit and inspection regimes has tended to follow departmental and service boundaries rather than reflect cross-cutting or joined-up objectives.

These issues have been located in broader contextual tensions between the requirement that different organisations continue to produce year-on-year efficiencies and the requirement that they collaborate to deliver broad policy outcomes on cross-cutting agendas. While there have been some attempts to develop cross-cutting performance indicators, the predominant focus of the external reviews of performance is on the efficiency of an organisation in delivering whatever happens to be its core business (managing housing stocks, catching criminals or educating young people). As a consequence, new policies – however broad in concept – have often resulted in a series of relatively small-scale projects based in different agencies. While each has had value in its own terms, these have tended to suffer from a lack of integration (each partner has shaped initiatives in a way which matched its own agenda) and a lack of continuity (projects were often based on short-term funding arrangements). However, government policy is only one variable in shaping the dynamics of partnership working. The next sections consider the impact of the organisations from which partnerships are formed, and the influence of practitioners.

Organisational cultures and professional identities

Understanding the dynamics of partnership means looking not only at what happens in collaborative arrangements but also at the dynamics of 'parent' organisations from which they are constituted. One of the problems is that developments in organisational theory are not very 'joined-up' with developments in theories of collaboration and partnership. They intersect around ideas of networked or virtual organisations, but little attention is paid to the impact of increased collaboration on mainstream, hierarchical organisations such as the professional bureaucracies of health, social services and local government. Various authors have highlighted factors that limit the collaborative capacity of such organisations. Benson notes the importance of the decision criteria which flow from an organisation's defence of its own interests in conditions of resource dependency (Benson 1975). Hardy et al. (1992) suggest a number of barriers to collaboration, arising from structural, procedural, financial and professional differences, but also follow Benson in highlighting the importance of status and legitimacy and the barriers to collaboration posed by an organisation's concern to deflect threats to its autonomy or domain of authority and influence.

The tensions between different imperatives noted in Figure 6.1 apply as much to the internal dynamics of organisations as to the dynamics of partnership. Organisational cultures are likely to be 'skewed' towards specific values. Cultures which value probity, accountability and control are unlikely to exhibit the flexibility required by partnership working. They may create tensions between the cultural values of boundary workers, seeking to pull the organisation towards flexibility and responsiveness, and the central control functions of the organisation. Collaboration also requires a degree of internal flexibility which may challenge traditional forms of control. This may lead to problems in securing legitimacy for partnership activity, leading in turn to difficulties in getting the organisation to 'sign up' to partnership decisions. The constraints imposed by the strategic centre of an organisation on partnership activity on the boundary – constraints of performance management, of delegation of power and authority, of sustained financial commitment – may closely replicate those imposed by government on local partnership bodies. The growth of the 'scrutocracy' of inspection and audit, described in Chapter 5, has intensified internal forms of organisational control, and increased the vulnerability of staff to charges of organisational or professional failure. An over-preoccupation with internal issues – securing accountabilities, building systems of control, developing skills and capacities – has tended to limit the ability of organisations to develop the kinds of network and partnership needed to respond to shifts in the external environment.

Analysis of partnerships and joined-up government have tended to focus on the difficulties created by the boundaries *between* organisations, producing differences in language, culture and perceptions of strategic interests. But boundaries *within* organisations have also changed as a result of government policies. The reconfiguration of professional boundaries in health around new models of patient care has offered greater potential for partnership working, especially in primary care. In local government there have been attempts to use the Best Value framework to create greater integration of services to specific client groups or localities. However, such shifts have affected only some parts of some organisations. Many mainstream hierarchies have remained strongly bounded, and the interconnections between core services and partnership initiatives have remained weak. This is in part due to a suspicion by agencies that such initiatives are a substitute for sustained expenditure in main programmes, and in part to the cultural gap existing between initiatives and the mainstream. For example, research by Stewart et al. suggests that the infrastructure had been in place from which connections between area-based initiatives and mainstream programmes might be developed, but that many local programmes had proceeded relatively independently from the processes of planning, strategy and objectives of mainstream programmes (M. Stewart et al. 2000). This suggests that any conclusion that there was an overall shift towards a new style or mode of governance is flawed. However, partnership working and network membership have had significant consequences for the experience and orientations of participants.

Professional roles, boundaries and identities

Considerable difficulties for practitioners are created by the gap between the idealistic language of policy documents, with their normative exhortations to find new ways of working across boundaries, and the realities of the day-to-day dilemmas which flow from competing policy imperatives. Discussions with practitioners from different sectors reveal widely different meanings of partnership, accompanied by significant differences of norms (how to do it) and values (whether collaboration is to be valued for its own sake). The response of practitioners to Labour's agenda has depended on their earlier experience of partnership working and the lessons learned, both positive and negative. Work with groups of senior managers suggests that responses have been contradictory: on the one hand, many are cynical about the repeated emphasis on partnership, impatient about the amount of time wasted on often fruitless meetings, and doubtful about the benefits. On the other hand, there has been a willingness to engage with the focus on innovation and to enjoy the new freedoms involved in some forms of partnership activity. For those engaged in the plethora of new projects and initiatives there has sometimes been a welcome release from traditional organisational constraints and the possibility of new career routes – or at least sources of motivation and satisfaction – opening up. This does not necessarily imply a narrow instrumentalism – there has been a match between new Labour values and the values of many public sector workers, leading to an enthusiasm for delivering aspects of the new agenda. At the same time there has been a suspicion about how far government intends to follow through on its attempts to deliver joined-up policy and practice, and a frustration with the continued lack of joining-up at the centre. For directors and chief executives there have been problems of balancing the drive to create momentum for change through collaboration while continuing to deliver on mainstream performance. And, while the former is often the source of new funding streams, there has been a strong perception that it is the latter that really counts in terms of league tables and core funding.

The responses of individual participants have been shaped by factors such as organisational culture, professional background, career aspirations and orientation to the political values of new Labour. For example, strongly hierarchical organisational cultures have been less likely to produce positive collaborative experiences for practitioners. Strong hierarchies also tend to be linked to narrow promotion criteria based on performance against core business (e.g. departmentally based policy work in the civil service) and militate against non-traditional career routes. Partnership activity has been viewed by many as a backwater away from the main arenas where promotion potential is judged. Occupations whose professional power base was perceived to be under threat have sometimes sought to dominate partnerships as a means of extending their arena of control. Some members of occupations with an uncertain future – for example, the probation service – responded by attempting to strengthen boundaries and reassert their territory, while others used opportunities presented by the new structures and roles of, say, Youth Offending Teams, to carve out new opportunities. Those with strong public service values that are viewed as aligned with Labour's policies tended to welcome what they perceived to be a shift away from the competitive ethos of New Public Management towards more positive frameworks of action. Partnership activity, then, carries the potential for important realignment of roles, boundaries and identities of those working in the public sector. Such realignments have taken place over a decade or more of experience of partnership working but have intensified with the new forms of legitimacy to such work accorded by the discourses and policies of Labour. It demands a shift from command and control and towards governing through influence and what Rhodes (1997) terms 'diplomacy' in conditions of uncertainty and ambiguity.

The way in which notions of partnership are incorporated within specific organisational cultures help constitute the identities of internal and external stakeholders. Whether these follow an optimistic model, based on reciprocity, trust and collaboration, or a so-called realistic model based on instrumentalism, bargaining and pragmatic compliance (Hudson et al. 1999) has profound consequences for the shaping of group cultures and individual identities. My emphasis on the constraints to partnership working should not detract from the importance of the power of those engaged in partnership working to shape agendas and to forge networks and alliances with the capacity to have a long-term impact. While 'joined-up government' may remain an aspiration rather than an achievement of Labour, this does not detract from its power as a discourse, a discourse that has produced important shifts in the languages and practices of public management and a reshaping of the notions of leadership, strategy and organisational culture on which it draws. The influence of this on roles, relationships and flows of power and influence have an impact far beyond the life-cycle of any particular partnership.

Towards a new governance?

The arguments of this chapter suggest that the explosion of the discourses of 'partnership' and 'joining up' under new Labour has not been matched by an expansion of network-based forms of governance. First, the policies used to promote partnerships have included a range of approaches giving rise to different trajectories of change, only some of which suggest a move to network forms of governance. In so far as Labour has represented a qualitatively different approach – an explicit use of partnership as a way of governing – this has been cross-cut by the continuance of forms of governance based on hierarchy and markets. The new paradigm has run alongside the old, rather than displacing it. The discourse of partnership, joining up and governance by steering has been traversed by others based on directive forms of coordination and control, as suggested by the quotation from Mottram earlier in this chapter.

Secondly, there has been a disjuncture between the language of policy documents and enacted policies. Notions of partnership carry normative connotations and have distinctly moral overtones. The optimistic and even idealistic language of partnership and collaboration can be contrasted with the reality of partnership working that results from the detail of policy proposals and implementation methods. Hudson et al. (1999) argue that Labour's approach represents a shift from an optimistic to a more realistic image of partnership:

> Exhortations to be decent about joint working have been replaced by a panoply of incentives and threats . . . and amount to a very different model – the realistic model. The basic assumption here is that individual and group interests are multiple and divergent, and that the net result is competition, bargaining and conflict. (Hudson et al. 1999: 199)

But rather than one model replacing another, it would seem that policy instruments have oscillated between exhortations towards partnership invoked by the optimistic model and the constraints imposed by the realistic model, leading to considerable difficulties for practitioners caught between them.

Thirdly, the politics of partnership have constantly evolved rather than remained static. Organisations have learned a new realism at the same time as government has developed a more pragmatic approach, based on the assessment of the potential costs as well as benefits of collaboration. There appeared to be an increasing emphasis on partnership and collaboration as tools to be used selectively – within the overall rubric of 'what works' – rather than as a universal panacea for defects in the design of policy and management systems. That is, partnership working became embedded as a politically legitimated but essentially *managerial* strategy to be selected as appropriate by government as it learned from its experience (about the costs as well as the benefits of partnership) and adopted new political priorities. The strategies for delivering mainstream services were relatively unaffected and integration between special projects and parent organisations tended to be weak. There may, then, be no sustained long-term shift in the mode of governing.

However, different questions can be raised about the proliferation of partnerships in the context of the changing role of the state. The 'new governance' literature tends to view networks in terms of their capacity to enlarge the range of actors involved in shaping and delivering policy. Individuals and communities with whom responsibility is shared may thus become 'empowered'. This perspective is strongly present in Labour's own discourse, for example in its talk of the involvement and empowerment of stakeholders outside government. But rather than partnerships being situated in a 'hollowing out' of the state, it may be that they can be viewed as a further dispersal and penetration of state power. The spread of an official and legitimated discourse of partnership has the capacity to draw local stakeholders, from community groups to business organisations, into a more direct relationship with government and involve them in supporting and carrying out the government's agenda. Partnership-based policies and programmes (especially those concerned with regeneration initiatives) have drawn community groups and organisations into new forms of collaboration and interpellated community leaders as actors in the public policy process. The impact of Labour's focus on joined-up government and partnership, then, may lie in constituting new kinds of legitimate subject and forms of relationship, and opening up new opportunities for engaging with and influencing the process of change. Partnership arrangements have enabled a wider range of actors to be discursively constituted as participants in the delivery of government policy. The government may have relinquished some forms of direct control (involved in governing through hierarchy) but may, in the process, have been 'purchasing wider *effective* control, an ability to manage, influence and manipulate local policy arenas and institutions more effectively' (J. Davies 2000: 20, original emphasis).

Labour's emphasis on holistic and joined-up government, and its use of partnerships as a means of delivering public policy, can be viewed as enhancing the state's capacity to secure political objectives by sharing power with a range of actors, drawing them into the policy process. From the perspective of the voluntary and community sectors, partnerships may represent 'dangerous liaisons' (Taylor 1998), implying a process of *incorporation* into the values of the dominant partner. The power to engage actors dis-cursively, and to draw them into the government's agenda, can be seen as complementing the apparent reduction in state power resulting from the break-up of the old bureaucratic hierarchies through which control over policy implementation was traditionally conducted. Such an analysis also leads to rethinking 'fragmentation' – the break-up of state power – in terms of a process of *dispersal* of power (Clarke and Newman 1997: Chapter 2 and Chapter 9 of this volume).

Questions can also be raised about the notions of partnership with users and communities which pervade the discourse but which get scant reference in analyses of central/local or inter-agency collaboration. Attempts to forge such partnerships open up debates about the nature of 'representativeness', issues of equality and diversity, and the problems and possibilities of enhancing public participation. The inclusion of users, communities and citizens in public policy decision-making networks and collaborative projects is of critical importance. It has a major impact on the sustain-ability, legitimacy and accountability of partnerships as a means of coordi-nating public policy and public services, and in the possible failure or success of networks as a mode of governance. These are discussed in the next chapter.

7 Public participation: the politics of representation

Modern Local Government: In Touch with the People. (title of a White Paper on local government, Department of the Environment, Transport and the Regions 1998)

'Men in suits make me fall silent'. (title of a paper on the experience of black and ethnic minority women in urban regeneration, Razzaque 2000)

In this chapter I explore recent policy developments around the themes of democratic innovation[1] and public participation,[2] and ask how far these can be viewed as signifying a form of governance adapted to an increasingly complex, diverse and dynamic society (Kooiman 1993). The governance literature highlights the development of a plural and differentiated set of connections between state, service deliverers, users, citizens and other stakeholders. These connections are viewed as providing greater flexibility and sophistication than the blunt instrument of party voting, especially since the dispersal of state power means that representative bodies can no longer control decision-making. New forms of connection between state and citizen are viewed as a means of responding to the fragmentation of authority and the problem of accountability in complex societies (Hirst 2000; Mulgan 1994; Peters 2000).

Democratic innovation and public participation, however, raise some significant theoretical and political challenges. First, direct public involvement in debate and decision-making cuts across the existing institutions of representative democracy, potentially undermining the role of officially elected representatives (MPs or local councillors). Secondly, such developments raise questions about our understandings of 'the people' who are to be consulted and involved, including questions about what notions of equality and difference are to be incorporated into the process of participation. Thirdly, new forms of decision-making can present challenges to state power, in both local and central forms. Such challenges centre on the issue of how discussions and decisions within new fora are connected to the policy processes of the state.

This chapter explores each of these challenges in turn. It begins by situating democratic innovation and public participation in the context of shifts in public policy and the politics of the Third Way. It goes on to discuss some of the developments in participatory democracy, and the challenges these raise for assumptions about representation and accountability. The chapter then traces the ways in which issues of equality, diversity and the politics of difference inflect debates about public participation. The final section returns to the question of how far the current emphasis on public participation can be viewed as signifying a form of governance adapted to an increasingly complex and differentiated society.

The Third Way and democratic renewal

The Third Way emphasises the importance of the public sphere in a revitalised social democracy. Giddens argued that:

> The Third Way . . . emphasises the core importance of active government and the public sphere. The public sphere does not coincide with the domain of the state. State institutions can diminish or discredit the realm of the public when they become oversized, bureaucratic or otherwise unresponsive to citizen needs. (Giddens 2000: 163–4)

State institutions, then, need to be renewed – made more open and responsive – in order to foster confidence in government. But, more than this, the public needs to be engaged in and involved since, in Blair's words, 'diverse democratic debate is a laboratory for ideas about how we should meet social needs' (Blair 1998b: 17).

An emphasis on public participation can be linked to a range of developments in public policy and management before the election of the Labour government in 1997, of which the most significant was undoubtedly the consumerist ethos of the late 1980s and the 1990s. This was influenced by changes in public management (the importation of business techniques into the public sector), by government reforms (e.g. the Citizen's Charter of John Major's administration), and by the rise of 'user' movements (Barnes 1997; Prior et al. 1995). Throughout this period public services were also experimenting with democratic innovation and public participation, involving the public in local decision-making fora, in the planning and commissioning of health and social care, in urban renewal initiatives and other arenas (Audit Commission 1999; DETR 1998; Stewart 1995, 1996, 1997; Seargeant and Steele 1998). New governance arrangements were established which gave tenants direct roles in the running of housing associations and which involved parents in school governing bodies. Some of these developments were based on experiments in Europe, the USA and elsewhere (Rao 2000a). There was much interest in the Scandinavian experiments with referenda, local self-government and community consultation. Citizen juries, panels and other consultative mechanisms in the USA had formed the basis for innovation in the NHS and local government in the UK (J. Stewart et al. 1994).

The Labour government built on and extended this agenda. The *Modernising Government* White Paper talked of 'responsive public services' that catered for the 'needs of different groups' (Cabinet Office 1999a) and the government introduced a range of direct consultative processes with stakeholders and citizens (see Chapter 4 of this volume). The Social Exclusion Unit (1998a) focused on the need for better strategies of public involvement as a means of building social capital and overcoming social exclusion. But the main emphasis was on the role of citizen and user involvement in the process of transforming local government. The White Paper introduced mandatory reforms of local government political structures, and made it a statutory duty for councils to consult and engage with local communities on a range of issues, including the production of local community plans, and talked of wishing to see consultation and participation 'embedded into the culture of all councils' (DETR 1998). In some policy documents the nature of participation was tightly prescribed (e.g. Best Value user satisfaction surveys), while in others there was ambiguity about what consultation meant, leading to considerable variation in both the scale and depth of participation (Leach and Wingfield 1999). But the requirement to find new ways of engaging the public in decision-making was clear.

Why did new Labour place so much emphasis on democratic innovation and public participation? A number of different themes can be traced in the discourse, including those of rebuilding trust between citizens and government, improving the policy process and enhancing the legitimacy of government and local government decisions. The 1995 Labour Party document *Renewing Democracy, Rebuilding Communities* and the Local Government White Paper of 1998 both talk repeatedly of councils keeping 'in touch with the people':

> Local Councils exist to serve and speak up for local people. They can only do that properly if they keep in touch with local people and local organisations. Democratic elections are the bedrock on which the whole system is built. . . . But the ballot box is only part of the story. It is therefore imperative that councils keep in touch with local views between elections. (Labour Party 1995: 13)

A key theme was the use of new forms of citizen and user involvement to enhance the accountability of local government and other providers directly to citizens. This underpinned the reform of political structures to make leaders more visible and accountable, and the move towards more direct forms of accountability to citizens for performance and quality. These were simultaneously viewed as a means of driving up standards. For example, the Local Government Act of 1999 required local authorities to consult local taxpayers, service users, partners and the 'business community' in the setting of performance targets. Local authorities were also encouraged to set up fora through which to explain council policies and to act as a setting for democratic debate.

Public consultation on local authority service plans and performance was viewed as an important means of continuing the shift of power away from the providers and towards community charge payers and service users

(DETR 2000). Both 'modernising government' and the Best Value legislation represent what Foley and Martin term a 'quasi-consumerist' model of participation:

> By virtue of the 'closeness to the community', user groups, citizen's panels and area/neighbourhood forums, are seen by ministers as an important means of exerting pressure for service improvements on public sector managers, professionals and frontline staff. (Foley and Martin 2000: 485)

Labour's drive to enhance public participation and involvement, then, may have been more about sharpening the accountability of the public sector downwards to citizens and users, eliciting pressure to drive up standards, than about new ways of engaging citizens in decision-making as a form of co- or self-governance. However, other themes were also strongly present, notably the importance given to local involvement in decision-making in area-based initiatives, the New Deal for Communities and other programmes. Such developments opened up new potential challenges to the institutions of representative democracy, challenges that are addressed in the next two sections of this chapter. These review a range of theories and critiques to help illuminate the subsequent discussion of Labour's approach in the final sections.

The challenge to representative democracy

Through the 1990s there had been a growing interest in viewing consumer *and citizen* involvement as twin strategies for enhancing service quality and enlarging public involvement in decision-making (Barnes 1997). Citizen-based participation developed alongside, rather than displacing, the consumerist focus of the 1980s and 1990s, and drew on many of the same techniques of market research. But it also flowed from critiques of liberal or representative democracy itself. This model of democracy is based on the role of free and equal citizens in electing representatives to a legislative assembly. Decision-making is based on the aggregation of individual preferences (voting) and is governed by an intricate body of rules and conventions. Knowing the rules is an important condition of being able to participate in decision-making, whether in parliament, the council chamber, or any of the host of organisations, from trades unions to the boards of many voluntary organisations, which have adopted the conventions of representative democracy. Participation through elections is viewed as the most legitimate form of engagement, and decisions by representative bodies as carrying super-ordinate legitimacy over decisions by non-elected bodies.

Barber (1984) views liberal democracy as 'weak' democracy in that its primary role is to ensure that citizens are able to remove tyrannical or ineffective governments. Advocates of 'strong democracy' seek the more active involvement of citizens in decision-making. The traditional institutions of representative democracy, while the ultimate guarantor of accountability, are also viewed as insufficient in complex and differentiated societies. More sophisticated methods are called for to enable decision-making bodies to respond to the multiplicity of views and interests which no longer – if they ever did – follow simple lines of class or party loyalty. There are, however, a number of perspectives on how to respond to these challenges. Hirst (1994) argues that existing political institutions lack accountability and fail to foster citizen participation because of the size of the state and the constraints of voting as a mode of communication between state and citizen. He advocates a move towards 'associative' democracy in which functions are taken out of state control and restored to citizens through the channel of associations controlled by their members. Fishkin (1991) argues that while democracy worked well in small, elite systems of government, mass suffrage has undermined the capacity of citizens to engage in deliberation and that the mass media has distorted the political process, and advocates the introduction of 'deliberative opinion polls'. Elster (1998) suggests that the aggregation of preferences through voting, while an ultimate arbiter where disagreements cannot be resolved, produces decisions that are inferior to those reached after dialogue and deliberation. The benefits of deliberative democracy are precisely those which governments interested in better policy decisions, 'community capacity-building' or 'social capital' might seek because they:

- Lessen or overcome the impact of bounded rationality.
- Help generate new alternatives rather than just debating existing ones.
- Induce a particular mode of justifying demands, based on rational discourse and recourse to the 'public interest' rather than secticonal interests.
- Produce Pareto-superior decisions.
- Produce better decisions in terms of distributive justice.
- Create a larger consensus and thus legitimates the ultimate choice.
- Have important process outcomes, e.g. educative effect on participants and on the bodies which sponsor deliberative fora.

(Based on the contributions to Elster 1998)

Elster follows Habermas in supporting the idea that democracy revolves around the transformation rather than the aggregation of preferences. While representative democracy is based on a relatively static notion of interests that can be aggregated, deliberative democracy assumes that interests can be reshaped or transformed as a product of engaging in dialogue with others. Miller (1992) takes this distinction further by arguing that liberal and participative democracy are based on different conceptions of human nature. He notes that while liberal conceptions stress the importance of giving due weight to each individual's preferences, participative democracy assumes that individuals can transcend particular interests or opinions in deference to common interests. Deliberation can also have a 'moralising' effect in that preferences regarded as narrowly self-regarding are likely to be eliminated from the debate. The transformative possibilities of deliberation and the 'responsibilisation' flowing from collective processes of decision-making are viewed as major benefits: 'Broadly speaking, discussion has the effect of turning a collection of separate individuals into a group who see one another as co-operators' (Miller 1992: 62).

While the transformation of preferences is a possible outcome of deliberation, this is not, of course, necessarily the case. Deliberative arenas are sites in which many different forms of power operate that may work to favour certain interests over others. The most obvious is the power of the sponsoring agency itself, which can set the agenda, decide how participants are to be selected and orchestrate the process of deliberation. Power differences between participants are less obvious because they tend to be masked by the dominant discourse of rationality and the unstated norms of public dialogue. These norms are worth a brief mention. Habermas (1987, 1989) talks of an 'ideal speech situation' based on communication directed towards mutual understanding in which questions of power are suspended. Information is conceived as an objective item of exchange rather than as something that is shaped and expressed within a set of power relations. Participants are assumed not to come as the delegates of others, but to be open to having their views transformed by the debate. The public sphere is conceived as one in which rationality dominates and in which status hierarchies are suspended. But as Nancy Fraser notes, 'declaring a deliberative arena to be a space where extant status hierarchies are bracketed and neutralised is not sufficient to make it so' (1997: 74). Individuals may express a narrow interest discursively constructed as the 'public interest'. The norms of rationality and the impersonal mode of discourse that are privileged in participative fora may marginalise cultural styles based on personal, affective or value-based modes of expression.

These debates highlight the importance of questions of power in the process of participation, and open up issues of how equality, diversity and difference are to be accommodated in democratic innovation and public participation. Those seeking to enhance participative democracy may be constrained by questions of 'how much' power is given to citizens rather than 'what forms' of power may be operating in the conduct of participative fora themselves. The 'how much' question is often expressed in terms of a ladder of participation, following Arnstein's work in the 1960s. This extends from weak delegation of power (e.g. information giving) at one end of the spectrum, through consultation and then involvement, to full citizen control at the other extreme. The question of *forms* of power is rather more challenging, covering agenda-setting power, normative power, discursive power, legitimising power as well as the more usual focus on decision-making power. Burns, Hoggett and Hambleton provide a helpful distinction between civic developmental conceptions of power and instrumental power (Burns et al. 1994). The civic developmental model views power as the property of the collective; the more who share in it, the greater it becomes. This conception of power often underpins the rhetoric of 'empowerment' frequently found in discussions of the capacity-building and social benefits of community-based participation. Opposed to this is an instrumental model that views power in terms of the capacity of one party or set of interests to dominate another. The instrumentalist view tends to deny the possibility of transformation, alliance-building or collectivities outside the interests that are officially recognised. While the former is captured by the phrase 'power to', the latter suggests 'power over'. Neither conception adequately captures the different forms and relations of power that operate in the interactions between public officials and citizens, inter-actions in which the 'rules' of engagement and the norms of behaviour are set by officials. For example, one challenge raised by some disability groups is that the state should seek to draw on the expert power of those with experience of disability in forming its policies and strategies rather than relying on professional expertise (Barnes 1997). This transforms the way in which the power relations between citizens and state are normally conceived: rather than seeking the crumbs from the table of the powerful, user groups have valuable resources to offer to the public realm. The issue is then raised about the costs (to users and citizens) of engaging in consultation or participation initiatives, and how they might be reimbursed for their contribution to the planning, improvement or evaluation of services.

Equality, diversity and the politics of difference

Innovations in public participation have developed in part from concerns about how far the institutions of representative democracy can adequately represent the multiplicity of identities and interests in complex and differ-entiated societies. The liberal conception of equality – institutionalised in the law, the electoral process and the administrative justice of the welfare state – has, however, been challenged from a number of different perspec-tives. First, the notion of citizenship on which formal equality is based has been shown to be both gendered (e.g. Phillips 1992) and racialised (e.g. Lewis 1998, 2000a, 2000b). Secondly, formal political equality has been shown to be insufficient as a means of redressing social inequality. For those – including the Labour government – concerned to tackle issues of social exclusion, other forms of participation which reach beyond the ballot box are viewed as vital. Thirdly, the 'un-representativeness' of those elected to parliament or local councils has become a topic of concern. Bias can arise in the selection of representatives and institutional discrimination may disadvantage 'non-typical' candidates who succeed in being elected. The institutions of political party fail to cope adequately with demands that elected representatives reflect the diversity of identities and interests in society (e.g. Rao 2000b), while the institutions of government fail to respond to the requirements of non-traditional representatives (Coote 2000). As a result there have been attempts by some political parties to broaden the representativeness of elected bodies. Women-only shortlists in the Labour Party significantly increased the proportion of women MPs in the House of Commons after the 1997 election, though the practice was subsequently abandoned. There have been continuing concerns about recruiting more black and ethnic minority representatives into public services and to stand for both local and national elections. There were reports of a 'row' following the selection of just one additional Labour party candidate from a black or minority ethnic group for the 2001 general election (*The Guardian*, 31 August 2000: 1), and dismay at the number of women MPs who had been elected for the first time in 1997 who had decided not to stand for re-selection.

If the mainstream institutions of representative democracy fail to reflect social diversity adequately, do the new participatory and dialogic forms of democracy offer a more promising source of change? The picture is, initially, not very promising. Many of the advocates of participatory democracy hark back to a 'pure' concept of democracy, based on the Athenian city state, which large-scale societies, mass communication and populist politics have distorted. Equality is viewed in terms of formal political equality, and the defects of the Athenian system (restricted citizenship) tend not to be much debated. Elster, for example, defines deliberative democracy as 'decision making by discussion among free and equal citizens' (1998: 1). Fishkin defines political equality as 'equal consideration to everyone's preferences' plus 'equal opportunity to formulate preferences on the issues under consideration' plus an 'effective hearing for the full range of interests that have significant followings' (1991: 30–2). These acknowledge different dimensions of influence but are underpinned by a traditional, rather than radical, form of pluralism. Feminism, black politics and the post-structuralist challenge to essentialist conceptions of identity have not happened in this world. However, participatory democracy is also associated with more radical perspectives which seek to engage citizens in deliberation as a means of challenging processes which reproduce patterns of social exclusion or power inequalities. Some organisations have tried to broaden inclusiveness by targeting initiatives at particular groups, perhaps co-opting members of such groups to conduct the consultation on the agency's behalf.

Participatory democracy has the capacity to build conceptions of difference into the political process, and to address the challenges to liberal democracy from the 'new social movements'. As Hirst comments: 'Citizens need a political community that will enable them to be different, not one which exhorts them to be the same' (Hirst 1994: 14). But conceptions of what is meant by difference, and how this relates to the political process, have tended to develop outside, rather than within, the disciplines of political science. It has been a common concern of feminist writers. Young, for example, talks of the value of heterogeneity, diversity and difference – the 'new pluralism' – and supports developments in deliberative democracy. However, she also suggests that their capacity to produce a general perspective is an 'establishment myth': the process of transcendence can mask subtle forms of control. She argues that citizenship may mean organising politically around group identities but then interacting with others (Young 1990). This is more fully developed by Fraser in her notion of 'counter publics'. She suggests that Habermas casts the emergence of additional publics, based on the new social movements, as 'a late development signalling fragmentation and decline' (Fraser 1997: 80). In contrast, Fraser views them as an essential element of the democratic process because of their capacity to formulate oppositional views, though they lack formal equality within the public sphere.

> History records that members of subordinated groups – women, workers, peoples of colour, and gays and lesbians – have repeatedly found it advantageous to constitute alternative publics. I propose to call these *subaltern counter-publics* in order to signal that they are parallel discursive arenas where members of subordinated social groups invent and circulate counter-discourses, which in turn permit them to formulate oppositional interpretations of their identities, interests and needs. (Fraser 1997: 81, original emphasis)

Although some such groups may be explicitly anti-democratic, '[i]n general, the proliferation of subaltern counter-publics means a widening of discursive contestation, and that is a good thing in stratified societies' (1997: 82). Such groups have a twin function: on the one hand as spaces of withdrawal and regrouping, on the other as bases for engagement with the wider public domain. 'It is precisely in the dialectics between these two functions that their emancipatory potential resides' (1997: 82).

Such 'counter-publics' are formed through collective processes of engagement and action, through which identities and interests are forged. They cannot be simply equated with fixed categories such as 'women', 'black and ethnic minority communities', 'the disabled', 'older people' and so on, categories which tend to be constructed by public agencies in their search for 'representative' forms of engagement with the public. Indeed, post-structuralist perspectives highlight the relational and fluid character of identity. Lewis, for example, highlights the difficulties involved in using categories such as 'black and ethnic minorities':

> While members of these groups still have a common experience of racial exclusion, there is also evidence of an increasing complexity of experiences and internal diversification. This suggests that any tendency to homogenizing categorisation may lead to an elision of differences among and within racialised populations of colour; and to the denial of the possibility and effects of agency on the part of members of these populations. (Lewis 2000a: 262)

The point about agency is significant. Squires (1998) views deliberative arenas as the sites in which identity is potentially constituted and mobilised, rather than as a site in which participants with fixed identities engage in political dialogue. This makes the task of trying to ensure 'representativeness' in a forum problematic. Commonality of experience or identity may facilitate discussion and produce a depth of understanding that a more 'representative' sample might not elicit. The authors of a DETR research report on public participation suggested that 'developing a range of participation methods to reach different citizens may, in many instances, be more important than seeking the elusive goal of "representativeness" within a specific initiative' (Lowndes et al. 1998: 4).

A further difficulty is that many of the experiments in democratic innovation and public participation are locality-based, and assume a commonality of interest and identity within a given community. The dominant image of community typically rests on un-gendered, un-racialised and non-antagonistic conceptions of 'the public' (Hughes and Mooney 1998). Differences of interest, of identity, and of social or economic position are dissolved in a general orientation towards inclusiveness. Despite successive challenges which have highlighted the significance of differences of interest and of identity within them, geographical communities still tend to be viewed as homogenous – a single entity which can be consulted with, engaged in dialogue or even have some forms of power delegated to it. Such conceptions have, rather than being challenged, been reinstalled in the communitarian ethos espoused by Labour in some policy documents (see Chapter 8 of this volume).

The existence of multiple lines of interest and identity, of overlapping and competing 'publics', are rendered invisible precisely through the attempt to constitute the public realm as a realm of equal subjects. But the public realm, in which people are invited to participate, cannot be viewed as an entity able to assimilate differences of interest and identity into a homogeneous whole. Rather, there is a need to recognise the multiplicity of sites in which dialogue is conducted and interests and identities shaped. Many of these are constituted outside the formally constituted political sphere. Concerns about lack of interest in politics (among the young, for example) reflect a concern about an unwillingness to participate in officially defined political spaces, perhaps linked to a disillusionment with formal political institutions. This could make the task of democratic innovation and public participation one based in part on the recognition of counter publics and the validation of informal political processes. Notions of participation which are drawn from formal models of representative democracy are unlikely to acknowledge the validity of challenges to dominant norms and discourses, and may seek to marginalise any 'oppositional interpretations' as being 'unrepresentative'.

New Labour, modernisation and the limits to public participation

The challenges outlined in the previous two sections highlight the importance of issues of power in the process of participation, and open up debates about the politics of equality, diversity and difference. The third challenge I want to highlight is the challenge to institutional power bases raised by new forms of public involvement and participation. Labour has drawn on many of the developments in participatory democracy, introducing citizen panels, focus groups, 'roadshows' which engage in direct debate with citizens, and other forms of innovation. It has also incorporated a limited view of diversity in the sense that it emphasises the need to cater for the needs of different groups. The *Modernising Government* White Paper, for example, talks of responding to the needs or problems of particular groups (of older people, of women, and, interestingly, of 'business'), while the Social Exclusion Unit has acknowledged the particular processes of exclusion which may be experienced by black and ethnic minority groups (Cabinet Office 1999a; Social Exclusion Unit 2000). But the increasing emphasis on public participation, and the limited acknowledgement of social diversity, was traversed by other shifts that limited organisational responses. The pressure on mainstream organisations (Health Authorities, civil service agencies) to deliver on targets cascading from government meant that their capacity to respond to local pressures or demands was severely constrained. The expansion of competitive bidding for special initiatives tended, as the lessons from SRB show, to produce fast and relatively unsophisticated consultation strategies in order to meet the tight timescales imposed by funders (M. Stewart 2000). As a result, many exercises in participation can be viewed as a response to isomorphic pressures, being more about presentation and legitimacy than about a genuine willingness to transform decision-making processes.

The traditional institutions of representation sit uneasily with the idea that the public should have direct involvement in decision-making. For example, many local authority members viewed public participation as undermining their representative role. Official guidance (e.g. Audit Commission 1999) sought to reassure them that the role of consultation and participation exercises, is to inform or influence their decisions rather than to supplant their role, and that councillors retained an important role in reconciling conflicting views and balancing public opinion against resource and other constraints. However, resistance to consultation, participation and new deliberative forms of citizen engagement (citizens juries, panels, fora) remained strong among both officers and members. Rather than heralding a new form of democracy, public participation was often viewed as anti-democratic in that the views expressed were constructed as 'unrepresentative' (Davis and Geddes 2000). But it is important to question what is meant by the term 'representative' in this context. What was at stake appeared to be an uneasy configuration of political notions of representation (based on liberal democracy) and the notions of statistical representativeness (based on population sampling) underpinning market research. Oscillations between these different notions of representativeness pervaded official documents (e.g. Audit Commission 1999) and discussions with managers and local authority members. Each may be challenged by alternative models derived from theories of diversity and difference.

Overall, organisational responses to the outcomes of participation tended to be weak. The DETR study on participation in local government found that strategies were predominantly informal and *ad hoc* (Leach and Wingfield 1999). While there were major developments in the number and range of initiatives, few organisations were able to highlight specific outcomes which have been directly influenced by the findings of participation exercises (Seargeant and Steele 1998). The Audit Commission study of participation initiatives in local government found that 'Many authorities report that much of the consultation they carry out is not used effectively. Nearly three-quarters of authorities surveyed for this paper thought that a failure to link the results of consultation with decision making prevented the results from being used effectively' (Audit Commission 1999: 34). The DETR research also highlighted the gap between public and 'official' perspectives on participation: for example, while the public viewed the council as remote and bureaucratic, the council viewed the public as ill-informed and prone to unrealistic expectations; and while the public were unaware of opportunities to participate, the council viewed the public as unwilling to participate or uninterested in participation (Lowndes et al. 1998).

These findings raise important issues about the relationship between institutional power and the political process. Public participation is a site of contestation. Political disagreement about appropriate channels of participation occurred between, on the one hand, 'modernisers' seeking to introduce greater transparency and responsiveness and, on the other, those seeking to defend the primacy of existing channels of decision-making. Conflicting views about appropriate forms of participation arose between 'marketeers' importing the techniques of consumer feedback and market research from the private sector and those seeking to develop innovative and more focused ways of engaging with citizens and communities. Different views about who should participate, and through what methods, were frequently found among stakeholders in partnership initiatives, for example between voluntary and statutory sectors. Problems also arose in the gap between the expectations of organisations sponsoring consultation and those whom they were consulting about the goals and intended outcomes of participation. Exercises in community participation sometimes exacerbated, rather than resolved, tensions between different interests and identities. As the previous section argued, the expectation that there would be a neat homogeneity of views expressing a 'community perspective' is rarely, if ever, realised.

However, participation processes also opened up new spaces which could be 'captured' by user groups, voluntary organisations and community groups seeking to claim a stronger role in decision-making. More usually, however, such groups presented challenges to which the sponsoring organisations were unable, or unwilling, to respond. The gap between agency expectations and those of the public were often considerable. Groups who felt that they did not fit the notion of the public whose views were valued

('This is not for people like us'), who did not trust the agency concerned ('They didn't take any notice last time so it's not worth bothering now') or who were defined by the agency concerned in what are perceived to be stigmatising terms ('I may be short of money but don't see myself as socially excluded') sometimes refused to participate on the agency's terms. This reinforced a 'vicious circle' in which agencies concluded that the public were apathetic about participation, or did not have the necessary skills to engage in dialogue with them. Participation may, then, worsen relationships between users and providers, between communities and public bodies, between citizens and government, rather than enhance them. Better techniques, for example communicating clearly about the aim and scope of any exercise in consultation, and giving feedback about the outcomes, are clearly important. But the political tensions in the process, and the potential conflicts these give rise to, cannot be massaged away: more effective management cannot solve problems in the political domain.

Towards a new form of governance?

Kooiman regards new forms of state/society interaction, based on co-steering or the emergence of self-steering systems, as a response or adaptation to societies characterised by greater complexity, diversity and dynamic processes of change. The proliferation of new democratic sites and fora might be linked to the reconfiguration of state/society interactions and to what Kooiman terms 'communicative governing' (Kooiman 2000: 150). The arguments of this chapter, however, suggest that only rarely is public participation allowed to challenge existing norms and established power structures. More often it can best be viewed not in terms of a new form of governance but as an adjunct to traditional forms of decision-making or models of service delivery. Rather than a shift in the mode of governance, the arguments of this chapter suggest that public involvement and participation is a site in which tensions between different discourses and practices are played out. Some of these can be mapped using the governance framework introduced in earlier chapters (see Figure 7.1). As previously emphasised, this is not intended as a typology of forms of participation but as a means of exploring the dynamics of institutional change.

The bottom left-hand corner, the *hierarchy model* of governance, is strongly associated with the formal processes of representative democracy. Accountability flows upward through clear lines of responsibility to the elected representatives. The model is based on formal notions of citizenship and individual equality. This model was strengthened by the modernisation agenda, which had introduced greater rules and norms designed to safeguard legitimacy (e.g. standards committees and scrutiny committees in local government). Modernisation also, however, produced a pull towards the two right-hand quadrants: the lower right-hand quadrant to demonstrate

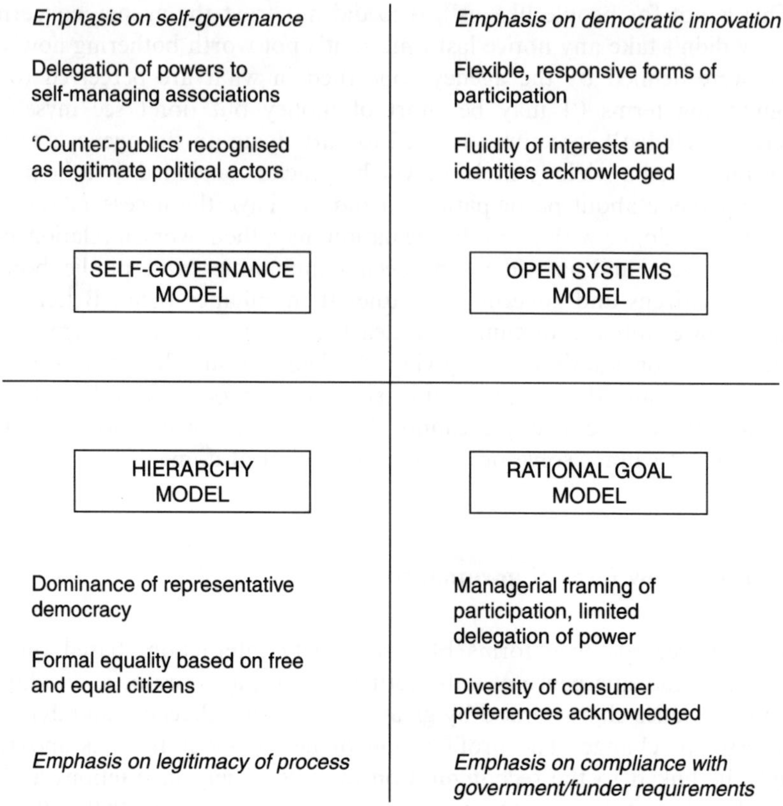

Emphasis on self-governance	*Emphasis on democratic innovation*
Delegation of powers to self-managing associations	Flexible, responsive forms of participation
'Counter-publics' recognised as legitimate political actors	Fluidity of interests and identities acknowledged
SELF-GOVERNANCE MODEL	OPEN SYSTEMS MODEL
HIERARCHY MODEL	RATIONAL GOAL MODEL
Dominance of representative democracy	Managerial framing of participation, limited delegation of power
Formal equality based on free and equal citizens	Diversity of consumer preferences acknowledged
Emphasis on legitimacy of process	*Emphasis on compliance with government/funder requirements*

FIGURE 7.1   *Democratic innovation and public participation: models of governance*

compliance with the requirement of legislation and competitive funding regimes; the upper right-hand quadrant to demonstrate responsiveness to the public and to address issues of social exclusion.

The bottom right-hand quadrant – the *rational goal model* – captures a range of responses, from service-based consultations to token consultations conducted at speed in order to meet the requirements of funders. Organisations tend to reach out to existing groups or community leaders already known to them in order to demonstrate that consultation has been built into a funding bid (M. Stewart et al. 2000). This can, however, lead to difficulties in building longer-term, more sustainable, involvement since those excluded from the process may not trust the groups or individuals brought in. Issues of diversity are acknowledged in the form of attempts to respond to the diversity of consumer choices and preferences, but more expansive or collective conceptions of diversity are not easily accommodated within the framework of 'representative sampling' linked to managerial technologies of consultation.

The *open systems model* – the upper right-hand quadrant – suggests the development of multiple and responsive forms of contact between state and citizen to enable the state to adapt to growing social complexity and diversity. Formal systems – voting and market research techniques – are supplemented by a range of informal strategies designed to enhance the connections between state and citizen. Issues of representation are of marginal concern; what matters is capturing a diversity of voices and perspectives and fostering dialogue. The transformation of citizen views through dialogic techniques is valued. Many of the new participatory techniques belong most readily to this model. However, they can open up challenges which organisations may resist on the grounds that those making them lack legitimacy or 'representativeness'.

The final model – *self-governance* – presents even more significant challenges to traditional conceptions of the relationship between state and citizen in that it involves real delegation of power and the recognition of 'counter-publics'. The language of some of the government's policy documents – notably those of the Social Exclusion Unit – suggests a focus on capacity-building and community empowerment representing a shift (however partial) towards this model. However, as Chapter 4 argued, the limits to delegation within a highly centralised state mean that this model of governance has a very marginal presence. Symbolic compliance with the government's requirement to engage communities in decision-making is unlikely to produce substantial change.

This framework can be used to highlight the relationship between different political imperatives – those of modernising local government political management, of improving the relevance and accessibility of services, of educating and involving citizens, of improving the legitimacy of decisions and of restoring trust between government and citizen. Not all are incompatible but some of these ambitions produce tensions which are extremely difficult to reconcile. For example, an internal focus on political management reform has produced a tendency to centralise power, which may be in tension with developing responses to the diversity and complexity of citizen views, a diversity which cannot easily be aggregated through the simple mechanism of party voting. Tensions also arise between conceptions of the public as consumers and as citizens. These imply different forms of engagement with decision-making: the former often drawing on market research, the latter on more direct forms of engagement in decision-making.

There is a great deal of emphasis in the policy literature, and among practitioners, on selecting techniques which are 'fit for purpose' (Audit Commission 1999; Lowndes et al. 1998). There is also a frequently found suggestion that representative and participatory democracy can be viewed as complementary (Leach and Wingfield 1999; Rao 2000a). While not arguing against these common-sense propositions, I do want to raise questions about the relationship between managerial and political forms of engagement, and between consultation and the new techniques of citizen engagement in decision-making. These are not necessarily easily reconcilable in that they invoke different images of the public which are located in conflicting political philosophies, incorporate diverse conceptions of difference, and rest on different models of governance.

Public participation and democratic innovation open up a set of difficult questions about the nature of power and decision-making, about how different political values can be reconciled, about social inclusion and exclusion, and about the process of institutional change. Such developments present potential challenges to traditional conceptions of democracy, of the public sphere and of equality/difference. However, such challenges are subject to a range of responses through which they may be contained, managed, resisted or deflected. One strategy of containment has been to focus innovation primarily around local initiatives or marginal innovations rather than to use new dialogic or participative techniques to look at mainstream policies, budgets or political priorities. A second has been the constitution of citizen participation within a consumerist discourse, with enhanced public accountability being viewed as a lever to drive up public sector performance 'from below'. However, democratic innovation and participatory democracy open up the possibility of challenges to the political process itself through questioning dominant forms of discourse and rules of engagement, and by challenging the boundaries of 'what counts' as formal politics. It is through such challenges that *political* renewal may be carried forward.

Notes

1 This chapter uses the term 'democratic innovation' to denote experiments in participatory democracy, such as citizen's juries, rather than to refer to constitutional change or to the reform of political structures in local government. These latter topics were discussed in Chapter 4.

2 'Public participation' refers to a range of initiatives, from consultation to user or citizen panels and through to the involvement of the public in decision-making bodies.

8   Remaking civil society: the politics of inclusion

We seek a diverse but inclusive society, promoting tolerance within agreed norms, promoting civic activism as a complement to (but not a replacement for) modern government. An inclusive society imposes duties on individuals and parents as well as on society as a whole. Promoting better state and civic support for individuals and parents as they meet their responsibilities is a critical contemporary challenge, cutting across our approach to education, welfare and crime reduction.

(Blair 1998a: 12)

This chapter explores the involvement of civil society in the process of governance. It traces Labour's attempt to remake the relationships between state, citizen and community in the search for a new social settlement. Such a settlement invoked an image of a modern society in which conflicts around class, 'race' and gender had largely been resolved. The constitution of new subjects – self-reliant and responsible, moral and familial, community-oriented and at the same time seeking new opportunities for themselves as individuals – can be viewed as an important strand of Labour's political project.

Labour attempted to resolve the fracturing of the postwar social settlement that took place under the neo-liberal regime of Conservative governments of the 1980s and early 1990s. This postwar settlement was based on particular assumptions about work (based on male full employment), the family (based on a sharp division between male breadwinner and female homemaker) and nation (based on the legacy of Britain's imperial role and particular conceptions of 'race') (Williams 1993). These assumptions had not only underpinned particular social policies (e.g. policies on unemployment and welfare benefits based on the centrality of the male breadwinner), but had also played a wider ideological role. They had produced a unifying imagery of 'the people', based on a clearly defined conception of Britishness and on a notion of citizenship that combined a nominal equality of access to universal welfare services and benefits with collective investment in the nation's future. The notions of universalism and equality in this relationship had been challenged from a number of directions, with feminism highlighting the limitations of class-based notions of equality and anti-racist movements pointing to the contested and limited equation of citizenship with nationality (Hughes 1998; Hughes and Lewis 1998). But the postwar welfare settlement had come under more sustained challenge in the period of neo-liberalism and the new right. Conservative governments in the UK had dismantled the collective basis of the welfare system and promoted self-provision of welfare through the market. At the same time, Conservative ideology had promoted a re-moralisation of a society viewed as having been undermined by the 'progressivism' of the 1960s culture and the dependency induced by the welfare state itself. It had also attempted to install a dominant conception of an English/British 'way of life' based on a repertoire of traditional imageries of nationhood and people.

These attempts by successive Conservative governments to forge new stabilising assumptions about the composition, character and ways of life of 'the people' had foundered in the face of both internal conflict (between economic neo-liberalism and neo-conservative morality) and external changes. This 'unfinished business' from the break-up of the old regime included sharp social, political and cultural tensions which were exemplified in conflicts around both the redistribution of resources and the recognition of social or political identities (Clarke and Newman 1997: Chapter 7; Hughes 1998; Williams 1996, 2000). Such conflicts continued under Labour. But Labour attempted to manage them through the construction of a new social settlement around the modernisation of the welfare state, and to forge a new social settlement based on a modernised image of civil society.

Renewing civil society

Labour's focus on renewing civil society marked out a terrain fundamentally different from both the economism of neo-liberalism and the welfarist associations of 'old' Labour. Its policies reflected a substantial attempt to redress the economic inequalities and the social fragmentation resulting from the Conservative reforms of the 1980s and 1990s. Labour pledged to end child poverty and to address the problems of poor neighbourhoods through its Sure Start scheme and the New Deal for Communities programme. It adopted a minimum wage and sought to support low-income families through the tax and benefits systems. It invested major resources into the health and education services in an attempt to develop long-term solutions to the problems of ill health, unemployment, poor education attainment, crime and disorder. These are issues which both exacerbate inequalities and place demands on public services (health and social services, and the criminal justice system) and the public purse (through the payment of welfare benefits). It radically reformed many areas of welfare policy by targeting benefits, producing what Taylor-Gooby terms a 'new individualism' in policy, with responsibility for meeting need placed on the individual (Taylor-Gooby 2000: 335). Labour attempted to engage individuals and communities as partners in the prevention and solution of social problems through voluntary and community-based activity, self-help and responsible lifestyle choices. To foster such engagement, the government sought, through its policies on neighbourhood renewal and social exclusion, to build 'social capital', to promote 'community leadership' and to enhance 'community capacity'. It also attempted to set out a new quasi-contractual relationship between state and citizen, based on responsibilities and obligations as well as rights, in a 'modernised' welfare state (Barnes and Prior 2000; Lund 1999). The old focus on redistribution through the tax and benefit system was rejected in favour of a 'redistribution of opportunity' through education, training and paid employment (Lister 1999: 2).

Labour's programme of modernisation, then, was directed towards social and cultural as well as institutional change. Its discourses and ideologies invoked a set of images through which civil society could be re-imagined (Hughes 1998). Blair constantly spoke in terms of the 'national community' and 'shared values', and his discourse was constructed through the inclusive concepts of 'we', 'us' and 'together' (Fairclough 2000: 34). The 'we' was one in which citizens (in families and communities) were constituted as partners in the governance of society. The 'third sector' of voluntary associations and self-help groups took on a new importance as a means of complementing – or replacing – state provision. Community leaders and 'social entrepreneurs' were to become the catalysts for overcoming the problems of run-down neighbourhoods. Parents and victims were addressed as partners in the search for solutions to problems of crime and disorder.

This focus on cultural change was directed towards redressing the perceived impoverishment of civil society caused by the political ideologies of both left and right:

> In deciding where to act on behalf of the national community, whether as regulator or provider, governments must be acutely sensitive not to stifle worthwhile activity by local communities and the voluntary sector. The grievous twentieth century error of the fundamentalist Left was the belief that the state could replace civil society and thereby advance freedom. The New Right veers to the other extreme, advocating wholesale dismantling of core state activity in the cause of 'freedom'. The truth is that freedom for the many requires strong government. A key challenge to progressive politics is to use the state as an enabling force, protecting effective communities and voluntary organisations and encouraging their growth to tackle new needs, in partnership as appropriate. (Blair 1998a: 4)

This extract takes us beyond the conventional conception of the Third Way as an idea that transcends the old ideological debates about state versus market. Rather than transcending ideology, Blair drew on intensely ideological images of 'truth' and 'freedom' in order to legitimate a set of ethical and moral values drawn from communitarianism and Christian socialism. Social integration and social order were coupled together in the concept of civility:

> My politics are rooted in the belief that we can only realise ourselves as individuals in a thriving civil society, comprising strong families and civic institutions buttressed by intelligent government. (Blair 1998a: 3)

Notions of family, community and citizenship were central to the government's imagery of modernity, while the discourses of partnership, self-help and responsibility underpinned Labour's approach to economic renewal and welfare reform. Rather than the Third Way representing a break from the politics of the new right, it recurrently revived a neo-conservative conception of community, family, responsibility and the importance of moral order.

Labour's policies on unemployment, ill health, poor educational achievement, crime and community safety, were underpinned by a focus on 'persuading people to think, believe, care and behave differently' (Perri 6 1998b: 52). All of this highlights the significance of discourse and ideology to Labour's political project. Post-structuralist theory can help understand the workings of the forms of knowledge and power in its approach to governance:

> Government concerns not only practices of government but also practices of the self. To analyse government is to analyse those processes that try to shape, sculpt, mobilise and work through the choices, desires, aspirations, needs, wants and lifestyles of individuals and groups. . . . One of the points that is most interesting about this type of approach is the way it provides a language and a framework for thinking about the linkages between questions of government, authority and politics, and questions of identity, self and person. (Dean 1999: 12–13)

Rather than ideas of individual and community responsibility representing a withdrawal of state power, they may suggest its extension through new discursive strategies in which citizens and other categories of actor are conceived as 'subjects of responsibility, autonomy and choice' (Rose 1996a: 54).

In the next sections I explore the notions of community and individual responsibility in the development of Labour's approach to governing civil society and modernising the welfare state. Before doing so, however, it is worth inserting a health warning. In the field of social welfare it is particularly important to stress the way in which discourses do not operate merely at the level of language and culture, but are also embedded in technologies and practices: the assessment of benefit claims, the funding of community organisations, the targeting of 'poor neighbourhoods' for special interventions, the treatment of offenders. Conceptions of the rights and obligations of citizens, of the centrality of the family to the social and moral order, of the need for social integration, are not of merely academic interest. They have real and very material consequences for welfare claimants, for lone mothers, for young people excluded from school and for others directly affected by Labour's social and welfare policies.

Re-building community capacity

Labour policy documents repeatedly stressed the importance of community as both a source of social integration and the locus of self-governance. The appeal of community lay not only in its roots in a particular philosophy, but also as a 'common-sense' idea in both public consciousness, political rhetoric and practical policy-making. Concepts of community in political rhetoric were of course not new. They have provided a recurrent reference point across a range of public services – Community Care, Community Safety, Community Health Councils, Community Planning and many others. The centrality of community in Labour discourse was based in part on this status as a practical concept which, because of its roots in 'common-sense' understandings of the world, seems to require little analysis or refinement. Community had a multi-faceted appeal precisely because it draws on diverse sets of images, not all of them compatible. It evoked a conception of sturdy and self-reliant communities, based on a nostalgic conception of Britain's past – traditional working-class communities based on key industries such as coal mining or shipbuilding, or traditional rural communities based in networks of mutual dependence, obligation and deference. Both of these images were profoundly nostalgic and had at their centre the idea of community as reproducing tradition – that is, a sense of moral order, of which the family was viewed as the foundation. A different set of images, and somewhat in tension with the first, derived from community activism. Here community was viewed as the basis for self-provisioning through 'active citizenship'. This idea was most forcefully expressed in the idea of the 'social entrepreneur', acting as a catalyst for local initiatives and providing leadership for local forms of action (Leadbeater 1997). The idea of community self-help was central to Labour's conception of the renewal of the social domain:

> The most powerful resource in turning around neighbourhoods should be the community itself. Community involvement can take many forms: formal volunteering; helping a neighbour; taking part in a community organisation. It can have the triple benefit of getting things done that need to be, fostering community links and building the skills, self-esteem and networks of those who give their time. (Social Exclusion Unit 1998a: 68)

These 'benefits' illuminate different strands of new Labour's agenda. The first is 'getting things done' without and beyond the state. While the new right viewed the market rather than the state as the best way of delivering services, Labour assumed a greater role for civil society. It emphasised the importance of a renewed and revitalised voluntary sector, delivering services outside the confines of the state, introducing innovative forms of provision and acting as a focus of community activity. This sector played a leading role in new Labour's partnership model of social and public policy. A second strand of Labour's agenda illustrated in the SEU quotation is that of 'fostering community links' as part of a set of strategies concerned with addressing social exclusion. Self-help was viewed as a 'vital ingredient in sustainable change in a deprived neighbourhood' (Social Exclusion Unit 2000: para 6.36). The state was viewed as a facilitator and enabler, with an emphasis on the need for community capacity-building to foster and support self-help, to develop skills and to build self-esteem.

Labour's policies on crime and the family acted as lines of continuity with the neo-conservative strand of new right politics under Thatcher, but also harked back to an older, paternalistic form of Labourism evident in the concept of 'ethical socialism' (Dennis and Halsey 1988). But the pervasiveness of community in the Labour lexicon derived in part from its early associations with communitarian philosophies and ideas (Driver and Martell 1998). Communitarianism both provided an alternative to neo-liberalism and served to distance the party from its postwar social demo-cratic past. Etzioni represents community as the third – or middle – way between statism (old left) and individualism (new right), or 'authoritarians' and 'radical individualists' (Etzioni 1995). His philosophy combines moral, social and civil agendas in its focus on the need to build consensus, foster trust and strengthen mutual ties of reciprocity and obligation. These moral and authoritarian components of communitarianism are traceable in formulations of the Third Way by Giddens and others close to new Labour (e.g. Giddens 1998a) and in the speeches of Blair himself. Communitarian-ism also formed the basis for many areas of policy reform. Policies on community policing, community safety and the 're-integrative public shaming' involved in, for example, restorative justice projects, can all be linked directly to Etzioni's ideas (Hughes 1996; Hughes and Mooney 1998). More generally, communitarianism evoked an image of a strong civil society in which the state acts as investor, enabler and empowerer, an image radically different from the socialist associations of old Labour.

Not all of the conceptions of community enshrined in central or local government policy evoked the conservative representations of Etzioni's communitarianism. Some government and local government documents recognised the difficulty of reconciling differences of values, interests and identities, while others acknowledged a more politicised conception than the concept of 'self-help' encompasses. Activist conceptions of community overlapped with some of the developments around local governance which had developed outside the Labour Party but which had been acknowledged and incorporated (albeit unevenly) into Labour policy in office. But the dominant conception of community returned to the moral and social inflections of communitarianism. The idea of community was strongly linked to very particular notions of civic responsibility and citizenship, notions that informed Labour's attempt to overcome social exclusion and reform the welfare state.

Remaking welfare subjects

Underpinning these reforms was a strategy designed to 'modernise' the welfare state in a way that distanced new Labour from many of the assumptions on which the postwar welfare settlement had been based. A key theme running through Labour's approach to welfare was the attempt to construct a 'new deal' between state and citizens based on the duties and obligations of citizens or, in Rose's terms, the creation of 'responsibilised' citizens (Rose 1996a). This was spelled out by Blair in his speech at the 1997 Labour Party conference: 'a decent society is not based on rights. It is based on duty. Our duty to each other. To all should be given opportunity, from all responsibility demanded.' This theme continued, with notions of the 'responsible society' central to the speeches of both the Home Secretary Jack Straw and of the Prime Minister (e.g. in Blair's speech in his constituency on 1 December 2000). These ideas did not emerge fully blown under Labour but developed out of long-standing debates about the post social democratic state from writers and thinkers who were influential to Labour. Dwyer (1998), for example, traces the theme of 'conditional citizenship' in the works of Giddens, Etzioni, Roche and Selbourne. He notes that one common strand is the assertion that individual responsibility is a priority for any meaningful notion of citizenship in future Western societies. Selbourne distinguished between civil and political rights on the one hand and social rights on the other, the latter being secondary and not imbued with equivalent legal status (Selbourne 1993). A second strand, more closely linked to Roche and Giddens, is the allied belief that the role of the state as a major provider of welfare services is limited. Giddens argues that the faith in the power of professionals, and of the state itself, to solve social problems had been undermined, partly through a decade or more of state failure and partly because of the rise of increasingly informed and sceptical citizens (Giddens 1998a, 2000).

Such ideas informed Labour's attempt to break away from the 'tax and spend' associations of old Labour and the welfare settlement of the postwar years. Its welfare reform was based on a determination to appeal to a middle-class electorate by limiting taxation and placing an emphasis on economic 'prudence'. There was a desire not to return to the (limited) universalist conceptions of citizenship which had characterised the postwar welfare state and the relationship between state and citizen that it had embodied. The collective rights and responsibilities underpinning the social democratic settlement of the welfare state, were, under Labour, recomposed around notions of equality of opportunity, and, more specifically, equal opportunity to work. The programme of welfare reform centred on the promise of 'salvation through work': work was to prevent poverty, improve health, reduce public spending, create role models for children, provide a sense of identity and a social life, and promote social inclusion. At the same time it was expected that government would overcome some of the impediments to inclusion and active participation in the economy by encouraging investment and training. Labour's policies on pre-school children (Sure Start), its focus on school standards and the expansion of post-16 education and training, the establishment of the Learning and Skills Council and other developments all testify to Labour's emphasis on creating equality of opportunity. But the policies on social exclusion, education and welfare invoked a quasi-contractual relationship between state and citizen in which opportunities were to be matched by responsibilities. The 'modernisation' of welfare was structured around the norm of the active, working citizen, availing him or herself of the opportunities to become part of the new information-based economy and equipped with the skills and capacities to do so.

The norm of active, working citizens differed from previous Labourist conceptions of work in that women as well as men, and those previously marginalised through disability, single parenthood or long-term unemployment, were expected to become fully integrated members of the working population. Labour had registered some of the challenges to the idea of the white, male, heterosexual, able-bodied breadwinner/citizen of the Beveridgean welfare settlement. Its response was to insist that anyone could be (and should be) a breadwinner. The articulation of rights and responsibilities carried profound moral resonances and provided a fertile ground for 'disciplinary' approaches to social welfare. If the government made a reasonable offer of a route to social inclusion through training or employment, people who refused it would be excluding themselves from society. They would be guilty of a moral failure – a failure to recognise their responsibilities – as well as experiencing economic penalties through the possible withdrawal of benefits. Moral and economic discourses interacted most obviously in the construction of welfare to work policies in terms of a 'new deal'. But they also underpinned notions of parenthood, as spelled out in a 1997 speech by Frank Field, then Minister for Welfare Reform:

> Our reform agenda is dominated by a new emphasis on responsibilities as well as rights: the responsibilities of parents, absent and present, to care, emotionally and materially, for their children; the responsibility of adults of working age to work; the responsibility of welfare recipients to take opportunities to escape from dependency. (Field 1997, cited in Lister 1998: 222)

There was a strong moral agenda here, not least in the reference to 'parents, absent and present', and in the negative construction of those in receipt of welfare benefits as being in a state of 'dependency'. It was not only about reining in welfare expenditure but also about addressing social exclusion and constructing citizens through a discourse of moral responsibility rather than one of rights and entitlements, bringing about a fundamental change in the 'culture, attitude and practice of the welfare state' (Blair 1998a: 222). One element of this involved transforming the welfare state into one that promoted personal responsibility and individual opportunity, in contrast to the 'passivity' of the old welfare state. The other side of the coin was the attempt to constitute welfare subjects as responsible and participating subjects, fulfilling the duties of citizenship, here defined expansively in terms of employment and responsible parenthood rather than the more traditional and limited duties of citizenship such as obeying the law and paying tax. This theme was frequently found in the writings and speeches of Blair himself, backed up by a subtle threat of enforcement:

> Strong communities depend on shared values and recognition of the rights and duties of citizenship. . . . In the past we have tended to take such duties for granted. But where they are neglected, we should not hesitate to encourage and even enforce them. (Blair 1998a: 12)

These processes of remaking individual subjectivities and recasting social identities were conducted both symbolically and materially. Symbolically, they took place through new uses of language (e.g. the emphasis on a value-imbued language of community, reciprocity and mutual responsibility), and through the reworking of traditional ideas into a 'modern' context (e.g. the reframing of 'equal opportunities' as 'equal opportunity to work'). These new discursive practices were developed within a broader ideological framework in which ideas of globalisation, economic prudence and modernisation formed super-ordinate narratives. However, discourses do not just involve the realm of symbols, narratives and ideas; they also involve material practices. Changes in the welfare system challenged the universalism of the past, with a shift to a more targeted provision evident in policies on lone parents, disability and pensions.[1] The reforms also aimed to reduce the welfare bill by curtailing long-term 'dependence' on benefits – including that of the long-term unemployed, lone mothers, the disabled – by encouraging those on state benefits into employment. The discourse of 'responsible citizenship' was embedded in the coercive elements of the New Deal and Welfare to Work programmes. The dominant discursive constructions of 'community' (as locality-based and partnership-oriented) were reinforced by the pattern of funding offered for neighbourhood renewal and for the host of locality-based initiatives described in previous chapters.

It is easy to overestimate the impact of change in the welfare system – the early welfare team of Harriet Harman and Frank Field failed to deliver on the reform programme and a number of proposals, including the abolition of child benefit, were not implemented. Indeed, the welfare programme of new Labour involved rather more redistribution, albeit selective, targeted and means-tested, than was first envisaged. However, the discourse of rights and obligations remained powerful, and the contractual elements of the New Deal have been strongly enforced, despite emerging concerns about its effectiveness (*Observer*, 2 April 2000: 5). This discourse was coupled with that of social exclusion in the process of welfare reform.

From equality to social inclusion

A distinctive feature of Labour's approach was its challenge to the neo-liberal silence about issues of poverty (Lister 1998). There was however, an attempt to de-couple notions of poverty from the politics of social rights and redistribution. While poverty and inequality were treated as legitimate issues of public concern, they were reconstituted in terms of processes of social exclusion (Levitas, 1998; Stepney et al. 1999). The concept of social exclusion was not an invention of new Labour but was a core element of European economic and social policy based on the experience of the European Anti-Poverty Programmes. The concept appeared widely in the European Union's Social Chapter as well as in the UK's Commission on Social Justice. It is a multi-dimensional concept which embraced 'a variety of ways in which people may be denied full participation in society and full effective rights of citizenship in the civil, political and social spheres' (Lister 1998: 2). In viewing poverty and inequality as a product of more complex social as well as economic processes, the concept of social exclusion drew on some of the challenges to the dominance of class-based politics that arose from the new social movements of the late twentieth century. However, there were different discourses of social exclusion. That elaborated by Giddens, and on which much of Labour's policy on welfare and poverty was based, suggested that it is not so much restricted access to material goods that constitutes poverty or inequality, but the capability to make effective use of such resources. Equality and inequality revolved around self-realisation: 'What matters isn't economic deprivation as such, but the consequences of such deprivation for individuals' well being' (Giddens 2000: 88). He suggests that the experience of poverty or unemployment was shaped by membership of groups, communities and cultures. While acknowledging the need for a continued focus on redistribution, Giddens argues that social and cultural factors constituted not only the way in which poverty or inequality was mediated, but also formed basic elements of inequality itself.

The focus on social exclusion was developed early in Labour's policy programme through its deliberations about how to address the problems of 'poor estates'. The establishment of the Social Exclusion Unit (SEU) in 1997 marked an attempt to reconfigure the policy process in order to tackle a series of interacting problems on a locality basis. The Unit later began to develop targeted policies directed to reducing the perceived problems created by particular groups – rough sleepers, teenage parents, young people excluded from school and 16–18 year olds not in education, employment or training. The SEU's discourse drew on two different, but interrelated, conceptions of social exclusion: one based on a *category of person* (or even an *area*); another based on *social and economic processes* of exclusion. The former implied the targeting of special measures or policies on a particular group of people, while the latter directed attention towards interacting processes in the wider society. Labour policy slipped between the two as its moral, economic, social and cultural agendas interacted. The focus on education, training and employment reflected new Labour's agenda of building a flexible workforce equipped for the information age. But the discourse highlighted a cultural, as well as an economic, set of causes of social exclusion, emphasising attitudes to risk, long-term dependency and a 'poverty of expectations' (a term much used by two Secretaries of State, David Blunkett and Alistair Darling). While the reports and documents of the SEU talked of a range of different processes, these tended to be presented as lists of interacting factors that together contributed to multiple forms of deprivation.[2] The nature of the interactions was not, however, much debated. In particular, the relationship between economic factors (material poverty), policy agendas (housing, education, access to services) and socio-cultural attributes of groups or individuals was, at best, ambiguous.

Labour discourse of social exclusion worked in two main ways. First, it created a distinction between the 'socially excluded' and mainstream society, the latter operating as the norm from which other groups differed. The cultures of groups defined as socially excluded were viewed in terms of deficits (of aspiration, confidence, willingness to take risks, and so on) or a surfeit of 'troubling' characteristics (e.g. school truancy, drug addiction, anti-social behaviour). Such defects might be implicitly attributed to the characteristics of particular ethnic groups. For example, Lewis's analysis of the SEU report *Truancy and School Exclusion* (1998b) notes its recognition of the racialised dynamics within schools that result in a disproportionate number of pupils from African-Caribbean descent being excluded. However, the solutions focused on redressing the deficits of such students through behaviour management, coupled with better data collection on the performance and behaviour of different pupil groups. She comments: 'By identifying the nodal points for intervention as the pupils' families and communities, the report is suggesting that the problem – and solution – to exclusions and underachievement lies in these locations' (Lewis 2000a: 272). A later SEU report on the first two years of the work of the Unit acknowledged the 'special problems' faced by ethnic minorities which include racist crime (Social Exclusion Unit 2000: para 6.11) and described the ways in which public services were characterised by 'an inadequate recognition and understanding of the complexities of ethnic minority groups, and hence *services that fail to fit their circumstances*' (Social Exclusion Unit 2000: annex B, page 2, my emphasis). Institutional and policy change were clearly on the agenda. The overriding emphasis, however, was on the need to integrate ethnic minorities as 'active citizens' within the process of neighbourhood renewal. While the report highlighted the need for services to be sensitive to special needs, the possibility of institutional discrimination by schools, employers, the police and other bodies was a subordinate theme. The cultural and moral dimensions of social exclusion were at the forefront, with personal transformation as well as access to opportunities central to the government's strategy. As with 'race', issues of gender and disability were included in a complex set of configurations. They appeared not as a set of processes producing inequality, but in terms of the categorisation of 'lone mothers' or 'the disabled' as groups likely to be marginalised from mainstream society (defined here as the world of work). The problem of social exclusion appeared to be defined predominantly in terms of a *category of person* (the excluded), not in terms of *process of exclusion* (institutional discrimination by schools, employers, public services, or even the welfare benefits system).

The second important feature of Labour's discourse of social exclusion was the form of governance that it invoked. The socially excluded became the target of 'influencing' forms of government policy alongside, or instead of, a focus on institutional reform or the redistribution of material resources. Intervention for particular groups – parents of young children in particular geographical areas, rough sleepers, school truants – became a question of better coordination of existing policies and the development of network-based forms of governance. Intervention to address the problem of run-down estates became less a matter of capital expenditure and more a matter of influencing others – shops, businesses, schools, service providers – to contribute to the regeneration process. The solution to the problems of social exclusion was viewed as largely a matter of an 'enabling' role for the state coupled with 'self-governance' by individuals and communities participating in their own salvation by setting up self-help groups, finding leaders from within the community to develop entrepreneurial solutions, or seeking escape through education and employment. As Franklin comments, 'By focusing on people in families and communities and sharing responsibility for social exclusion between different agencies, there has been a tendency to disregard the significance of wider social and economic forces and the inequalities they produce' (Franklin 2000: 17). Similar points were made in Chapter 4 concerning the 'localisation' of social problems within Labour's policy approach. These strategies served to distance new Labour from old Labour's traditional focus on social class and structural forms of inequality. But the concepts of inequality that replaced it are extremely limited. The next section traces the way in which Labour has selectively appropriated, incorporated and resisted notions of equality and diversity in its imagery of a modern British people.

A modern British people?

It is possible to trace twin strands running through Labour's approach to civil society. The first was based on an image of a modern society in which inequalities had largely been overcome (with residual categories dealt with through policies on social exclusion); in which the old divisions around class, 'race' and gender had been reconciled; in which old prejudices (e.g. around disability or gay lifestyles) had been overcome; and which was characterised by mutual understanding and tolerance. This strand of Labour's discourse was represented in its commitment to deal with long-term issues of poverty and to heal the divisions resulting from two decades of neo-liberal economic policies. Labour was also more attentive to notions of difference and diversity than Conservative governments had been. There was a greater degree of acknowledgement of changes in gender relations, of 'multi-culturalism' and anti-racism, of sexuality, disability and other issues raised by the 'new social movements' of the 1960s, 1970s and 1980s.

The existence of ethnic minorities was acknowledged in the reform proposals around health and education services and in policies developed to tackle social exclusion. As I noted earlier, difference was usually conceived as the possession of special needs discursively positioned by their relationship to the normal/universal needs of the majority. But Labour also addressed issues of racism (e.g. through the establishment of a new category of racially aggravated crime, and new legislation that outlaws discrimination in public services and places a duty on public bodies to promote race equality). It adopted a positive public stance on disability, with the establishment of a Minister for the Disabled and the setting-up of the Disability Rights Commission. It made a commitment to repeal section 28 of the Local Government Act (banning the 'promotion' of homosexuality)[3] and to reduce the age of consent for gay relationships. It celebrated the achievement of greater equality for women represented in the sharp increase of women MPs in the 1997 parliament.

The second strand of Labour's approach was, however, based not on overcoming inequality or celebrating diversity but on the attempted installation of a homogenous, consensual representation of the people:

> The goal of the new social democracy is consensus, to calm down and resettle a society agitated by the individualism of the 1980s. The tacit argument now is that 'old style' social democratic arguments for equality, equal opportunities and social justice, can stir up discontent and political activity which needs to be contained in the interests of social order, within a politics that manages dissent and aims to share the best of what we have in a fair and responsible way. (Franklin 2000: 17)

This was particularly sharply represented in the discourses of nation and family around which issues of 'race' and 'gender' were constellated.

Labour operated in an imaginary 'post-feminist' world in which conflict around gender issues was viewed as yesterday's agenda. While distancing itself from feminist politics, it did, however, develop policies in line with a supposed new consensus around gender issues. It put in place policies likely to deliver, in the longer term, considerable improvements in women's lives: the minimum wage, increase in child benefit, childcare tax credits, the New Deal for lone parents, the national childcare strategy, the introduction of parental leave legislation and its attempt to influence employers to introduce more 'family friendly' working conditions. The focus on health and education tended to correspond to issues high on many women's agendas. These achievements, however, were carried through in the name of the family rather than from an explicit consideration of continued forms of gender inequality (notably the continued disparity of incomes between women and men, coupled with inequalities of disposable time). While acknowledging changes in gender roles and household composition, the family was viewed as fundamental to the renewal of community and society, and Labour was concerned to assert the value of stable, two-parent families for social issues from child development to crime reduction. Labour explicitly attempted to strengthen the family, producing a consultation document on *Supporting Families* (Home Office 1999), setting up a policy forum on parenting and establishing the National Family and Parenting Institute. A Family Policy Unit within the Home Office supported a ministerial group on the family and coordinated policy across government. Moral and social agendas interacted in these initiatives, with notions of 'good parenting' and government initiatives designed to 'strengthen marriage' interacting with a more social (and progressive) agenda of persuading employers to introduce 'family-friendly' employment practices and arguing for a more 'child-friendly' society. This familial discourse intersected with the equal opportunity to work discourse in a rather uncomfortable way. Government attempts to get lone mothers off state benefits and into the labour market was somewhat in tension with new Labour's conception of traditional family values (Edwards and Duncan 1997). Should women, as parents (single or otherwise) be encouraged to move off benefits and into the workplace, or should they focus their energies on building strong families and acting as 'responsible' parents? Such tensions were not new, but refracted the continuation of tensions between the neo-liberal and neo-conservative strands of the policies of Conservative governments through the 1980s and early 1990s. But Labour's links with communitarianism tended to strengthen the moral and conservative emphasis on the family, and of women's role in the building of the 'responsible society'. Although not adopting Etzioni's philosophy wholesale, the links between 'poor parenting' and crime and delinquency were repeatedly affirmed, and the 'problem' of single parenthood much debated.

Many areas of social policy under Labour – from schooling to pensions, from care of the elderly to the Sure Start programme for young children – were presented in a gender neutral way but had a profoundly differential impact on women and men. The family under new Labour was one in which parents were supposedly actively involved in preventing truancy and contributing to community safety, supervising homework, getting involved in the governance of schools, and contributing to the creation of thriving communities. The gendered division of labour, on which much of this activity is based, was hardly compatible with the prospect of women competing equally with men in the waged economy. Blair acknowledged the growing importance of women's role in the labour force in his pamphlet on the Third Way, but went on to comment that: 'Reconciling such changes and opportunities to the strengthening of the family and local communities is among the greatest challenges of contemporary public policies' (Blair 1998a: 6). It is a challenge to which Labour has yet to find a successful response.

In the same way that the family formed a crucial, albeit unstable, link in the construction of an imaginary unity of the 'modern people', concepts of a multi-cultural Britain characterised by tolerance and harmonious relations were central to Labour's imagery. Progressive policies on race and race relations operated alongside, and in tension with, Labour's attempt to appeal to a traditional, conservative constituency:

> Contemporary policy documents define the central issue facing central and local government as how to promote and reconcile ethnic diversity and *simultaneously* resurrect (and become the keeper of) an older version of the British nation – one which is seen as ethnically homogenous, benign and 'tolerant'. How, in other words, to align the pursuit of a (narrowly conceived) 'multi-culturalism' with a recourse to 'tradition' and an unchanged Britain. (Lewis 2000a: 265)

Hall has provided a cogent analysis of the way in which Labour was oriented towards 'middle England': an imagined community in the south or centre of the country, peopled by home owners, and 'commitedly suburban, anti-city, family-centred, devoted to self-reliance and respectability' (Hall 1998: 14). It was also essentially white. Racialised minorities were placed outside conceptions of 'the people' as a modern nation (Lewis 1998). They might aspire to be admitted to it, but they did not form the elements from which it was composed. The inclusive and consensual imagery of community and 'the people' served to mask exclusions, with clear limits to how far communities of identity – of 'race', of culture, of sexuality – could be incorporated.

Nevertheless the boundaries of Britishness were constantly being challenged, redefined or restated. Since new Labour was elected such challenges clustered around two main themes: the political fights around asylum seekers and the arguments following the murder of the young black teenager Stephen Lawrence and the subsequent Macpherson report of 1999. The political and cultural upheavals produced by the death of Stephen Lawrence and the subsequent enquiry led to a number of government initiatives. The Crime and Disorder Act of 1998 included, for the first time, a category of 'racially aggravated offences'. The Home Office set out a code of practice for recording racist incidents and set staff employment targets for the Home Office and the prison, police, fire and probation services. A consultation process on strengthening the black and ethnic minority voluntary sector infrastructure was also initiated. But the alignment of the Home Secretary with the project of modernising the police force and other public bodies to eradicate institutional racism stood in stark contrast to the policies of the same government department on asylum seeking and the defence of British nationality. The presentation of government policies on asylum seeking were depicted as 'racist' and divisive by the Church of England and the Commission for Racial Equality, among others.

Such policies carried implicit messages about the nature of what it meant to be included in dominant conceptions of Britishness. They were also the site of struggle by those who were excluded from such conceptions, providing discordant notes in the consensual imagery at the heart of new

Labour's conceptions of a modern British people. Fundamental to the images and representations of 'the people' were the ways in which conceptions of diversity, difference and equality were (sometimes) incorporated or managed, and how contestation and resistance was (unevenly) appropriated or deflected. For example, some challenges to the dominant conception of multi-culturalism were included in the Runnymede Trust's *Report on the Future of Multi-Ethnic Britain* (Runnymede Trust 2000). The publication of the report produced what one of its contributors characterised as a 'torrent of misquotation and abuse' (Hall, cited in The *Observer*, 15 October 2000). Despite massive media coverage, the dominant messages from the Trust remained largely unreported and undebated, even though issues of race continued to carry a high political salience.

Sharp conflicts continued to pervade the politics of new Labour in its attempt to establish a new conception of the 'modern people'. They indicated the limits of Labour's struggle to displace issues of poverty and inequality by a new, more contained and manageable set of distinctions based on the idea of social exclusion and inclusion. This struggle included an attempt to subsume conflicts about 'race' within a conception of a multi-cultural Britain, and issues of gender within an image of a post-feminist society in which gender inequalities had largely been resolved.

The politics of inclusion

This chapter has explored Labour's capacity to shape a new social settlement in the aftermath of the fracturing of the postwar settlement that took place under the neo-liberal regime of Conservative governments of the 1980s and early 1990s. It has traced Labour's attempt to remake civil society around a powerful set of images of family, community and responsible citizenship. It has highlighted the uneasy balance between modern, progressive policies on 'race', gender and other structural forms of inequality and Labour's traditional – and deeply conservative – conceptions of civil society.

David Marquand has argued that new Labour's conception of the 'people' is an inclusionary and consensual one: 'New Labour speaks and acts as though it embodies a national consensus – a consensus of the well-intentioned, embracing rich and poor, young and old, suburbs and inner-cities, black and white, hunters and animal rights campaigners, successful and unsuccessful' (Marquand 1998: 19). In this sense, everyone had – or would have – the opportunity to be a part of 'the people'. This inclusionary view, however, rested on the distinctions that Marquand identified as being non-antagonistic. The 'people' could include differences, so long as those differences did not make a difference. As long as everyone was indeed 'well-intentioned' – disposed to take their opportunities, observe their responsibilities and generally behave reasonably – anyone could join. But as Lister comments, inclusion into an unjust and unequal society could be viewed as a 'less than inspiring vision' (Lister 1998: 2).

Marquand himself identifies the inevitable economic antagonisms between 'winners' and 'losers' that result from processes of social change. However, those categories are gendered and racialised as well as based on economic or class identities. The legacy of the old social settlement and its dislocation was the most significant set of contradictions and contestations that was addressed – though not resolved – by new Labour's vision of a modern society. The limits to consent and the constraints of who could be included became starkly evident as Labour faced a series of challenges around gender, race and sexuality in its first years of office. Labour's discourse delineated multi-culturalism as a valid policy goal but tended to struggle where issues of 'race' and racism were invoked. It was sympathetic to its gay constituencies but oscillated around legislative change, in one case amending the clause of the Local Government Bill repealing Section 28 in order to secure support in the House of Lords, in another invoking the Parliament Act to align the homosexual and heterosexual age of consent after this had been repeatedly blocked by the House of Lords. It included (at least symbolically) 'women's issues' within the political agenda, in part through its policies on employment but also by foregrounding policies concerned with education, health, community safety and family poverty. However Labour's attempts to engage with women's agendas – for example by establishing a separate Minister for Women, setting up a series of consultation exercises and even launching its own magazine – remained largely symbolic.

Labour's attempt to forge an inclusive society was based on the delineation of new patterns of exclusion – beggars, economic migrants, asylum seekers – through which the (troubling) boundaries of citizenship and nation were reaffirmed. Distinctions were opened up between 'irresponsible' parents and 'responsible' families, between the socially excluded and mainstream society, distinctions through which what Morris terms the 'legitimate membership of the welfare community' was defined (Morris 1998). The homeless were redefined as 'rough sleepers' or 'beggars' and became subject to new strategies of containment and control. It was around these new discursive categories and practices of inclusion and exclusion that Labour attempted to forge its new social settlement. But its inclusiveness was both partial and conditional. It embodied the contradictions and fault lines inherited from the break-up of the old social settlement and attempted to make them settle around the 'responsible' working citizen. But the forms of social inequality and social differentiation that dominated the patterns of social change in the last thirty years undercut Labour's attempt to build an inclusive, consensual society. Such changes and challenges could hardly be reconciled in new Labour's contradictory assemblage of ancient and modern social images, where authority, order, discipline and familial stability were juxtaposed with mobility, autonomy, diversity and change. The 'social' still refused to be settled.

Notes

1 This was based in part on critiques of social welfare emerging from academics close to new Labour. Research by Le Grand and others had begun to raise questions about 'who pays, who benefits' from universal welfare provision, pointing to the way in which health and education provision tended to benefit the middle classes rather than the poorest sections of society (Le Grand 1992).

2 Policy Action Teams were established by the SEU to improve access to employment and education, the dominant themes in Labour's discourse on exclusion, but also to extend provision of the arts and sport, shops, information technology and financial services. Teams were also established to address 'anti-social behaviour' and to foster 'community self-help'.

3 The repeal of this clause of the 1988 Local Government Act was dropped in response to the potential defeat of the new Local Government Bill in the House of Lords. The clause was, however, repealed in Scotland.

9   Conclusion: the politics of governance

In this final chapter I review the arguments of the book and suggest how they contribute to an understanding of the political project of new Labour. I begin by asking how far Labour's reforms reflect a shift in the way in which the UK is governed, and argue that the 'new governance' narrative, while illuminating some aspects of Labour's approach, fails to capture the dynamic tensions within its policies and strategies. The chapter moves on to explore the nature of governance as a constructed and contested domain of ideas and practice, reviewing the contribution of cultural and post-structural forms of theory to the analysis of the changing role of the state. These forms of analysis are then used to assess the capacity of Labour to construct a new social and political settlement based on the politics of the Third Way. Finally, I discuss the discursive constructions of 'the modern' that inform Labour's programme of modernisation, and raise some possible alternative conceptions of, and routes through, modernity.

New Labour and governance

At the beginning of this book I asked the question: 'How far do the 1997 Labour government's reforms represent a shift in the governance of the UK?', and set out a number of propositions against which such a shift might be assessed (see Table 9.1).

Labour's approach to governance seems to reflect many of these propositions. The 'pragmatic' politics of the Third Way, described in Chapter 3, were based on an explicit rejection of both predominantly hierarchical and predominantly market-based modes of coordination. There are considerable overlaps between governance theory and the Third Way conception of moving beyond the alternatives of state and market. Labour emphasised the value of partnership as a way of delivering services, stressing both the need for collaboration between the public and private sectors and the importance of voluntary and community-based organisations working in partnership with the statutory sector. In Chapter 4 I argued that Labour's approach to the policy process sought to involve a wider range of actors in the process of tackling social and economic issues, drawing existing policy networks closer to the heart of government and promoting the development of new networks. There was evidence of 'governing at a distance' by steering and coordinating a plurality of actors in Labour's initiatives on crime and disorder, the New Deal for Communities, the Sure Start programme

TABLE 9.1 *Governance shifts: propositions (from Chapter 1)*

The literature suggests that we are witnessing:

1 A move away from hierarchy and competition as alternative models for delivering services towards networks and partnerships traversing the public, private and voluntary sectors.
2 A recognition of the blurring of boundaries and responsibilities for tackling social and economic issues.
3 The recognition and incorporation of policy networks into the process of governing.
4 The replacement of traditional models of command and control by 'governing at a distance'.
5 The development of more reflexive and responsive policy tools.
6 The role of government shifting to a focus on providing leadership, building partnerships, steering and coordinating, and providing system-wide integration and regulation.
7 The emergence of 'negotiated self-governance' in communities, cities and regions, based on new practices of coordinating activities through networks and partnerships.
8 The opening-up of decision-making to greater participation by the public.
9 Innovations in democratic practice as a response to the problem of the complexity and fragmentation of authority, and the challenges this presents to traditional democratic models.
10 A broadening of focus by government beyond institutional concerns to encompass the involvement of civil society in the process of governance.

and other locality-based initiatives. The government also attempted to build the capacity of the public policy system to act in a more reflexive and responsive way. For example, the Treasury attempted to introduce longer planning cycles and to use the leverage of funding to secure more joined-up and outcome-based policy development and delivery, while the Cabinet Office and the units within it acted as a force for policy innovation. There was evidence of different tiers of government – in Scotland, Wales and Northern Ireland, at regional, city and local levels – engaging in what in proposition 7 is termed 'negotiated self-governance'. Labour's emphasis on public participation and democratic renewal, discussed in Chapter 7, appears to provide strong support for propositions 8 and 9. Finally, the book has described ways in which the government attempted to involve civil society in the process of governance, both through its emphasis on community as the source of solutions to social problems and through its framework of citizen rights and obligations in a modernised welfare state.

However, this kind of summary simplifies complex and often contra-dictory processes. Rather than a coherent and unidirectional change from markets and hierarchies towards governance through networks, I have argued that the process was uneven and ambiguous, and was cross-cut by strong counter-pressures. In Chapter 4 I suggested that there were severe limitations to the process of decentralisation and to the development of a more plural, inclusive policy process. There were significant tensions within the Labour Party and government around regional government, and the development of multiple tiers of governance was accompanied by sub-stantial conflict over political power. Labour's espousal of a more inclusive policy process was matched by the exercise of greater central control over party and government policy – its new inclusions were more than matched by new exclusions. Alongside the partial decentralisation, the Labour administration was characterised by a clear recentralisation of political control.

The governance literature suggests a growing dominance of decentralised, network forms of governance in which the role of the state is to influence and steer a wide range of policy actors. While there was some evidence of this in Labour's approach, there was also an intensification of a 'command and control' style of governing, as power became concentrated. In Chapter 5 I described a range of measures, from the growth of audit and inspection to the threat of removal of powers for 'failing' schools, hospitals and local authorities. In Chapter 6 I argued that partnerships were positioned in a field of interactions between centralising and decentralising tendencies, and that partnerships as a policy approach must be distinguished from network forms of governance. In Chapter 7 I suggested that the prescriptive policy climate in which participation exercises took place meant that the scope for participation to contribute to a more open and reflexive style of governance was limited.

Overall, then, it is not possible to assert that Labour's approach represents a shift (or extension of earlier shifts) towards a new form of governance. The process of realigning and dispersing state power interacted with, rather than displaced, a process of concentration and the exercise of more coercive and direct forms of control. This produces particular challenges for understanding the process of change. Rather than asserting or rejecting the notion that there has been a fundamental shift, it is necessary to ask how different processes – of centralisation and dispersal, of enabling and controlling, of loosening and tightening – coexisted, and what might the consequences be?

The paradoxes of modernisation

In Chapter 2 I talked of the difficulty of analysing change through the lens of binary oppositions between the old and the new. Social change can be viewed as a process in which different – and not necessarily coherent – trends and tendencies interact in combination, producing fields of tension within the process of governing. Such tensions are not confined to governance under new Labour, but are played out in particular ways in its approach. They highlight some of the paradoxes at the heart of its political project. Labour sought to create both a new social settlement based on consensus and inclusion, and a more coercive and conditional welfare regime. It attempted to ensure the consistency and efficacy of policy delivery by setting and enforcing performance standards, while at the same time seeking to institutionalise new forms of co-steering and co-governance through partnerships and community capacity-building. It sought to send out a strong and consistent set of messages from the centre while also fostering public participation and drawing a wider range of actors into the policy process.

To help conceptualise the dynamic interplay of different sets of tensions, the book has developed a framework through which the interaction between multiple models of governance might be explored. This set out four models of governance, representing different flows of power and authority, forms of relationship and conceptions of social action. Each model is based on distinctive discourses, embodying specific forms of language, practice and relationship. Each is associated with particular logics of decision-making that guide and coordinate action, and with specific forms of authority and conceptions of responsibility and accountability. These are not readily compatible. For example, the form of accountability embodied in hierarchical governance – upward through vertical, departmental chains of command to the relevant minister, with an emphasis on accounting for expenditure – forms one of the institutional barriers to joined-up government and an open, reflexive approach to policy. The devolution of power and responsibility implied by the 'self-governance' model is not readily compatible with the managerial forms of power at the core of Labour's policies and strategies.

This way of representing the process of modernisation does more than suggest the existence of multiple discourses or conflicting policy styles. It can be used to examine specific lines of tension and their possible impact on the process of implementation. At first sight it seems possible to map different elements of Labour's programme of modernisation as 'belonging' to a particular model in terms of its dominant focus or orientation. But it quickly becomes apparent how different modes of governance might coexist within discrete policy areas. For example, the centrally-driven modernisation of services such as health, education and criminal justice belongs predominantly to the rational goal model, but it also includes elements of the open system and self-governance models where services are linked to 'cross-cutting' initiatives, policy innovation or the development of new forms of collaboration with users or communities. The promotion of 'joined-up government' and 'partnership' appear to belong to the open systems model, though not all partnership working represents an open system, network-based approach. The introduction of new forms of public participation suggests a possible shift towards the self-governance model, but where government tightly prescribes methods of participation, this tends to produce a focus on hierarchy or rational goal models. For example, the compulsory introduction of local referenda on elected mayors may be considered as a strategy to legitimate a hierarchically imposed change in the process of local government rather than as part of an open, participative style of governance. I have argued that overall the dominant pull was towards vertical integration, centralising power to government. But this process of tightening central control was uneven, being weakest in areas of policy innovation and strongest in relation to the control of mainstream professional or quasi-professional services (health, education, social services and probation). Here the partial softening of market imperatives – based on a reliance on the market as a self-regulating system – was accompanied by a search for strategies through which to exercise more consistent regulation of what have tended to be perceived as recalcitrant professionals.

Despite this, change in many areas has been slower and harder to deliver than the government anticipated, much to the frustration of ministers and of the prime minister himself. Was this just a case of government will meeting professional obstruction and organisational inertia, or is something more at stake here? This book has attempted to conceptualise the process of change in rather more complex ways than the traditional public administration focus on the policy-implementation nexus. I established the approaches to theorising change on which this book has drawn in Chapter 2. The next section reviews the contribution of these strands of theory for developing the analysis of political, social and cultural change.

Governance as a constructed and contested domain

New Labour was as much about a struggle to establish new political ideas (the 'Third Way', 'modernisation') and representations of the nation ('the people' as a consensual unity; organisations as partners in 'joined-up' government) as it was about new policies, institutions and practices. The government attempted to establish the super-ordinate importance of the global economy as the context in which economic, welfare and social policies must be shaped (Chapter 3). It attempted to reconfigure representations of the social around ideas of social inclusion and exclusion, rights and responsibilities (Chapter 8). The public realm was re-imagined through the imagery of communities and citizenship, of democratic renewal and public participation, an imagery overlaid on the individualised metaphor of the consumer which had gained dominance in the Thatcher years. A central theme of the book has been an exploration of the symbolic and cultural forms of governance through which Labour attempted to build consent and to constitute 'self-regulating' subjects. The interface between intention and realisation, between the formation of the new and the continuance of the old, was articulated through a struggle for ideas.

The Third Way was a relatively new ideology whose emergence reflected an attempt within the UK and other nations to forge a new political settlement. However, many of the discourses on which it drew were not new, but were appropriated, extended and reworked into new formations. 'Joined-up government', for example, was not a phrase invented by Labour. It describes a set of practical problems that many governments have attempted to resolve. However, as a discourse, 'joined-up government' also played a crucial role in Labour's narrative about the consequences of the fragmenting effects of neo-liberalism, against which the idea of the Third

Way was constructed. It was coupled with other discourses – inclusion, participation and partnership, for example – in a cluster of ideas signifying a reconfiguration of relationships and a new approach to governing. Such a reconfiguration was also indicated in Labour's reworking of the discourse of partnership. Partnership carries strong ideological connotations, signifying a harmonious, non-conflict-based form of relationship. Examples included prime ministerial talk of 'partnership' between government and health professionals in the modernisation of the NHS; the ministerial discourse of 'partnership' between central and local government; or the local government discourse of forging 'partnerships' with local communities. The language of partnership was also adopted in place of the language of competition to re-label contractual or outsourcing arrangements between the public and private sectors. These constructions, together with those of 'community', 'responsibility' and 'inclusion', formed part of the ideological glue through which disparate elements of the Third Way were seemingly held together.

Discursive negotiations

However, the new discourses and ideologies promulgated by Labour were not necessarily successful. Cultural analysis helps illuminate the processes and practices through which ideas are produced, struggled over, become incorporated into 'official' government discourse or perhaps form the basis of new counter-narratives legitimising alternative forms of action. Public participation, for example, can be viewed as the site of struggle between traditional and emergent conceptions of democracy. As I suggested in Chapter 7, it formed a site in which the traditional discourses of 'representation' and 'representativeness' inhibited the extent to which new forms of public participation and involvement, of dialogue and inclusion, were able to challenge the norms of practices of state institutions.

New discourses had to negotiate or displace the residues of those installed under social democratic and neo-liberal governments, now deeply embedded in institutional norms, entrenched interests, cultural values and organisational or professional identities. The tensions between new and old discourses were partly resolved through the strategies of co-option, displacement, subordination and appropriation. We have already seen how the ideology of the Third Way *co-opted* existing discourses into its own legitimating narrative, attempting to draw into itself those interests and values from which earlier discourses were shaped. For example, those with past experience of working in ways now legitimated by Labour (perhaps on local partnership initiatives or on cross-cutting policy areas) became the source of important forms of knowledge and experience, and their activities incorporated into Labour's success stories. Labour also attempted to selectively appropriate elements of the discourses of gender equality, disability, multi-culturalism and other ideas linked to the new social movements of the late twentieth century (Chapter 8).

The *displacement* of old discourses by new is harder to recognise in Labour's strategy since its very essence was one of reconciling seemingly irreconcilable strands of the old and the new. Chapter 8 described the way in which the social democratic discourse of equality was superceded by a discourse of 'equal opportunity to work', and the traditional Labour discourse of class reworked as 'social inclusion'. Whether these emergent discourses will be successful in displacing concepts so central to the core ideas of social democracy remains to be seen. *Subordination* is a more usual outcome where new discourses are overlaid on old ones and are reinforced through the agency of the state. In Chapter 2 I told the story of how, in the late 1980s and early 1990s, managerialism partly displaced bureau-professional power as neo-liberal ideology gained pre-eminence. Labour can be viewed as continuing and intensifying this process. It did so through an emphasis on the rational goal model of governance, and through its managerial, pragmatic style of politics (Newman 2000a; and Chapter 4 of this volume). The arguments of Chapter 5 suggest that Labour's concern to standardise performance and subordinate professional power bases can be viewed as continuing an uncompleted part of the Thatcherite programme of public sector reform.

It is, however, also possible for managers, professionals, staff, user groups and others to *appropriate* parts of Labour's own discourse in their pursuit of other interests and agendas. For example, some local authorities adopted the vocabulary of 'democratic renewal' or 'social inclusion' to legitimise a range of initiatives, while professionals began to appropriate the language of 'what works' to challenge aspects of Labour's policy programme. Public participation, democratic innovation and other discourses were appropriated as legitimating narratives for those working for change as advocates of particular groups. Such conditions created spaces within which counter-discourses might be elaborated. Labour policies opened up new pathways of change as the emphasis on innovation and experimentation, coupled with greater devolution in some areas, provided those responsible for implementing policy more room for manoeuvre. New networks spanning organisational boundaries created new subject positions and enabled the development of alternative patterns of identification. Both the language and practice of partnership working also opened up the possibility of new sources of meaning and identity for those delivering public services, and a new language of legitimation for those working to shape public and social policy around alternative possibilities. Boundary-spanning workers developed new skills and cultural orientations, and alternative routes for career development. Community and voluntary groups became more directly involved in developing solutions within the new partnership arrangements, to some extent being 'incorporated' into official institutions but also presenting challenges to dominant cultures and ways of working. Ideas and values which formerly existed on the margins of mainstream services, commanding low status and limited recognition – health promotion, crime prevention, community development, public involvement – took on a new significance at the hub of many projects and initiatives. Patterns of disadvantage and discrimination were highlighted as government and local government officials became involved in working on initiatives developed under the Social Exclusion Unit, Sure Start programme, Better Government for Older People Initiative and others. The proliferation of experiments created opportunities for actors to draw on a range of cultural ideas, some of which conflicted with the orthodoxies of government discourse.

My use of cultural perspectives has, then, opened up questions about meaning, identity and subjectivity that help illuminate the process of institutional change and the complexity of social action. The discourses of 'partnership', 'participation' or 'inclusion' created new understandings of what it meant to be a public service worker under Labour, much as 'consumers', 'contracts' and 'competition' had done under Thatcher. These discourses provided new, legitimate subject positions and identities for social actors, even though they did not directly determine social action. Patterns of relationship and hierarchies of knowledge were being reshaped, and new spaces and sites of action that could not be controlled from the centre opened up.

The dispersal of power

This view of power as productive, drawn from post-structuralist theories of governmentality, provides a sharp contrast with the governance literature. In Chapter 1, I suggested that arguments about the 'hollowing out' of the state or the 'fragmentation' of power fail to capture the ways in which state power has been realigned. Rather than the reduction of government, the shifts examined in this book can be viewed as the dispersal of state power across new sites of action, augmented by new strategies and technologies. The process of devolving power to public sector organisations and their managers, associated with the New Public Management regime of the 1980s and 1990s, continued under Labour. It was accompanied by a range of strategies and techniques used to regulate activity. Some were overtly coercive: for example, the capacity of government to take over 'failing' organisations. However, Labour also installed a range of strategies for 'governing at a distance': the intensification of the discourse of failure, the expansion of the audit and inspection culture, the proliferation of standards and quality regimes and the introduction of incentive-based funding regimes. In Chapter 5 I noted the capacity of these discourses and practices of modernisation to constitute 'self-regulating' organisations and actors. They produce particular forms of calculation and control within organisations and prioritise particular forms of judgement and action. They have the capacity to produce shifts of power within organisations (e.g. from professionals to managers, or between internal regulators and front-line staff). My argument here is not about whether these strategies have positive or negative consequences: it is about whether the dispersal of power across a plurality of organisations delivering public services is best understood as a withdrawal or an extension of state power.

In Chapters 6 and 7 I traced a rather different set of processes through which the range of actors involved in shaping policy and delivering services had been enlarged. The growth of partnerships and the extension of public participation in decision-making might, in the governance literature, be regarded as evidence of a shift towards co- or self-governance. In political or managerial discourse, such shifts might be described as the 'empowerment' of individuals, communities and organisations. Post-structuralist theory, however, would view them not in terms of empowerment but as an enlargement of the range and penetration of state power. As I suggested in Chapter 6, the government may have given up some forms of direct control, but, by drawing a wider range of actors into a more direct relationship with government, may have enhanced its capacity to extend its influence and control.

The dispersal of power, then, did not mean the erosion of power. Post-structuralist theories of governmentality (see Chapter 1) highlight the importance of discourse and its role in the constitution of new forms of subjects: as responsible citizens in the 'modernised' welfare state; as organisations in the new partnership arrangements for the delivery of public policy; and as communities charged with the responsibility of solving their own problems. It is possible to trace the attempt to constitute new forms of subject through a series of dualities: between active, working citizens and the 'socially excluded', or between responsible (job-seeking) recipients of welfare benefits and those who did not deserve state support. The category of 'consumer' as empowered subject was amplified through the discourse of modernising services. At the same time, notions of community were invoked in discussions of the moral citizen, constituted in relationships of mutuality and reciprocity with others, and taking responsibility for social problems.

However, Labour's approach to governing cannot be understood through the concepts and propositions of either governance theory or post-structuralist forms of analysis alone. Though each offers important insights, both forms of theory are rooted in attempts to analyse *long-term* and *transnational* shifts in the governance of Western states in the late twentieth century. While the UK Labour government can be located in the context of global economic trends and long-term shifts in the role of nation states, it also represented a specific political conjuncture. This was shaped in the context of the historical trajectory of UK politics, the specificity of the UK state, and the pattern of political alliances and interests from which Labour as a political party attempted to remake itself. As well as describing and analysing Labour's discourses, it is necessary to ask why *these* discourses in *this place* at *this time*? (Clarke and Newman 1998): that is, to situate them in Labour's strategies to forge a new political and social settlement in the aftermath of neo-liberalism.

Towards a new political settlement?

The Third Way was an attempt to blend the legacies of neo-liberalism with a focus on social cohesion. It was not confined to the UK, but its form and focus in the UK were distinctive. It attempted to appeal to highly disparate political constituencies within the UK in the mid-1990s: to the financial sector, to business, to 'middle England', to women, to the young, as well as to traditional Labour voters. It sought to accommodate the promise of devolution to the populations of Scotland and Wales while at the same time attempting to hold on to conventional images of nationhood and tradition. It was forced to operate on a terrain defined by the new right while seeking to heal at least some of the divisions that resulted from their long period of hegemony. So, new Labour was situated within a political terrain in which the idea that there can be no going back on the economic restructuring of the Thatcher years, and the reframing of social welfare that accompanied it, was taken for granted. In this sense, Labour represented a kind of consolidation of Thatcherism. It was subject to the same economic and political contradictions that underpinned Thatcherism itself (Hay 1996). Yet Labour also represented something rather different in its concern to build consensus and heal social divisions, to reinstall a notion of civil society, and to draw (albeit in a highly limited and selective way) on the political shifts of the late twentieth century.

I argued in Chapter 3 that the Third Way, in its attempt to combine neo-liberalism with a renewal of civil society, represented an 'unstable' political settlement. Two further areas of instability have been suggested by the arguments of subsequent chapters. One lay in Labour's attempt to forge a new *social* settlement which articulates elements of the radical politics of the late twentieth century's 'new social movements' together with the moral orthodoxies of Christian socialism, communitarianism, ethical socialism and old Labour paternalism (Chapter 8). A second area of instability arose from conflicts over power resulting from the partial constitutional changes that had been introduced, and from the uneasy interaction between forms of centralisation and decentralisation.

Neither 'good governance' nor 'well-managed government' could resolve the contradictions and tensions around the proper role of government and the appropriate boundaries of governance. New discourses and practices involved conflict between different tiers of government as the strong drive to centralise clashed with the rhetoric of, and claims for, local control and flexibility. The interaction between different levels and sites of power – local and central government, the voluntary and statutory sector, the front-line delivery office and the headquarters – can be understood as sites of conflict and resistance rather than as components of self-managing systems. Conflict arose where what Cooper (1998) terms 'excessive governance' – the attempt by state agencies to enlarge their domain of power or influence – met the agency of individuals, groups and organisations seeking to defend or enlarge their territory, ideologies or traditions. Such points often occur on the boundaries of what constitutes the proper business of government and serve to highlight the changing agenda of governance.

In these terms, the interaction between Westminster, Scotland, Wales, Europe and the English regions can best be understood not as the evolution of a new, decentralised form of governance, but in terms of a struggle over who should govern and with what areas of authority and autonomy. Other areas of struggle over the terms and processes of governance were intensified under Labour: those between 'rural' and 'urban' constituencies; between back-bench MPs and ministers; between parliament and the House of Lords; between professionals in public services and regulators such as Ofsted; and between local and central government. The outcomes will depend in part on the working through of contradictions and the shaping of new alliances between established political formations (based on trades unions, party officials, local councils and so on) with those seeking to shape a new political agenda (anti-racists, the green movement, community activists and others).

But the interplay of forces within Labour's unstable political settlement will also depend on the way in which government exercises its power. Jessop argues that: 'The state reserves to itself the right to open, close, juggle and rearticulate governance not only in terms of particular functions but also from the viewpoint of partisan and global political advantage' (Jessop 1998a: 39). This is an important point. It reminds us that any government will not only be concerned with shaping the activities of the state to respond to the challenges of governing in more complex and dynamic societies, but will also strive to retain political support, win consent for its programme and be re-elected to office. It is not only concerned with building processes to support effective governance but also with reproducing its own power to govern. These two goals may be in considerable tension.

Reconceptualising governance

A normative concern with appropriate or effective governance tends to overlook the specifically political dimensions of the state. By 'political dimensions' I do not mean just the politics of a multi-levelled, multi-tiered or dispersed set of government institutions. I also use it to highlight the politics of the wider public realm, and the patterns of inclusion and exclusion on which it is based (see Chapter 8). It is noticeable that theories of governance fail to deal adequately with the issues of diversity and the patterns of inclusion and exclusion through which notions such as 'citizens' and 'communities' are constituted. The conceptualisation of governance and the analysis of the institutions of government tend to take little account of the dissolution of the postwar social settlements around gender, race and class. This dissolution has led to a broader set of issues around diversity, complexity and dynamics than that conceptualised by Kooiman and his colleagues in the governance literature (Newman, forthcoming).

I want to suggest the importance of rethinking 'governance' as a gendered and racialised domain. Notions of 'the public', 'community' and 'citizenship' are structured around particular (gendered) notions of family and the public and (racialised) notions of nation and citizenship. Other lines of division – around disability, age, sexuality, class and so on – are equally significant. Feminist, anti-racist and other 'new social movements' ask important questions of governance at two different levels of analysis. One level concerns questions about 'who governs'. Liberal ideology claims that those elected to representative assemblies are un-gendered and un-racialised beings, able to represent the totality of the population they serve in a non-partisan way. Radical politics disputes this claim and highlights the disproportional exclusion of women and of black and ethnic minorities, claiming that this matters in both symbolic terms (the capacity of different groups to identify with 'government') and in material terms (the impact of policy and financial decisions on different groups).

A second, and less visible, level at which notions of the new governance fail to acknowledge issues of diversity lies in the inclusionary and exclusionary practices on which it is based. In Chapter 6 I noted that networks and informal partnerships are notoriously difficult for some groups to access, while I argued in Chapter 7 that public participation initiatives, while formally claiming to be open to diverse interests and identities, may be delimited by the individualising norms of consumerism or the rule-bound rational discourse of liberal democracy. Challenges from 'outside' these norms may easily be deflected or incorporated. The emerging practices of governance through public involvement may also serve to reproduce dominant understandings of race and gender by replicating biological and essentialist group categorisations (Lewis 2000b). Feminist perspectives highlight the problems resulting from the sharp separation between notions of 'public' and 'private' with many of the concerns or agendas of significance to women being marginalised in, or excluded from, the public realm (Phillips 1992). Women's disproportionate contribution to the informal political domain of community and social action may remain unrecognised (see, for example, Lowndes's analysis of the gendered nature of social capital: Lowndes 2000).

The governance literature is typically silent on such issues. Yet they are of central importance to the analysis of Labour as it attempted to reconcile divergent strands of politics. The politics of gender, 'race', disability and sexuality informed Labour's attempt to build on critiques of both neo-liberalism and social democracy arising from the 'new social movements', and to carve out a distinctive style of politics which engaged with social and cultural agendas. Yet these forms of politics became increasingly marginalised as Labour attempted to hold together its fragile alliance of progressive and conservative forces, and to appeal to 'middle England' as well as its new cosmopolitan, metropolitan supporters, not to mention its traditional constituencies. As I argued in Chapter 8, notions of gender, ethnicity, sexuality and nationhood were crucial points of disruption for

Labour as it attempted to forge a politics that could reconcile tradition and modernity.

Re-imagining modernisation

This conception of governance as a site of conflict, alliances, negotiations and accommodations offers a *political* reading of the dynamics of change. This is rather different from the institutional dynamics highlighted earlier in this chapter. It is specific to this political formation (the Labour government of 1997) at this time (following a long period of Conservative party dominance) and in this place (the UK, with its specific history, traditions and its own external conditions and internal tensions). It suggests a reading of the Third Way not as providing a clear basis for policy choices and the foundation of a distinctive approach to governance, but as an unstable alliance between different political groupings based on the juxtaposition of disparate ideologies and values. The instability of this political formation creates spaces within which the discourse of modernisation might be renegotiated or appropriated, and perhaps attached to alternative political trajectories.

New Labour's reform programme was driven by a commitment to modernisation – the need to align outdated public and welfare services with the new conditions, demands and challenges of the 'modern world'. The concept of modernisation that was used to legitimise the reform of the welfare state offered particular conceptions of citizenship (empowered as active, participating subjects or marginalised as the 'socially excluded'); of work (as the source of opportunity, economic renewal and responsible citizenship); of community (non-antagonistic and homogeneous); and of nation (setting out Britain's place in the changing global economy). It was through such conceptions that Labour attempted to build a new political alliance across fractions of 'old Labour' and the centre left and right. But Labour's modernisation was based on a highly selective appropriation of trends and tendencies of the modern world. It treated globalisation, work and consumerism as forming a unified conception of the modern. At the same time it espoused social and cultural traditionalism in the realm of family, community and social authority. This juxtaposition of neo-liberal and neo-conservative strands has, as this book has repeatedly argued, formed a key line of instability within the discourses and politics of the Third Way. But rather than merely noting this juxtaposition of neo-liberalism and neo-conservatism, I want to suggest that new Labour was profoundly shaped by the need to negotiate other conceptions of the modern. In what follows I explore areas of struggle over what is, and is not, included in Labour's image of the modern world.

Despite its repeated emphasis on the new, much of Labour's approach can be understood in terms of a rather old-fashioned modernity, associated with an industrial age dominated by scientific rationalism and Fordist production methods. This old-fashioned modernity was evident in Labour's attempt to standardise practice, in its belief in scientific solutions and in its emphasis on rational management, evidence-based practice, standardisation, audit, measurement and control. The rationality on which this version of modernity drew is based on what Wheeler terms 'a model of individual action and self-interest which is supposedly "coolly" calculated and opposed to the "hot" impulses of the heart' (Wheeler 1998: 177). Alongside this old-fashioned modernity, Labour invoked a new or late modernity characterised by the complexity of the social domain, post-modern cultural forms, and by a focus on knowledge and information in the post-Fordist elements of the economy (see, for example, Lash (1993) and Beck (1997) on 'reflexive modernisation', Lash and Urry (1994) on 'reflexive accumulation', and Andrews (1998) on the left, new Labour and post-modernism). The tensions between these repeatedly caused problems for the government. Its economic discourses and policies were based on the imperatives of the global market place, the need to produce a more flexible, skilled labour force, the necessity of working in new ways, and training in new skills. There was a strong imperative to abandon 'old-fashioned' practices that did not fit with the image of a modernised economy (see Chapter 3 in this volume). But the economic problems associated with old-style industrial production stubbornly refused to go away. The withdrawal of BMW from car production at Longbridge in April 2000, followed by General Motors' withdrawal from production in Luton in December, sent shock waves through the UK, not least because the Longbridge crisis was met by incautious comments from the minister concerned, suggesting that car production (the superordinate symbol of Fordist production) was somehow less central to Labour's political project than its support for the new knowledge-driven economy. Later that year the political crises produced by the blockade of oil refineries provided a timely reminder of the difficulties of exerting control over flexible, contractual labour forces and the vulnerabilities created by 'just in time' production and delivery methods. Labour's social policies also reflected an uncomfortable attempt to straddle different conceptions of modernity. As I argued in Chapter 8, a clear strand of Labour's approach to re-imagining the social was its emphasis on traditional conceptions of community and family as the basis for moral order. The blend of Christian socialism, communitarianism and an older Labourist authoritarianism invoked a 'pre-modern' image of the past. This image sat uncomfortably alongside its emphasis on the need for a flexible, mobile and feminised labour force adapted to a modernised economy.

Labour's programme of modernisation can be viewed as an attempt to straddle these different conceptions. Its project was to forge a politics for a nation in which Fordism and post-Fordism coexist, and which is cross-cut by pre-modern, modern and post-modern cultural forms. Some of these issues were articulated in contemporary debates over the future direction of social welfare. In an article tellingly entitled 'This is the modern world' (2000), David Miliband, head of the Number Ten policy unit, argued that new technologies, a changing labour market and the reconceptualisation of the role of government and public services required a new approach to welfare provision. He noted the significance of globalisation in the dismantling of the old welfare settlement based on the universal, 'Fordist' principles enshrined in the Beveridge era and set out one set of alternative principles on which a future welfare state might be based. The first was that of legitimacy, based in part on the quality of public services. The second was sustainability, based on the foundation of work as a source of opportunity. The third was based on the need to 'set clear priorities and see them through' (Miliband 2000: 12) rather than attempting to tackle multiple problems at once. The fourth was concerned with the modernisation of the delivery of services to support a model in which 'the Government is changing its role from provider of many separate services to the designer and broker of an integrated programme geared to individual choices and demands. At every stage decentralisation is matched by accountability for the organisation, and opportunity by responsibility for the individual' (2000: 13).

I have cited these principles at length both because they reflect many of the 'new governance' themes discussed in earlier chapters, but also because, in articulating one version of modern welfare, Miliband excludes others. Along with Giddens, the way forward was conceptualised in terms of empowering individuals rather than in overcoming structural inequalities. Other conceptions of a modernised welfare system have drawn rather different critiques of the past and offered alternative images of the future. While Miliband's principles of legitimacy and sustainability are important, they exclude other possible principles based on ideas such as social rights or social justice. Elsewhere, Fiona Williams (2000) has outlined the principles through which 'recognition and respect' might be incorporated into social welfare. They include the principle of interdependence (between welfare users and providers); of identity (based on cultural recognition and respect); of voice (based on a call for a democratisation of the welfare system); and of transnational welfare (calling for social rights that transcend the boundary of the nation state). Williams's principles combine a focus on overcoming cultural forms of injustice with an explicit acknowledgement of the need for a continued redistribution of material resources to overcome social and economic forms of inequality, and form the basis from which alternative conceptions of a modern society and modern welfare system might be articulated.

Debates about the future of the welfare state raise difficult issues about what might constitute the basis for a modern conception of citizenship. Images of tradition and modernity were uncomfortably juxtaposed in Labour's attempt to re-imagine citizenship in the context of the redrawing of national boundaries and the creation of supra-national boundaries such as the European Union (EU). At present, the UK is engaged in big debates about national identity. These debates oscillate around a number of concerns: around the uncertainties of Britishness given regional and national

devolution within the UK; around the difficulties of reconciling multi-
culturalism with images of a historically defined English identity; and
around fears of a European 'superstate'. Each of these take as their base-
line a nineteenth-century image of the sovereign nation state, free from
interference, able to operate in the world as a unified, autonomous actor.
This image no longer matches the complexity of governance in the modern
world. It is not a clear basis for national identity, nor a good enough basis
for social, civil and political rights.

Europe offers many examples of democratic innovation and initiatives to
combat social exclusion on which the UK might draw. It also offers the
possibility of new conceptions of citizenship. Patterns of European migra-
tion, based in part on the flow of 'guest workers' between nations, have
created a potential basis for what Soysal terms a 'post-national' model of
citizenship in which political and social rights are no longer vested solely in
the nation state:

> The model of national citizenship, anchored in territorialised notions of cultural
> belonging, was dominant during the period of massive migration at the turn of the
> century, when immigrants were expected to be moulded into national citizens. The
> recent guestworker experience reflects a time when national citizenship is losing
> ground to a more universal model of membership, anchored in deterritorialised
> notions of persons' rights. This new model, which I call postnational, reflects a
> different logic and praxis: what were previously defined as national rights become
> entitlements legitimised on the basis of personhood. (Soysal 1994: 3)

Yet questions of 'race' and racism, often institutionalised in political parties
included in coalition governments in continental Europe, repeatedly undermine such a possibility. As I write this final chapter, European leaders are
meeting at Nice to discuss the enlargement of the EU and debate the issues
raised by the inclusion of twelve prospective new member states. An
enlarged Europe may well be one that continues historical lines of inclusion
and exclusion drawn around cultural and religious lines, with Eastern and
Mediterranean member states marginalised or subordinated (Hadjimichalis
1997). It may be one in which nationalism continues to be reinforced
through the conflation of citizenship with white, Christian Europeanness
(Delanty 1995). Such debates repeatedly open up questions about what kind
of multi-cultural settlement a future political settlement might embrace.

Labour's conceptions of a modern economy, modern welfare system and
modern citizenship potentially close off alternative conceptions of modernity
which have developed both within and beyond the Labour Party. Such issues
challenge the inclusive, consensual, post-ideological conception of a modern
politics that Labour attempted to install. In Chapter 8 I described Labour's
attempt to construct a new social settlement based on a 'modern' conception
of the people in which old lines of division (e.g. around class, gender and
'race') had been resolved. The limits to the discourses of inclusion and
consensus became starkly evident as Labour faced a series of challenges in its

first years of office. These clustered around Labour's response to charges of institutional racism in the police service; around its policies on asylum seekers; around its stance on benefits for lone mothers; around the moral authoritarianism of its stance on 'beggars', 'rough sleepers' and other vulnerable groups; and around its oscillations on legislative reform on issues of sexuality. Labour's difficulties in handling these issues derived from the way in which the Third Way was discursively constructed in opposition to the class politics of the old left. In the process, it also marginalised other forms of politics which challenged understandings of inequality and difference embedded in the social composition of the 'nation'. The strands of the left which articulated a politics of diversity based on the 'new social movements' were present in neither the image of the 'old' that was being rejected nor in the formulation of the 'new' in the guise of the Third Way. Rustin (1999a) notes the way in which Labour selectively appropriated some of the ideas emerging from the new left, as represented in the 'New Times' debate conducted in *Marxism Today*:

> What New Labour has taken from the 'New Times' position is an insistence on the need for a new political project – and new vocabularies and images for this – a rejection of merely statist or as we might also now say 'Fordist' programmes, a critique of simplistic class politics, an attention to feminist agendas, and a commitment to democratic renewal, via constitutional reform. The 'post-material' agendas of environmental conservatism, and attention to cultural meaning and expressive style are also part of the package. (Rustin 1999a: 11)

But, as I argued in Chapter 8, the conflicts that produced these movements are now assumed to have been settled. For example, while feminist thinking provides part of the political imagery and vocabulary on which Labour drew, the need for a continued feminist politics was explicitly rejected.[1] Coote notes the profound 'unease' about new Labour's stance on women's politics, and the way in which the Third Way excluded feminist perspectives on social and political agendas. Despite the increase in women MPs after the 1997 election, women remained marginal to the political centre of government:

> Old labour had its roots in male dominated trades-unionism and old-style industrial politics. . . . New Labour was forged in highly charged, deeply embattled times. It sought to rid itself of associations with the past, tighten discipline and close ranks against adversity on all sides. This has given rise to a closed political culture of elite insiders. In Downing Street's inner sanctum, the occupants are predominantly young, male, white graduates: a generation who grew up feeling that the gender issue was sorted (perhaps by their own mothers) and are inclined to think feminism is yesterday's politics. (Coote 2000: 2–3)

The inclusion of women as active participants in national politics and in the rebuilding of local communities was, then, conditional on the exclusion of overtly feminist perspectives. The image of modernity was one in which old conflicts are assumed to have been settled.

The patterns of inclusion and exclusion in Labour's imagery of the modern people also inscribed patterns of *political* inclusion and exclusion, through which alternative visions and forms of political agency might be de-mobilised and dismissed. Several commentators have highlighted the limitations of Labour's consensus-based, inclusive conception of modernity. Mouffe (1998) suggests that Labour's consensual imagery marks out an apolitical terrain, or a politics without antagonism. Lewis argues that 'They [Labour] attempt to proceed as if all inequalities deriving from the constitution of differences around axes of "race"/ethnicity, gender, class, sexuality and disability are no longer sources of serious antagonism' (Lewis 2000a: 268). Franklin (2000), drawing on Beck (1997), argues that: 'New distinctions have been identified to supplant the politics of difference in late modern society: inclusion and exclusion, insider/outsider, conflict/consensus, safe/unsafe, rights/responsibilities, order/disorder. They draw a veil over old configurations that haven't necessarily disappeared and set alternative patterns for decision-making. The acceptable choice of consensus, responsibility and cohesion coincides with the communitarian approach, and leads to a framework that is not conducive to social change and can have a dulling effect on political agency' (Franklin 2000: 18).

However, Labour's efforts to treat differential inequalities and the struggles over them as 'settled' – allowing a view of equalised opportunities tempered by pockets of exclusion – were not wholly successful. On the contrary, alternative versions of a modern Britain and a modern people continued to circulate and challenge those of new Labour. Some of these reflected struggles around paid work: the level of the minimum wage, the (disputed) effects of the New Deal programmes; the tensions around the UK's adoption of European legislation on parental leave and the extension of employment rights for women returning to work after maternity leave; and issues concerning racism and other forms of discrimination in the workplace. Some were represented in debates about environmental and green politics. Some reflected the struggles of those marginalised in the consensual imagery of the nation for access to the social, political and economic rights of citizenship. Some were embedded in conflicting visions of Britain, Europe and the world.

Towards a modern governance?

New Labour was highly selective in its approach to the dynamics, diversity and complexity of the modern world. Its governance practices struggled with the problem of how to install one (vision of) modernity while having to negotiate other dimensions that it seeks to repress or contain. Any attempt to re-imagine modernity outside the current political project of new Labour is likely to produce charges of idealism. It is also difficult, as Williams acknowledges, to articulate alternative values when the (stigmatised) old left appears as the only alternative to neo-liberalism and the Third Way (Williams 2000). Yet I want to conclude by suggesting alternative ways of imagining a modern governance. I begin by looking towards Europe, not because it offers a set of institutions on which nation states might model themselves (many of its institutions are deeply flawed), but because it is the source of alternative political ideas and models of citizenship. The European Union offers a form of governance and politics with which the UK is profoundly uneasy. It is one in which many different layers of governance – regional, local, national, supra-national – are overlaid on each other. It is based on politics of compromise and coalition-building, of understanding shifting balances of power rather than the emergence of clear winners and losers. It is one that recognises the need for complexity rather than offering simple choices. This very complexity is one of the reasons why UK governments have found it so difficult to gain support for any deepening of political or economic links with the EU among the British media and electorate. Yet this style of governance and politics offers many parallels with the kind of governance required for a complex, diverse and dynamic world. Amin (1997), for example, argues that it will not be possible to govern in the new Europe in a way that is based on the old rules of hierarchy and central control. He proposes a 'European Social Model' based on imaginative region-building, a democratic and interactive pluralism that draws in both state and non-state institutions, and an extension and deepening of egalitarianism and participatory democracy.

Within the UK, a form of governance responsive to the increasing complexity, diversity and dynamic character of the public realm might include a much less ambiguous and constrained devolution of power to regional, local and national governments. The loosening of the stranglehold of tight political control in what remains a highly centralised state could foster a more diverse and responsive process of policy development adapted to local interests, needs and priorities, coupled with a more reflexive process of innovation and adaptation. It would, as Labour has claimed, be based on flexible, knowledge-based and iterative processes of policy development (evident in the proliferation of pilots and experiments that Labour has introduced, and its emphasis on networks and 'co-production' with communities and users). But such developments would not be repeatedly undercut as shifting political imperatives produce a return to a model of governance based on centrally imposed solutions from above.

A modern governance would be based on responsive institutions, open to challenge and debate in order to generate new ideas, broaden political involvement and encourage political agency, even where this might present challenges to the status quo. It would offer a broadened conception of democracy that enabled minority and excluded voices to be heard in a range of decision-making fora that complemented, but also challenged, the traditional institutions of representative democracy. These traditional institutions would themselves be modernised through proportional representation and positive action initiatives to enable minority or excluded voices to be heard at the centres of power.

These ideas invoke an image of modernity that transcends the moral conservatism and old-style nationalism that continue to shape many aspects of Labour's social policy agenda, and which constrain its responses to questions of diversity. Such images offer conceptions of citizenship and identity that transcend conservative assumptions about the pre-eminence of the nation state. A modern governance might offer the possibility of a reshaping of democracy, enabling the possibility of challenges that move forwards, beyond the Third Way, rather than back to an old form of left politics. It might recognise the need for a continued array of feminist, anti-racist, gay and disability politics that articulates issues of recognition and redistribution. It would be based on a wider conception of politics that could enable the mobilisation of interests and collective identities outside the boundaries of political parties and formal political institutions. It would offer a richer basis for democratic renewal than the election of municipal mayors coupled with consumer-based models of public consultation. The settlement of the social, in all its diversity and complexity, can never be a once-and-for-all political achievement, but, in 'modern' societies, must be the focus of continuing debate and sometimes dissent. Such is the clay from which political renewal is constructed.

Note

1 Indeed, in December 2000 it was reported that Labour was intending to replace the Women's Unit with a new organisation representing both males and females discriminated against because of their gender. A senior government source was cited as saying 'the debate has moved on', while the minister was cited as suggesting that, under the 'new feminism', we should be worried about inequalities affecting either sex (*Observer*, 18 December: 15; *The Guardian*, 19 December: G2, page 9).

Bibliography

Alcock, P., Craig, G. and Thornton, P. (1998) 'Evaluating local authority anti-poverty initiatives', in R. Griffiths (ed.), *Social Exclusion in Cities: the Urban Policy Challenge*. Bristol, University of the West of England.

Amin, A. (1997) 'Tackling regional inequality in Europe', *Soundings*, Special issue, 'The Next Ten Years'.

Amman, R. (2000) 'Foreward', in H.T. Davies, S.M. Nutley and P.C. Smith (eds), *What Works? Evidence-based Policy and Practice in Public Services*. Bristol, Policy Press.

Andrews, G. (1998) 'Shifting to the bright – in search of the intellectual left', in A. Coddington and M. Perryman (eds), *The Moderniser's Dilemma: Radical Politics in the Age of Blair*. London, Lawrence and Wishart.

Armstrong, H. (1998) Interview in D. Calpin, 'Moving modernisation forward', *Municipal Journal*, 7 August, p. 13.

Ashworth, R., Boyne, G. and Walker, R. (1999) 'Regulatory problems in the public sector: theories and cases'. Paper presented to the ESRC Seminar *New Labour and the Third Way in Public Services*, University of Manchester, December.

Audit Commission (1986) *Making a Reality of Community Care*. London, HMSO.

Audit Commission (1990) *We Can't Go On Meeting Like This: the Changing Role of Local Authority Members*. London, HMSO.

Audit Commission (1997) *Representing the People*. London, HMSO.

Audit Commission (1999) *Listen Up! Effective Community Consultation*. London, HMSO.

Bacchi, C. (1999) *Women, Policy and Politics: the Construction of Policy Problems*. London, Sage.

Baines Report (1972) *The New Local Authorities: Study Group on Local Authority Management Structure*. London, HMSO.

Barber, B. (1984) *Strong Democracy: Participatory Politics for a New Age*. Berkeley, CA, University of California Press.

Barker, A. (2000) 'May the force be with you', *The Stakeholder*, 3, 6.

Barnes, I., Dudley, J., Harris, P. and Petersen, A. (1999) 'Introduction: themes, context and perspectives', in A. Petersen, I. Barnes, J. Dudley and P. Harris (eds), *Postructuralism, Citizenship and Social Policy*. London: Routledge.

Barnes, M. (1997) *Care, Communities and Citizens*. London, Longman.

Barnes, M. and Prior D. (2000) *Private Lives as Public Policy*. Birmingham, Venture Press.

Beck, U. (1997) *The Reinvention of Politics: Rethinking Modernity in the Global Social Order*. Cambridge, Polity Press.

Benson, J.K. (1975) 'The inter-organisational network as a political economy', *Administrative Science Quarterly*, June.

Benyon, J. and Edwards, A. (1999) 'Community governance of crime control', in G. Stoker (ed.), *The New Management of British Local Governance*. Basingstoke, Macmillan.

Bewes, T. (1998) 'Who cares who wins? Postmodernisation and the radicalism of indifference', in A. Coddington and M. Perryman (eds), *The Moderniser's Dilemma: Radical Politics in the Age of Blair*. London, Lawrence and Wishart.

Bichard, M. (1999) 'The Outsider v. the Club', interview with C. Price, *The Stakeholder*, 3, 4, September–October, p. 7.

Blackman, T. and Palmer, A. (1999) 'Continuity or modernisation? The emergence of New Labour's welfare state', in H. Dean and R. Woods (eds), *Social Policy Review 11*. Luton, Social Policy Association.

Blackwell, T. and Seabrook, J. (1993) *The Revolt against Change: Towards a Conserving Radicalism*. London, Vintage.

Blair, T. (1998a) *The Third Way: New Politics for the New Century*. London, Fabian Society.

Blair, T. (1998b) *Leading the Way: a New Vision for Local Government*. London, Institute for Public Policy and Research.

Blair, T. (2001) 'Third Way, Phase Two', *Prospect*, March.

Blunkett, D. (1999) 'World class education for all', in G. Kelly (ed.), *Is New Labour Working?* London, The Fabian Society.

Bogason, P. and Toonen, T.A.J (1998) 'Introduction: networks in public administration', *Public Administration*, 76, Summer.

Boseley, S. (2000) 'Bitter pills to swallow', *The Guardian*, 19 April, pp. 6–7.

Boyne, G. (1999) 'Introduction: processes, performance and best balue in local government'. *Local Government Studies*, 25, 2, Summer.

Burns, D., Hambleton, R. and Hoggett, P. (1994) *The Politics of Decentralisation: Revitalising Local Democracy*. London, Macmillan.

Burr, V. (1995) *An Introduction to Social Constructionism*. London, Routledge.

Cabinet Office (1999a) *Modernising Government* (Cmnd 4310). London, The Stationery Office.

Cabinet Office (1999b) *Professional Policymaking in the 21st Century*. London, The Cabinet Office.

Campbell, C. and Wilson, G.K. (1995) *The End of Whitehall: Death of a Paradigm?* Oxford, Blackwell.

Carter, J. (ed.) (1998) *Post-modernity and the Fragmentation of Social Welfare*. London, Routledge.

Carter, N. (1989) 'Performance indicators: "backseat driving" or "hands-off" control', *Policy and Politics*, 17, 2.

Carter, N., Klein, R. and Day, P. (1992) *How Organisations Measure Success: the Use of Performance Indicators in Government*. London, Routledge.

Chaney, D. (1994) *The Cultural Turn*. London, Routledge.

Clarence, E. (1999) 'New Labour discourse and collaborative working'. Paper presented to the ESRC Seminar *Recent Developments in the New Public Management*, Aston University, November.

Clarke, J. (1999) 'Coming to terms with culture', in H. Dean and R. Woods (eds), *Social Policy Review 11*. Luton, Social Policy Association.

Clarke, J. (2000) 'Globalisation and welfare states: some unsettling thoughts', in R. Sykes, B. Palier and P. Prior (eds), *Globalisation and the European Welfare States: Challenges and Change*. London, Macmillan.

Clarke, J. and Cochrane, A. (1998) 'The social construction of social problems', in E. Saraga (ed.), *Embodying the Social: Constructions of Difference*. London, Routledge.

Clarke, J. and Newman, J. (1996) 'The tyranny of transformation'. Paper presented to the first *International Research Symposium on Public Management*, Aston University, March.

Clarke, J. and Newman, J. (1997) *The Managerial State: Power, Politics and Ideology in the Remaking of Social Welfare*. London, Sage.

Clarke, J. and Newman, J. (1998) 'A Modern British People? New Labour and the reconstruction of social welfare'. Paper presented to the *Discourse Analysis and Social Research Conference*, Copenhagen Business School, September.

Clarke, J., Gewirtz, S., Hughes, G. and Humphrey, J. (2000) 'Guarding the public interest? The rise of audit and inspection', in J. Clarke, S. Gewirtz and E. McLaughlin (eds), *New Managerialism, New Welfare?* London, Sage.

Clarke, M. and Stewart, J. (1999) *Community Governance, Community Leadership and the New Local Government.* York, Joseph Rowntrees Foundation.

Clegg, S.R. (1990) *Modern Organisations: Organisation Studies in the Postmodern World.* London, Sage.

Cochrane, A. (1993) *Whatever Happened to Local Government?* Buckingham, Open University Press.

Cochrane, A. (2000) 'Local government: managerialism and modernisation', in J. Clarke, S. Gewirtz and E. McLaughlin (eds), *New Managerialism, New Welfare?* London, Sage.

Cook, D. (1999) 'Putting crime in its place: the causes of crime and New Labour's local solutions', in H. Dean and R. Woods (eds), *Social Policy Review 11.* Luton, Social Policy Association.

Cooper, D. (1998) *Governing Out of Order: Space, Law and the Politics of Belonging.* London: Rivers Oram Press.

Coote, A. (2000) 'Introduction', in A. Coote (ed.), *New Gender Agenda.* London, Institute of Public Policy Research.

Cope, S. and Goodship, J. (1999) 'Regulating collaborative government: towards joined-up government?', *Public Policy and Administration*, 14, 2, Summer.

Corera, G. (1998) 'More by default than design: the Clinton experience and the Third Way', *Renewal*, 6, 2, Spring.

Corry, D., Le Grand, J. and Radcliffe, R. (1997) *Public/Private Partnerships: a Marriage of Convenience or a Permanent Commitment?* London, Institute of Public Policy Research.

Corvellec, H. (1995) *Stories of Achievement: Narrative Features of Organisational Performance.* Malmo, Lund University Press.

Coulson, A. (1998) 'Trust and contract in public sector management', in A. Coulson (ed.), *Trust and Contracts: Relationships in Local Government, Health and Public Services.* Bristol, Policy Press.

Cousins, C. (1987) *Controlling Social Welfare.* Brighton: Wheatsheaf Books.

Cropper, S. (1996) 'Collaborative working and the issue of sustainability', in C. Huxham (ed.), *Creating Collaborative Advantage.* London, Sage.

Dahrendorf, R. (1999) 'Whatever happened to liberty?' *New Statesman*, 6 September.

Davies, C. (2000) 'The demise of professional self-regulation: a moment to mourn?', in G. Lewis, S. Gewirtz and J. Clarke (eds), *Rethinking Social Policy.* London, Sage.

Davies, H.T.O, Nutley, S.M. and Smith, P.C (2000) 'Introducing evidence-based policy and practice in public services', in H.T.O. Davies, S.M. Nutley and P.C. Smith (eds), *What Works? Evidence-based Policy and Practice in Public Services.* Bristol, Policy Press.

Davies, J. (2000) 'Local regeneration partnerships under New Labour: a case of creeping centralisation'. Paper presented to the ESRC seminar *The Third Way in Public Services – New Forms of Partnership*, York University, April.

Davis, H. and Geddes, M. (2000) 'Deepening democracy or elite governance? New political management arrangements in local government', *Public Money and Management*, 20, 2, April–June.

Dean, M. (1999) *Governmentality: Power and Rule in Modern Society.* London, Sage.

Delanty, G. (1995) *Inventing Europe.* Basingstoke, Macmillan.

Dennis, N. and Halsey, A.H. (1988) *English Ethical Socialism.* Oxford, Oxford University Press.

Department of the Environment, Transport and the Regions (1998) *Modern Local Government: In Touch with the People.* London, The Stationery Office

Department of the Environment, Transport and the Regions (2000) *Coordination of Area-based Initiatives: Research Working Paper*. London, The Stationery Office.

Department of Health (1997) *The New NHS: Modern – Dependable* (Cmnd 3807). London, The Stationery Office.

Department of Health (1998a) *Our Healthier Nation: A Contract for Health* (Cmnd. 3852). London, The Stationery Office.

Department of Health (1998b) *Modernising Social Services: Promoting Independence, Improving Protection, Raising Standards* (Cmnd 4169). London, HMSO.

Department of Health (1998c) *Partnerships in Action – a Discussion Document*. London, Department of Health.

Department of Social Security (1998) *New Ambitions for Our Country: a New Contract For Welfare* (Cmnd 3805). London, The Stationery Office.

DiMaggio, P.J. and Powell, W.W. (1991) 'Introduction', in W. Powell and P.J. diMaggio (eds), *The New Institutionalism in Organizational Analysis*. Chicago, University of Chicago Press.

Dobson, F. (1999) 'A modernised NHS', in G. Kelly (ed.), *Is New Labour Working?* London, The Fabian Society.

Douglas, M. (1987) *How Institutions Think*. London, Routledge.

Driver, S. and Martell, L. (1997) 'New Labour's communitarianisms', *Critical Social Policy*, 17, 3, pp. 27–46.

Driver, S. and Martell, L. (1998) *New Labour: Politics after Thatcher*. Cambridge, Polity Press.

Driver, S. and Martell, L. (1999) 'Left, right and the Third Way'. Paper presented to the ESRC Seminar *New Labour and the Third Way in Public Services*, London School of Hygiene and Tropical Medicine, April.

Dunleavy, P. and Hood, C. (1994) 'From old public administration to new public management', *Public Money and Management*, 14, 3.

Dwyer, P. (1998) 'Conditional citizens? Welfare rights and responsibilities in the late 1990s', *Critical Social Policy*, 18, 4, November.

Edwards, R. and Duncan, S. (1997) 'Supporting the family: lone mothers, paid work and the underclass debate', *Critical Social Policy*, 17, 4, November.

Elster, J. (1998) 'Introduction', in J. Elster (ed.), *Deliberative Democracy*. Cambridge, Cambridge University Press

Etzioni, A. (1995) *The Spirit of Community*. London, Fontana.

Exworthy, M. and Halford, S. (eds) (1999) *Professionals and the New Managerialism in the Public Sector*. Buckingham, Open University Press.

Fairclough, N. (1992) 'Introduction', in N. Fairclough (ed.), *Critical Language Awareness*. London, Longman.

Fairclough, N. (2000) *New Labour, New Language*. London, Routledge.

Falconer, P.K. (1999) 'The new public management today: an overview'. Paper presented to the ESRC Seminar *Recent Developments in the New Public Management*, Imperial College London, May.

Ferlie, E., Pettigrew, A., Ashburner, L. and Fitzgerald, L. (1996) *The New Public Management in Action*. Oxford, Oxford University Press.

Fishkin, J.S. (1991) *Democracy and Deliberation*. New Haven, CT, Yale University Press.

Flynn, N. (1994) 'Control, commitment and contracts', in J. Clarke, A. Cochrane and E. McLaughlin (eds), *Managing Social Policy*. London, Sage.

Foley, P. and Martin, S. (2000) 'A new deal for the community? Public participation in regeneration and local service delivery', *Policy and Politics*, 28, 4.

Franklin, J. (2000) 'After modernisation: gender, the Third Way and the new politics', in A. Coote (ed.), *New Gender Agenda*. London, Institute of Public Policy Research.

Fraser, N. (1997) *Justice Interruptus: Critical Reflections on the 'Postsocialist' Condition*. London, Routledge.

Gamble, A. (2000) 'Economic governance', in J. Pierre (ed.), *Debating Governance: Authority, Steering and Democracy*. Oxford, Oxford University Press.

Giddens, A. (1998a) *The Third Way: the Renewal of Social Democracy*. Cambridge, Polity Press.

Giddens, A. (1998b) 'After the left's paralysis', *New Statesman*, 1 May.

Giddens, A. (2000) *The Third Way and its Critics*. Cambridge, Polity Press.

Glendinning, C. and Clarke, J. (2000) 'Old wine, new bottles? Prospects for NHS/ local authority partnerships under "New Labour"'. Paper presented to the ESRC Seminar *The Third Way in Public Services – New Forms of Partnership*, York University, April.

Glennerster, H. (1999) 'A Third Way?', in H. Dean and R. Woods (eds), *Social Policy Review 11*. Luton, Social Policy Association.

Grant, D., Keenoy, T. and Oswick, C. (1998) 'Introduction', in D. Grant, T. Keenoy and C. Oswick (eds), *Discourse and Organisation*. London, Sage.

Habermas, J. (1987) *The Theory of Communicative Action* (translated by T. McCarthy). Boston, MA, Beacon Press.

Habermas, J. (1989) *The Structural Transformation of the Public Sphere* (translated by T. Burger and F. Lawrence). Cambridge, MA, MIT Press.

Hadjimichalis, C. (1997) 'What kind of Europe?', *Soundings*, 6, Summer.

Hall, S. (ed.) (1997) *Representation: Cultural Representation and Signifying Practices*. London, Sage.

Hall, S. (1998) 'The great moving nowhere show', *Marxism Today*, November/ December.

Hall, S. and du Gay, P. (eds) (1996) *Questions of Cultural Identity*. London, Sage.

Ham, C. (1999a) 'The Third Way in health care reform: does the emperor have any clothes?', *Journal of Health Services Research Policy*, 14, 3, July.

Ham, C. (1999b) 'A modernised NHS: commentary', in G. Kelly (ed.), *Is New Labour Working?* London, The Fabian Society.

Hardy, B., Turrell, A. and Wistow, G. (1992) *Innovations in Community Care Management*. Aldershot, Avebury.

Hay, C. (1996) *Re-stating Social and Political Change*. Buckingham, Open University Press.

Hay, C. (1999) *The Political Economy of New Labour: Labouring under False Pretences?* Manchester, Manchester University Press.

Held, D., McGrew, A., Goldblatt, D. and Perraton, J. (1999) *Global Transformations: Politics, Economics and Culture*. Cambridge, Polity Press.

Hill, M. (1997) *The Policy Process in the Modern State* (3rd edition). Harlow, Prentice-Hall.

Hillyard, P. and Watson, S. (1996) 'Postmodern social policy: a contradiction in terms?', *Journal of Social Policy*, 25, 3.

Hirst, P. (1994) *Associative Democracy*. Cambridge, Polity Press.

Hirst, P. (2000) 'Democracy and governance', in J. Pierre (ed.), *Debating Governance*. Oxford, Oxford University Press.

Hirst, P. and Thompson, G. (1999) *Globalisation in Question: the Myths of the International Economy and the Possibilities of Governance* (2nd edition). Cambridge, Polity Press.

Hoggett, P. (1996) 'New modes of control in the public services', *Public Administration*, 74, 1, Spring.

Home Office (1999) *Supporting Families*. London, The Stationery Office.

Hood, C. (1991) 'A public management for all seasons?', *Public Administration*, 69, 1.

Hood, C. (1998) *The Art of the State: Culture, Rhetoric and Public Management*. Oxford, Clarendon Press.

Hood, C., Scott, C., James, O., Jones, G. and Travers, T. (1999) *Regulation Inside*

Government: Waste Watchers, Quality Police and Sleaze Busters. Oxford, Oxford University Press.

Hudson, B., Hardy, B., Henwood, M. and Wistow, G. (1999) 'In pursuit of inter-agency collaboration in the public sector: what is the contribution of theory and research?', *Public Management: an International Journal of Research and Theory*, 1, 2.

Hughes, G. (1996) 'Communitarianism and law and order', *Critical Social Policy*, 16, 4, November.

Hughes, G. (ed). (1998) *Imagining Welfare Futures*. London, Routledge.

Hughes, G. and Lewis, G. (eds) (1998) *Unsettling Welfare: the Reconstruction of Social Policy*. London, Routledge.

Hughes, G. and Mooney, G. (1998) 'Community', in G. Hughes (ed.), *Imagining Welfare Futures*. London, Routledge.

Hughes, M. and Newman, J. (1999) 'From new public management to new labour: from "new" to "modern"'. Paper presented to the third *International Symposium on Public Management*, Aston University, Birmingham, March.

Hutton, W. (2000) 'The control-freak gets his comeuppance', *Observer*, 13 February, p. 29.

Huxham, C. (ed.) (1996) *Creating Collaborative Advantage*. London, Sage.

Huxham, C. and Vangen, S. (1996) 'Working together: key themes in the management of relationships between public and non profit organisations', *International Journal of Public Sector Management*, 9, pp. 5–17.

Huxham, C. and Vangen, S. (1999) 'New ways to think about leadership in collaboration'. Paper to the third *International Symposium on Public Management*, Aston University, Birmingham, March.

Jacobs, M. (1999) 'Introduction', in G. Kelly (ed.), *Is New Labour Working?* London, Fabian Society.

Jervis, P. and Richards, S. (1997) 'Public management: raising our game', *Public Money and Management*, April–June.

Jessop, B. (1998a) 'The rise of governance and the risks of failure: the case of economic development', *International Social Science Journal*, 155.

Jessop, B. (1998b) 'Reflections on globalisation and its (il)logics', in K. Olds et al., *The Logic of Globalisation*. London, Routledge.

Jessop, B. (2000) 'Governance failure', in G. Stoker (ed.), *The New Politics of British Urban Governance*. Basingstoke, Macmillan.

Johnson, T. (1973) *Professions and Power*. London, Macmillan.

Jordan, A.G. and Richardson, J.J. (1987) *British Politics and the Policy Process*. London, Unwin Hyman.

Jospin, L. (1998) *Modern Socialism*. London, The Fabian Society.

Keen, L. and Scase, R. (1998) *Local Government Management: the Rhetoric and Reality of Change*. Buckingham, Open University Press.

Kickert, W. (1993) 'Autopoeisis', *Organisational Studies*, 14.

Kirkpatrick, I. and Martinez Lucio, M. (eds) (1995) *The Politics of Quality in the Public Sector*. London, Routledge.

Kitchen, H. (ed.) (1997) *A Framework for the Future: an Agenda for Councils in a Changing World*. London, Local Government Information Unit.

Kooiman, J. (ed.) (1993) *Modern Governance: Government–Society Interactions*. London, Sage.

Kooiman, J. (2000) 'Societal governance: levels, models and orders of social-political interaction', in J. Pierre (ed.), *Debating Governance: Authority, Steering and Democracy*. Oxford, Oxford University Press.

Kooiman, J. and van Vliet, M. (1993) 'Governance and public management', in K.A. Eliassen and J. Kooiman (eds), *Managing Public Organisations: Lessons from Contemporary European Experience*. London, Sage.

Labour Party (1995) *Renewing Democracy, Rebuilding Communities*. London, Labour Party.

Lash, S. (1993) 'Reflexive modernisation – the aesthetic dimension', *Theory, Culture and Society*, 10, 1.

Lash, S. and Urry, J. (1994) *Economies of Signs and Spaces*. London, Sage.

Leach, S. and Wingfield, M. (1999) 'Public participation and the democratic renewal agenda: prioritisation or marginalisation?', *Local Government Studies*, 25, 4, Winter.

Leadbeater, C. (1997) *The Rise of the Social Entrepreneur*. London, Demos.

Legge, K. (1995) 'HRM: rhetoric, reality and hidden agendas', in J. Storey (ed.), *Human Resource Management: a Critical Text*. London, Routledge.

Le Grand, J. (1992) *The Strategy of Equality*. London, Allen and Unwin.

Leonard, P. (1997) *Postmodern Welfare: Reconstructing an Emancipatory Project*. London, Sage.

Levitas, R. (1998) *The Inclusive Society? Social Exclusion and New Labour*. Basingstoke, Macmillan.

Lewicki, R.J. and Bunker, B. (1996) 'Developing and maintaining trust in work relationships', in R.M. Kramer and T.R. Tyler (eds), *Trust in Organisations: Frontiers of Theory and Research*. London, Sage.

Lewis, D. (1997) *Hidden Agendas: Politics, Law and Disorder*. London: Hamish Hamilton.

Lewis, G. (1998) 'Coming apart at the seams: the crisis of the welfare state', in G. Hughes and G. Lewis (eds), *Unsettling Welfare: the Reconstruction of Social Policy*. London, Routledge.

Lewis, G. (2000a) 'Discursive histories, the pursuit of multiculturalism and social policy', in G. Lewis, S. Gewirtz and J. Clarke (eds), *Rethinking Social Policy*. London, Sage.

Lewis, G. (2000b) *'Race', Gender, Social Welfare: Encounters in a Post-colonial Society*. Cambridge, Polity Press.

Lister, R. (1998) 'From equality to social inclusion: New Labour and the welfare state', *Critical Social Policy*, 18, 2.

Lister, R. (1999) 'To Rio via the Third Way: New Labour's "welfare" reform agenda'. Paper to the first ESRC Research Seminar Programme on *New Labour and the Third Way in Public Services*. London, April.

Lowndes, V. (1996) 'Varieties of new institutionalism: a critical appraisal', *Public Administration*, 74, 2, Summer.

Lowndes, V. (1999) 'Management change in local government', in G. Stoker (ed.), *The New Management of British Local Governance*. Basingstoke, Macmillan.

Lowndes, V. (2000) 'Women and social capital: a comment on Hall's "Social Capital in Britain"', *British Journal of Political Science*, 30.

Lowndes, V. and Skelcher, C. (1998) 'The dynamics of multi-organisational networks and partnerships: an analysis of changing modes of governance', *Public Administration*, 76, 2.

Lowndes, V. et al. (1998) *Guidance on Enhancing Public Participation in Local Government*. London, Department of the Environment, Transport and the Regions.

Luke, J.S. (1998) *Catalytic Leadership: Strategies for an Interconnected World*. CA, Jossey-Bass.

Lund, B. (1999) 'Ask not what your community can do for you: obligations, New Labour and welfare reform', *Critical Social Policy*, 19, 4, November.

Mackintosh, M. (1997) 'Economic culture and quasi-markets in local government: the case of contracting for social care', *Local Government Studies*, 23, 2, pp. 80–102.

McLaughlin, E. and Muncie, J. (2000) 'The criminal justice system: New Labour's new partnerships', in J. Clarke, S. Gewirtz and E. McLaughlin (eds), *New Managerialism, New Welfare?* London, Sage.

Macpherson, W. (1999) *The Stephen Lawrence Inquiry: Report of an Inquiry by Sir William Macpherson of Cluny.* The Stationery Office.

March, J. and Olsen, J. (1976) *Ambiguity and Choice in Organisation.* Bergen, Norway, Universitetsforlaget.

March, J. and Olsen, J. (1989) *Rediscovering Institutions: the Organisational Basis of Politics.* New York: Free Press.

Marquand, D. (1998) 'The Blair paradox', *Prospect*, 30, pp. 19–24.

Marr, A. (2000a) 'Arise, the city state', *The Guardian*, 12 March, p. 28.

Marr, A. (2000b) 'The tyranny of numbers', *Observer*, 16 April, p. 28.

Marsh, D. and Rhodes, R.A.W. (eds) (1992) *Policy Networks in British Government.* Oxford, Clarendon Press.

Marsh, D. (ed.) (1998) *Comparing Policy Networks in British Government.* Oxford, Clarendon Press.

Martin, S. (2000) 'Implementing "best value": local public services in transition', *Public Policy and Administration*, 78, 1, March.

Massey, D. (2000) 'Editorial: opening up debate', *Soundings*, 15, Summer.

Maud Report (1967) *Committee on the Management of Local Government Report*, vols 1–5. London, HMSO.

Mawson, J. and Spencer, K. (1997) 'The origins and operation of the government offices for the English regions', in J. Bradbury and J. Mawson (eds), *British Regionalism and Devolution.* London, Jessica Kingsley.

Metcalfe, L. and Richards, S. (1990) *Improving Public Management.* London, Sage.

Meyer, J.W., Boli, J. and Thomas, G.M. (1994) 'Ontology and rationalization in the Western cultural account', in W.R. Scott and J.W. Meyer, *Institutional Environments and Organisations: Structural Complexity and Individualism.* London, Sage.

Meyer, J. and Rowan, B. (1977) 'Institutional organisations: formal structure as myth and ceremony', *American Journal of Sociology*, 83.

Meyer, J. and Rowan, B. (1991) 'Institutionalised organisations: formal structure as myth and ceremony', in W. Powell and P. diMaggio (eds), *The New Institutionalism in Organisational Analysis.* Chicago: University of Chicago Press.

Miliband, D. (2000) 'This is the modern world', *Fabian Review*, 111, 4, Winter.

Miller, D. (1992) 'Deliberative democracy and social choice', *Political Studies*, XL, Special issue.

Mintzberg, H. (1983) *Structures in Fives: Designing Effective Organizations.* Englewood Cliffs, NJ, Prentice-Hall.

Morgan, K., Rees, G. and Garmise, S. (1999) 'Networking for local economic development', in G. Stoker (ed.), *The New Management of British Local Government.* Basingstoke, Macmillan.

Morgan Report (1991) *Safer Communities: the Local Delivery of Crime Prevention through the Partnership Approach.* London, HMSO.

Morris, L. (1998) 'Legitimate membership of the welfare community', in M. Langan (ed.), *Welfare: Needs, Rights and Risks.* London, Routledge.

Mottram, R. (2000) 'Government for the twenty-first century', *Public Management and Policy Association Review*, 8, January.

Mouffe, C. (1998) 'The radical centre: a politics without adversary', *Soundings*, 9, Summer.

Mulgan, G. (1994) *Politics in an Anti-political Age.* Cambridge, Polity Press.

National Health Service Executive (NHSE) (1999) *Seven Underpinning HAZ Principles.* HAZ Development Team, Quarry House, Leeds.

Newman, J. (1998a) 'The dynamics of trust', in A. Coulson (ed.), *Trust and Contracts: Relationships in Local Government, Health and Public Services.* Bristol, Policy Press.

Newman, J. (1998b) 'Managerialism and social welfare', in G. Hughes and G. Lewis (eds), *Unsettling Welfare: the Reconstruction of Social Policy*. London, Routledge.

Newman, J. (2000a) 'Beyond the new public management? Modernising public services', in J. Clarke, S. Gewirtz and E. McLaughlin (eds), *New Managerialism, New Welfare?* London, Sage.

Newman, J. (2000b) 'The dynamics of partnership'. Paper presented to the seventh *International Conference on Multi-organizational Partnerships and Strategic Collaboration*, Leuven, July.

Newman, J. and Clarke, J. (1994) 'Going about our business? The managerialisation of public services', in J. Clarke, A. Cochrane and E. McLaughlin (eds), *Managing Social Policy*. London, Sage.

Newman, J., Raine, J. and Skelcher, C. (2000) *Innovation and Best Practice in Local Government*. London, Department of the Environment, Transport and the Regions.

Newman, J., Richards, S. and Smith, P. (1998) 'Market testing and institutional change in the UK civil service: compliance, non-compliance and engagement', *Public Policy and Administration*, 13, 4, Winter.

Newman, J., Richards, S. and Smith, P. (2000) 'Modelling institutional change: the making of markets', in R. Rhodes (ed.), *Transforming British Government: Changing Roles and Relationships* (vol. 2). London, Macmillan.

Newman, J. (forthcoming) 'New Labour, governance and the politics of diversity', in J. Barry et al. (eds) *Gender and the Public Sector*. London: Routledge.

North, D. (1990) *Institutions, Institutional Change and Economic Performance*. Cambridge, Cambridge University Press.

Nutley, S. and Webb, J. (2000) 'Evidence and the policy process', in H.T.O. Davies, S.M. Nutley and P.C. Smith (eds), *What Works? Evidence-based Policy and Practice in Public Services*. Bristol, Policy Press.

Ozga, J. (2000) 'New Labour, new teachers', in J. Clarke, S. Gewirtz and E. McLaughlin (eds), *New Managerialism, New Welfare?* London, Sage.

Parsons, W. (1995) *Public Policy*. Aldershot, Edward Elgar.

Performance and Innovation Unit (2000a) *Wiring It Up: Whitehall's Management of Cross-cutting Policies and Services*. London, The Stationery Office.

Performance and Innovation Unit (2000b) *Reaching Out: the Role of Central Government at Regional and Local Level*. London, The Stationery Office.

Perri 6 (1998a) *Holistic Government*. London, Demos.

Perri 6 (1998b) 'Problem-solving government', in I. Hargreaves and I. Christie (eds), *Tomorrow's Politics: The Third Way and Beyond*. London, Demos.

Perri 6, Leat, D., Seltzer, K. and Stoker, G. (1999) *Governing in the Round: Strategies for Holistic Government*. London, Demos.

Perryman, M. (ed.) (1996) *The Blair Agenda*. London, Lawrence and Wishart.

Peters, G. (2000) 'Comparative politics', in J. Pierre (ed.), *Debating Governance: Authority, Steering and Democracy*. Oxford, Oxford University Press.

Pettigrew, A., Ferlie, E. and McKee, L. (1992) *Shaping Strategic Change*. London, Sage.

Phillips, A. (1992) 'Must feminists give up on liberal democracy?', *Political Studies*, XL, Special issue.

Pierre, J. (2000) 'Introduction: understanding governance', in J. Pierre (ed.), *Debating Governance: Authority, Steering and Democracy*. Oxford, Oxford University Press.

Pierre, J. and Peters, B.G. (2000) *Governance, Politics and the State*. Basingstoke, Macmillan.

Platt, S. (1998) *Government by Task Force: a Review of the Reviews*. London, The Catalyst Trust.

Pollard, C. (1999) 'Freedom from fear: building a safer Britain: commentary', in G. Kelly (ed.), *Is New Labour Working?* London, The Fabian Society.

Pollitt, C. (1993) *Managerialism and the Public Services* (2nd edition). Oxford, Blackwell.

Pollitt, C., Birchall, J. and Putnam, K. (1998) *Decentralising Public Service Management*. Basingstoke, Macmillan.

Poole, L. (2000) 'Health care: New Labour's NHS', in J. Clarke, S. Gewirtz and E. McLaughlin (eds), *New Managerialism, New Welfare?* London, Sage.

Powell, M. (ed.) (1999) *New Labour, New Welfare State? The 'Third Way' in British Social Policy*. Bristol, Policy Press.

Power, M. (1994) *The Audit Explosion*. London, Demos.

Power, M. (1997) *The Audit Society*. Oxford, Oxford University Press.

Pratt, J., Gordon, P. and Plampling, D. (1998) *Working Whole Systems*. London, Kings Fund.

Prior, D., Stewart, J. and Walsh, K. (1995) *Citizenship: Rights, Community and Participation*. London, Pitman.

Quinn, R.E (1988) *Beyond Rational Management: Mastering the Paradoxes and Competing Demands of High Performance*. San Francisco, CA, Jossey-Bass.

Raine, R. (1998) 'Evidence-based policy: rhetoric and reality', *Journal of Health Services Research Policy*, 3, 4, October.

Rao, N. (2000a) *Reviving Local Democracy: New Labour, New Politics?* Bristol, Policy Press.

Rao, N. (2000b) 'Research report to the Nuffield Foundation on the political representation of councillors'. Unpublished.

Razzaque, K. (2000) 'Men in suits make me fall silent: black and minority ethnic women in urban regeneration'. Paper presented to the seventh *International Conference on Multi-organizational Partnerships and Strategic Collaboration*, Leuven, July.

Reynolds, D. (1999) 'World class education for all: commentary', in G. Kelly (ed.), *Is New Labour Working?* London, The Fabian Society.

Rhodes, R.A.W. (1994) 'The hollowing out of the state', *Political Quarterly*, 65.

Rhodes, R.A.W. (1997) *Understanding Governance*. Buckingham: Open University Press.

Rhodes, R.A.W. (1999) 'Foreword: governance and networks', in G. Stoker (ed.), *The New Management of British Local Governance*. Basingstoke, Macmillan.

Rhodes, R.A.W. (2000a) 'Governance and public administration', in J. Pierre (ed.), *Debating Governance: Authority, Steering and Democracy*. Oxford, Oxford University Press.

Rhodes, R.A.W. (2000b) *The Governance Narrative: Key Findings and Lessons from the ESRC's Whitehall Programme*. London, Public Management and Policy Association.

Richards, S. et al. (1999) *Cross-cutting Issues in Public Policy*. London, Department of the Environment, Transport and the Regions.

Richardson, J.J. (ed.) (1982) *Policy Styles in Western Europe*. London, Allen and Unwin.

Rose, N. (1996a) 'The death of the social? Re-figuring the territory of government', *Economy and Society*, 25, 3, August.

Rose, N. (1996b) 'Governing "advanced" liberal democracies', in A. Barry, T. Osborne and N. Rose (eds), *Foucault and Political Reason*. London, University College London Press.

Rose, N. and Miller, P. (1992) 'Political power beyond the state: problematics of government', *British Journal of Sociology*, 43, 2, June, pp. 173–205.

Ross, S. (1973) 'The economic theory of agency: the principal's problem', *Americam Economic Review*, 63.

Runnymede Trust (2000) *Report on the Future of Multi-Ethnic Britain*. London, Profile Books.

Rustin, M. (1999a) 'Editorial: a Third Way with teeth', *Soundings*, 11, Spring.

Rustin, M. (1999b) 'Review of Coddington and Perryman: *The Moderniser's Dilemma*', *Renewal*, 7, 1.

Sbragia, A. (2000) 'The European Union as coxswain: governance by steering', in J. Pierre (ed.), *Debating Governance: Authority, Steering and Democracy*. Oxford, Oxford University Press.

Scott, W.R. (1994) 'Institutional environments and organisations', in W.R. Scott and J.W. Meyer, *Institutional Environments and Organisations: Structural Complexity and Individualism*. London, Sage.

Scottish Office (1999) *Targeting Excellence: Modernising Scotland's Schools*. Edinburgh, The Scottish Office.

Seargeant, J. and Steele, J. (1998) *Consulting the Public: Guidelines and Good Practice*. London, Policy Studies Institute.

Selbourne, D. (1993) 'Civic duty first or we drown', *The Independent*, 25 November.

Skelcher, C. (1998) *The Appointed State: Quasi-governmental Organisations and Democracy*. Buckingham, Open University Press.

Smith, M. (1993) *Pressure, Power and Politics*. Hemel Hempstead, Harvester Wheatsheaf.

Smith, M. (1999) *The Core Executive in Britain*. London, Macmillan.

Social Exclusion Unit (1998a) *Bringing Britain Together: a National Strategy for Neighbourhood Renewal* (Cmnd 4045). London, The Stationery Office.

Social Exclusion Unit (1998b) *Truancy and School Exclusion* (Cmnd 3957). London, The Stationery Office.

Social Exclusion Unit (2000) *National Strategy for Neighbourhood Renewal: a Framework for Consultation*. London, The Cabinet Office.

Soysal, Y.N. (1994) *Limits of Citizenship: Migrants and Postnational Membership in Europe*. Chicago, University of Chicago Press.

Spencer, K. and Mawson, J. (1998) 'Government offices and policy coordination in the English regions', *Local Governance*, 24, 2.

Spencer, K. and Mawson, J. (2000) 'Transforming regional government offices in England: a new Whitehall agenda', in R.A.W. Rhodes (ed.), *Transforming British Government* (vol. 2). Basingstoke, Macmillan.

Squires, J. (1998) 'In different voices: deliberative democracy and aesthetic politics', in J. Good and I. Velody (eds), *The Politics of Postmodernity*. Cambridge, Cambridge University Press.

Stepney, P., Lynch, R. and Jordan, B. (1999) 'Poverty, exclusion and New Labour', *Critical Social Policy*, 19, 1, February.

Stewart, J. (1990) 'The government of uncertainty', in *Meeting the Needs of the 1990s*, Social Policy Paper No. 2. London, Institute for Public Policy and Research.

Stewart, J. (1995) *Innovation in Democratic Practice*. Birmingham, School of Public Policy.

Stewart, J. (1996) *Further Innovation in Democratic Practice*. Birmingham, School of Public Policy.

Stewart, J. (1997) *More Innovation in Democratic Practice*. Birmingham, School of Public Policy.

Stewart, J. (2000) *The Nature of British Local Government*. Basingstoke, Macmillan.

Stewart, J. and Stoker, G. (1988) *From Local Administration to Community Government*. London, Fabian Society.

Stewart, J. and Stoker, G. (eds) (1989) *The Future of Local Government*. Basingstoke, Macmillan.

Stewart, J., Kendall, E. and Coote, A. (1994) *Citizen's Juries*. London, Institute of Public Policy and Research.

Stewart, M. (2000) 'Collaboration and conflict in the governance of the city region'. Paper presented to the seventh *International Conference on Multi-organizational Partnerships and Strategic Collaboration*, Leuven, July.

Stewart, M., Hambleton, R., Purdue, D. and Razzaque, K. (2000) *Community Leadership in Area Regeneration*. York, Joseph Rowntrees Foundation.

Stoker, G. (1991) *The Politics of Local Government* (2nd edition). Basingstoke, Macmillan.

Stoker, G. (1998a) 'Governance as theory: 5 propositions', *International Social Science Journal*, 155.

Stoker, G. (1998b) 'Public-private partnerships and urban governance', in J. Pierre (ed.), *Partnerships in Urban Governance: European and American Experience*. London, Macmillan.

Stoker, G. (1999) 'Introduction: the unintended costs and benefits of new management reform for British local government', in G. Stoker (ed.), *The New Management of British Local Governance*. Basingstoke, Macmillan.

Stoker, G. (2000) 'Urban political science and the challenge of urban governance', in J. Pierre (ed.), *Debating Governance: Authority, Steering and Democracy*. Oxford, Oxford University Press.

Storey, J. (1999) 'Human resource management: still marching on, or marching out?', in J. Storey (ed.), *Human Resource Management: a Critical Text*. London, Routledge.

Storey, J. and Sissons, K. (1992) *Managing Human Resources and Industrial Relations*. Buckingham, Open University Press.

Straw, J. (1998) Speech to Conference on *The Renewal of Criminal Justice? New Labour's Policies in Perspective*. Leeds University, September.

Taylor, M. (1998) 'Dangerous liaisons'. Paper presented to the *Centre for Voluntary Organisations Symposium*, September.

Taylor-Gooby, P. (2000) 'Blair's scars', *Critical Social Policy*, 64.

Terry, F. (2000) 'Transport: beyond predict and provide', in H.T. Davies, S.M. Nutley and P.C. Smith (eds), *What Works? Evidence-based Policy and Practice in Public Services*. Bristol, Policy Press.

Vincent-Jones, P. (1999) 'Competition and contracting in the transition from CCT to best value: towards a more reflexive regulation?', *Public Administration*, 77, 2.

Walker, D. (2000a) 'You find the evidence, we'll pick the policy', *Guardian Higher*, 15 February, p. 3.

Walker, D. (2000b) *Central Command and Local Delivery: the New Shape of Local Governance*. London, Association of Chartered Certified Accountants.

Walsh, K. (1995) *Public Services and Market Mechanisms: Competition, Contracting and the New Public Management*. Basingstoke: Macmillan.

Walshe, K. (2000) 'NHS Trusts make a start on clinical governance', *Health Services Management Newsletter*, 6, 1.

Watson, S. (2000) 'Foucault and the study of social policy', in G. Lewis, S. Gewirtz and J. Clarke (eds), *Rethinking Social Policy*. London, Sage.

Weick, K.E. (1976) 'Education organisations as loosely coupled systems', *Administrative Science Quarterly*, 21.

Wheeler, W. (1998) 'Together again after all these years: science, politics and theology in the new modernity', in A. Coddington and M. Perryman (eds), *The Moderniser's Dilemma: Radical Politics in the Age of Blair*. London, Lawrence and Wishart.

White, S. (1998) 'Interpreting the Third Way: not one road, but many', *Renewal*, 6, 2, Spring.

Wicks, M. (1994) *The Active Society: Defending Welfare*. London, The Fabian Society.

Wilkinson, D. and Appelbee, E. (1999) *Implementing Holistic Government: Joined-up Action on the Ground*. Bristol, Policy Press.

Williams, F. (1993) 'Gender, "race" and class in British welfare policy', in A. Cochrane and J. Clarke (eds), *Comparing Welfare States: Britain in International Context*. London, Sage.

Williams, F. (1996) 'Postmodernism, feminism and the question of difference', in N. Parton (ed.), *Social Theory, Social Change and Social Work*. London, Routledge.

Williams, F. (1999) 'Good-enough principles for welfare', *Journal of Social Policy*, 28, 4.

Williams, F. (2000) 'Principles of recognition and respect in welfare', in G. Lewis, S. Gewirtz and J. Clarke (eds), *Rethinking Social Policy*. London, Sage.

Young, I. (1990) *Justice and the Politics of Difference*. Princeton, NJ, Princeton University Press.

Index